IRA,

Pleasure to see you again.
Thanks for bringing a touch of
the classic New England diner
into Manhattan.

Randy Garbin

Randy Garbin

STACKPOLE BOOKS

Copyright ©2005 by Stackpole Books

Published by
STACKPOLE BOOKS
5067 Ritter Road
Mechanicsburg, PA 17055
www.stackpolebooks.com

Printed in the United States of America

10 9 8 7 6 5 4 3 2 1

FIRST EDITION

Cover design by Caroline Stover

Library of Congress Cataloging-in-Publication Data

Garbin, Randy.
    Diners of New England / Randy Garbin.— 1st ed.
       p.   cm.
    Includes bibliographical references and index.
    ISBN 0-8117-3141-3
    1. Diners (Restaurants)—New England.   I. Title.
TX945.G28   2005
647.9574—dc22
                                       2004005477

Contents

Foreword

What is it about the diners of New England that we find so appealing? Why are we drawn to them? What makes them so special? There are as many ways to answer these questions as there are diners to explore. For some, it's the diner's structure and history. For others, it's the food. For still others, it's the people. For me, it's the whole package.

No two diners are the same: each is a distinctly different experience. Most diners are owned or independently operated by the people behind the counter, and while all diners have their own interesting physical characteristics, it's the people who bring them to life.

Over the past three decades, I've surveyed many closed and abandoned diners. An empty, nonoperating diner rarely speaks to me. When it does, it seems sad. It's missing those essential ingredients that complete a diner and make it what it is—a meeting place for people. Of course, diners exist to serve food, but people who love diners readily admit it's not necessarily the food that brought them there in the first place or causes them to return.

Much has been written about diner atmosphere. A good diner experience appeals to all of your senses. When I first discovered the wondrous world of diners back in the 1980s, I'm not sure I could have articulated what it was that drew me to them. Now I better understand why I love them. In a world dominated by and obsessed with speed, efficiency, cable TV, cell phones, the Internet, and fast food, I'm making a conscious effort to slow down. I go to a diner to sit down, take in the atmosphere, and enjoy the moment. I'm never in a rush when I go to a diner, so for me it's a calming place.

For some reason, I'm not comfortable dining alone at a formal restaurant. But I always feel comfortable sitting alone in a diner. If I feel like talking, I sit at the counter, and within minutes, I'm engaged in lively conversation with complete strangers. This interaction is often the high point of my day. If I want to sit alone to think or write or observe, I spread out at a booth and just take it all in. Diners seem to offer the traveler a friendly solitude that is unique. I'm not much for sitting in a bar where "everybody knows my name," although regulars at local diners experience that kind of camaraderie.

In my work as a documentary filmmaker, I've studied hundreds of hours of archival film footage of everyday life and have long recognized that though styles change, people do not. And the things that people are naturally drawn to are those things that never really change, such as opening a morning newspaper, that first cup of coffee, a hearty breakfast, and the sounds of conversation and laughter. No matter what happens in the outside world, the world inside the diner remains constant. The diner is like a friend who sticks with you through thick and thin. When I walk into a busy diner at 7:30 A.M., it just feels like home wherever I am. When I venture out on the roads of New England, I stop almost exclusively at the diners featured in this book. Like lighthouses dotting the roadside guiding my way, they are a destination and often the highlight of my travels.

Diners are like tiny time capsules. Upon entering an intact factory made diner, no matter when or where it was made, you are experiencing the decor of the day. It's a touchstone to the era in which it was made. My favorite diners were made in Massachusetts, where I was born. These were individually hand-crafted and combine porcelain enamel, Formica, glass block, and stainless steel with oak and mahogany booths, cabinets, and trim. A wondrous, eye-catching confluence of materials recalls the sturdiness of the American Arts and Crafts movement, the efficiency of the machine age, and the sexy lines of streamlined moderne industrial design. Over the years, I've come to appreciate those huge New Jersey–built stainless steel diners of the 1950s, the zigzag George Jetson–inspired creations of the 1960s, the Colonial Revival and Ranch wagon wheel themed units from the 1970s, and later those Mediterranean Romanesque mansard roof diners with angel stone monsters from the 1980s. They all have their own special appeal.

Some people believe the diner image is all about nostalgia and the past. I see it more as tradition and a very real part of the present. I was born in the 1960s, so what do I really know about life in the 1930s or 1940s or 1950s? And I'm not a hopeless romantic who believes things were so much better back then.

Although the diners celebrated on the following pages were very much a part of the past, they also are a part of our here and now. As Carly Simon sang, "These are the good old days." Enjoy.

Colin Strayer
Filmmaker
Toronto, Ontario

Acknowledgments

Every book, magazine article, website, or documentary that has appeared since 1978 on the history and culture of diners owes a debt of gratitude to Richard J. S. Gutman and John Baeder. This book is no exception. Their pioneering work to document the history of these roadside gems has directly and indirectly preserved countless diners for people to enjoy for years to come.

Thanks also to Larry Cultrera for generously sharing his considerable knowledge on this topic, and to Brian Butko, Kevin Patrick, Dave Hebb, Steve Harwin, Gary Thomas, Michael Engle, and Will Anderson for their contribution of information.

I especially thank the thousands of *Roadside* and *By the Way* magazine readers for their ongoing correspondence, support, and dedication to the cause. The diner owners who have seen fit to advertise in and distribute these magazines, published from 1990 to the present, also deserve my sincerest thanks. Of these, I have to single out Dennis "Skip" Scipione of the Blue Moon Diner for that first $150 in ad money, sight unseen, which funded the initial steps of this amazing journey.

Thanks also to the fine folks at Elcy's Coffee Shop in Glenside, Pennsylvania, for the coffee and brownies and for providing such a great environment to work on the first drafts.

This book never would have happened without the love and support of a core group of friends, enthusiasts, and family members who supplied information, places to stay, coffee to drink, food to eat, and advice to consider. Among this group, I must specifically thank Julie and George Lucey, Chris and Diane Carvell, Jerry Soucy, Gary "Weenieman" Zemola, Ron Dylewski, Joe Manning, and my mother, Elaine Garbin (hi, Mom!).

Teri Dunn, my collaborator and conscience, has soldiered with me through all the ups and downs and trials and tribulations of my broader roadside explorations.

My affable editor, Kyle Weaver, conceived and developed this series of diner guides and recruited me to write this New England volume. Thanks also to his diligent assistant David Reisch and meticulous copyeditor Joyce Bond.

Finally and foremost, I thank my ever-patient and loving wife, Louise, for bringing peace of mind and her steadfast support.

A Word about
Diner Manufacturers

Most of the diners listed in this book came from companies that specialized in their construction. For the purposes of helping you find a great meal during your travels or because of their historical value, this guide also includes several on-site or "stick-built" diners. I feel that to omit them for failing to meet the strictest definition of "diner" would do the reader a disservice—and cause me no small amount of grief from the legions of devoted regulars of these places.

One of the most frequently proposed stories people wanted to see published in *Roadside* magazine was a guide to identifying diner makes. Because of the numerous variations applied even to standard diner models, however, a comprehensive guide would inevitably get bogged down in mind-numbing details. How, for instance, would you describe the difference between a 1967 Mustang and a 1967 Camaro?

Nevertheless, some makes are easier to spot than others. In northern New England, for instance, you could safely bet that any diner with porcelain on the exterior likely came from Worcester Lunch Car. But outside New England, only about a dozen Worcesters exist, so you can generally eliminate that possibility.

Silk City diners built between the late 1930s and the mid-1950s varied only in the use of exterior cladding. Their shapes, sizes, and configurations mostly conformed to similar templates.

Mountain Views stand out because of their cowcatcher corners or scroll-like ornaments at the roofline. Kullmans, Paramounts, O'Mahonys, and Foderos—the most popular of the makes—become much more problematic to spot, especially in the later years. The companies often freely borrowed design elements as they saw fit, something they still do. When in doubt, look for the tag. If you can't find a tag, ask the owner.

Several of the descriptions that follow come directly from *Diners of Pennsylvania*, by Brian Butko and Kevin Patrick, altered here mainly for the sake of regional relevance. The basic list of manufacturers and the dates of operation were borrowed from Richard J. S. Gutman's *American Diner Then and Now*.

DeRaffele. 1933–present. Vertical fluting in the 1940s, fluted corners combined with streamline style in the 1950s, angular vestibule overhang starting about 1960, zigzag rooflines in the 1960s, arched windows with orange tile mansard in the 1970s.

Fodero. 1933–81. Either horizontal stainless or flat vertical porcelain fluting in the 1940s, both having rounded corners with stainless sunburst. The company used the name **National** from 1940 to 1945 and thereafter referred to those models as Foderos. Vertical stainless ribs below roofline in the 1950s.

Kullman. 1927–present. Vertical fluting in the 1940s, picture windows beginning in 1950, 5-foot-wide canopy starting in 1955. The company began making other structures in 1969, and by 1990 only 7 percent of its output was diners.

Master. 1947–circa 1957. Earlier diners featured fluted exteriors with stained-glass transom windows.

Mountain View. 1939–57. Distinctive rolling roofline and glass block corners after war, cowcatcher corners in the late 1940s to early 1950s, square roof corners in the early 1950s, and thin scrolls at roofline in the late 1950s.

Paramount. 1932 to present. Porcelain flutes in the late 1930s with rounded monitor roofs. Credited as the first maker to incorporate stainless steel interior surfacing. Completely stainless with burnished circles or verticle fluting in the 1940s. Large plate-glass windows and flared rooflines in the late 1950s to early 1960s.

Sterling. 1936–42. Former coach builder that retooled to build diners. Barrel-monitor hybrid style clad in porcelain panels. Its Streamliner was a dramatic bullet-nosed diner designed to evoke railroad imagery.

Swingle. 1957–88. Vertical stainless fluting along roofline on early models.

Tierney. 1905–33. Barrel roof, porcelain tile surfaces, and marble countertops.

Ward & Dickinson. 1923–circa 1940. Niagara-region manufacturer that sent diners throughout Pennsylvania, upstate New York, and Ohio. Its railcar-style diners were topped by high clerestories. Not a particularly popular make in New England, where only one known example remains in Willamantic, Connecticut.

Worcester Lunch Car. 1910–61. Builder of lunch wagons until the 1920s. From 1920s to early 1930s, most cars were barrel-roofed units with steel plate exteriors wrapping interiors that featured marble counters and porcelain tile. From 1930 to 1953, company built monitor-roofed deluxe models as well as larger, more elaborate barrel roof diners, and began using porcelain enamel panel exteriors. Immediately before World War II, began to construct streamlined diners, elaborate monitor roof diners with slanted ends. The company also built two circular diners with full bullet-ended streamlining, both now destroyed. From 1953 on, incorporated more stainless steel on its last eleven diners in an effort to compete with the New Jersey builders.

In addition, a few other companies are represented in the New England landscape: Lowell-based **Pollard** (1926–27) has two known examples; **Bixler** (1931–circa 1937) only one (and just barely, as it has been remodeled frequently) in Stamford, Connecticut; and three **Musi/Sunshine** (1966–present?).

Several manufacturers stamped the job number assigned during construction onto their builder plates. This included Worcester (from 1945 on), Mountain View, Silk City, and Sterling. O'Mahony and Swingle also gave their cars serial numbers but did not typically make them evident in the public areas.

Both Mountain View and Worcester diners were numbered consecutively, apparently indicating when an order was placed. Worcester would continue to use the original number when diners were returned to the factory for refurbishment. Worcester numbers spanned from 200 to 851 and Mountain View's ended at 533. The Route 66 in Springfield, Massachusetts, is 532.

Most Silk City and Sterling serial numbers corresponded to the year of construction, followed by a job number. Finely Fran's Diner, a Sterling, was 363, or the third diner built in 1936. Cassidy's Diner in Meriden, Connecticut, is 49212, or the 212th diner built in 1949 (a lot of diners for one year!). Though you won't find any in New England, early 1960s Silk City numbering seemed to abandon that scheme. A Silk City numbered 3071 was not built in 1930, but no one has yet discovered the reason for the change.

Swingle's numbering scheme similarly corresponded to the date of the diner's order but also included letters indicating the diner's configuration. The Parthenon Diner in Branford, Connecticut, is numbered 385DKDR, indicating that it was constructed in March 1985 and was a diner with kitchen and dining room. An L would represent an L-shaped dining area, and V a vestibule.

A Word about Diner Styles

The following are general categories of diner styles developed by the authors of *Diners of Pennsylvania* (Stackpole Books, 1999), Brian Butko and Kevin Patrick. The styles are based on traits typical for the era. Not all features are listed, and some styles overlap periods. Years are also approximate.

Barrel Roof (1910–35)

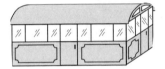

Exterior: Wood and porcelain enamel; sliding doors at front center and side.

Interior: Marble counter; porcelain enamel ceiling with vents; honeycomb tile floor; walls of 2-by-4-inch off-white and green tiles. Booths and restrooms are introduced. Cooking is done behind the counter.

Note: This category also includes the few monitor roof diners from the 1930s (usually Ward & Dickinsons).

Modern Stainless (1935–55)

Exterior: Large porcelain panels or vertical fluting in early years, stainless facade later; glass block, corners rounded in early years then getting squarer; monitor-style or rounded roof.

Interior: Booths at one end; stainless steel backwall behind counter, with sunburst pattern; Formica countertops and ceilings; 4-inch square-tile walls of yellow, pale blue, pink, or gray. Cooking is done behind the counter or in an attached kitchen or both.

Exaggerated Modern (1955–65)
Exterior: Stainless steel with colored horizontal bands of flexglas or anodized aluminum; large, canted windows; wide, flared canopies with zigzag shape and recessed lights; flat roof.
Interior: Booths at both ends and along front windows; terrazzo floor of pink or green; tiered ceiling with mirror strip. Cooking is seldom done behind the counter.

Environmental (1965–85)
Exterior: Stone or brick facade; brown or red mansard roof; colonial traits, such as coach lamps, or Mediterranean traits, such as pillars or arched windows.
Interior: Wood grain; curtains and carpeting; brown or avocado upholstery; stools with backrests; wagon-wheel or chimney-flue chandeliers; acoustic tile ceilings with faux wooden beams; copper fixtures. No cooking is done behind the counter.
Note: Many older diners have been remodeled in this style, some retaining their original interiors.

Postmodern (1985–present)
Exterior and interior. Reinterpretation of classic diner elements: quilted stainless steel, neon trim, black-and-white-checkered walls, chrome fixtures, glass block, boomerang Formica on tables and counters. No cooking is done behind the counter.
Note: The category also includes the late-modern style, a transition between environmental and postmodern typified by black or mirrored glass exteriors. Some older diners have been remodeled with postmodern elements.

ABBREVIATIONS USED ON MAPS

Barrel Roof = BR	Modern Stainless = MS
Exaggerated Modern = EM	Environmental = E
Postmodern = P	Remodeled = R
On Site = OS	Retro = Retro

NEW ENGLAND:
THE DINER MECCA

W hat more natural birthplace for the American diner than New England? Developed to serve the needs of hungry, late-shift mill workers in the expanding industrial towns in the last half of the nineteenth century, the diner's predecessor, the lunch wagon, became yet another ingenious method for ambitious men and women to achieve the American dream. With a little bit of money, a lot of determination, and plenty of luck, any Joe could open up his own diner.

And all of these "Joes" had Walter Scott to thank for sparking the idea. A budding entrepreneur in the age of Horatio Alger, Scotty noticed that all the restaurants in his native Providence, Rhode Island, closed after serving dinner. Meanwhile, the factories stayed open all night, and the workers inside still needed something to eat. Converting a horse-drawn freight wagon, he set up a mobile operation to dispense simple but hot meals on the street corner outside the offices of the *Providence Journal*.

Though Scotty hardly invented the idea of serving meals from a mobile structure, the stars aligned around his initiative, spawning imitators and an industry. The simple converted freight wagon evolved into an ornate, enclosed, rolling lunch counter, complete with seating. Competition by an expanding roster of builders brought more innovations to the trade. Builders constructed larger and more stylish, but still prefabricated and movable, structures that featured booth service, ceramic tile interiors, refrigeration, and toilets. The counter and the idea that the customer could get a good but inexpensive hot meal any time of the day have remained constants throughout the diner's 125-year evolution. The diner was actually America's first fast-food restaurant.

Providence rightly claims itself as the birthplace of the diner concept, but Worcester, Massachusetts, gets the credit for starting the industry of building diners. This centrally located industrial powerhouse, home of many firsts, saw Samuel Messer Jones set up shop building wagons for others under his employ to operate. After Jones came C. H. Palmer, then T. J. Buckley, Wilfred Barriere, and Charlie Gemme and his Worcester Lunch Car Company, who all built wagons or diners for sale to others. For a short while around the turn of the century, Worcester reigned supreme as the center of

Main Street, North Adams, Mass.

Around the turn of the century, many roving lunch wagons settled into more or less permanent locations, either due to city ordinance or because the operator recognized a good location when he saw it. This wagon appeared North Adams, Massachusetts, around the turn of the century.

the diner industry, with some builders churning them out by the dozens for use in towns and cities all over the industrial Northeast and beyond.

Soon lunch wagons appeared just about anywhere a crowd might gather. Early names included colorful terms such as dog wagon, White Eagle, and Night Owl. Many eventually were called diners, which capitalized on the romantic image of railroad dining and the similarity between the two structural forms. To this day, many people still propagate the myth born from simple marketing of diners as converted railroad cars. Building diners that looked like railcars hardly required much special engineering, given the comparable proportions, and indeed some railcar builders expanded into this field as a hedge against economic recession.

Worcester held its position as a diner-building center for only a short period. In a story that closely parallels that of the rest of American industrial history, the epicenter moved south, though only as far as New York and New Jersey. The faster-growing population and economy made this shift almost inevitable. Companies such as Tierney and O'Mahony soon displaced Worcester Lunch Car as the predominant builders, and those two companies led to the founding of many others.

The iconic image of the diner most people envision most likely came from those built in New Jersey. Handcrafted by meticulous artisans who perfected the form, the streamlined and stainless steel clad beacons along the roadside advertised the singular purpose of food service in a setting built with an unmatched level of workmanship. New England gave birth to the diner, but New Jersey took it to its logical extremes.

By the 1920s, most diner manufacturing had left the region, but a few makers lingered on. Lowell's Pollard Company built a small number of diners in that decade, of which only two still exist. In Springfield, Massachusetts, the Wason Manufacturing Company struggled through the Depression with few orders for its railroad cars, so it converted its line into diner building. Similarly, the J. B. Judkins coach builders in Merrimac, Massachusetts, jumped into diner construction after the demise of its coach-building markets. Judkins remains most notable for introducing the sectional diner and for its much-loved Sterling Streamliner, with its bullet-nosed end caps. None of these companies saw the end of World War II.

Until 1961, Worcester Lunch Car limped along as New England's sole representative in the industry. Unfortunately, its stubbornly Yankee reputation for sturdy but staid diners did not serve it well in a business that increasingly celebrated newer, shinier, and larger. The players all generally leapfrogged each other with new outlandish designs and advances in food service efficiency. While the Jersey builders churned out gleaming, streamlined, stainless, and Formica-clad structures, Worcester chugged along with

The diner at its nadir. The Central Square Diner left this Leominster, Massachusetts, location in 1986, and then spent some time in storage in Kensington, Connecticut. In 1989, a South Carolina restaurateur purchased it at auction for incorporation into a larger restaurant, but the plans fell through. Today it sits dismantled in a warehouse in Aiken, South Carolina.

This is how they move them. In 1995, Gary Zemola purchased this 1941 Silk City and removed it from its original location in Meriden, Connecticut. Zemola never got his venture off the ground, though he still heads up the Super Duper Weenie in Fairfield, Connecticut, serving up the finest hot dogs in the country. He has since sold the diner to restorer Steve Harwin of Cleveland, who fixed it up for the Gilmore Car Museum in Hickory Corners, Michigan.

its quaint, cozy, barrel roof diners, which appealed to an ever-shrinking local market.

Eventually the diner industry and the New England restaurant industry, for all intents and purposes, turned their backs on each other. Worcester Lunch Car closed up shop in 1961, delivering its last diner in 1957. The Jersey builders, increasingly threatened by the franchised chains, sent only a trickle of new units farther north than Fairfield County, Connecticut. The region's remaining diners, mostly small, aging facilities in declining neighborhoods, became increasingly marginalized. The restaurant industry's most successful players developed operations where the food now waited for its customers. Those customers, in turn, waited in line to order and pay for that food, often carrying it away for consumption in their cars.

With the concept of actual service marching slowly into obsolescence, the future for the diner, with its onerous overhead of servers, dining areas, and food prep, looked increasingly bleak. Baby boomers' families increasingly patronized fast-food establishments offering quick, cheap burgers and fries, seemingly without concern for nutrition or the economic and social impact of losing so many independently operated businesses.

But fortunately the diner survived and in some places even thrives. The wholesale demolition of diners has largely stopped, and even in New England, the numbers of diners in operation has increased by a small degree in the last fifteen years. Diner aficionados with an appreciation for a better class of comfort food can look to this region for standard-bearers. Yankee ingenuity lives on in a small number of classic gems run by culinary school graduates seeking to wipe the diner clean of its greasy-spoon image. Others have rediscovered diner operation as a difficult but ultimately rewarding vocation, where the little guy has an opportunity to make a positive impact on the local community.

The diner has finally come full circle, with the industry and society at large now appreciating this distinctly American restaurant form. To be sure, some diners are still lost to the bulldozer, obsolescence, and a lack of appreciation, but more often than not, someone will at least make an attempt to find the diner a new home, whether that means installation in a museum or movement to a new location to serve a grateful market.

HOW THE GUIDE WORKS

This guide delineates the region's geography along fairly subjective cultural designations, rather than the more convenient state borders. Grouping Rhode Island with southeastern Massachusetts, for example, acknowledges the influence of the Portuguese and French Canadian populations that overlap state lines and reflects operational styles of the diners in that area. This regional grouping also attempts to distribute the listings more evenly.

Anyone living in New England knows full well that southwestern Connecticut looks and feels more like New York Metro than New England, and not surprisingly, the size and style of the region's diners support that perception. Diners in Fairfield County tend to be newer, larger, and almost universally Greek-owned.

Nevertheless, some of the smaller, cozier places still attract people with a dream, not only to serve good food, but also to serve as a strong thread binding their local communities. With their owners actually working in the diner, if not right behind the counter, customers know instinctively that an O'Rourke's Diner is most likely owned by someone named O'Rourke and that, more often than

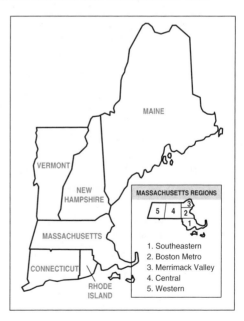

not, they can ask for him by name. This remains a characteristic of almost every diner, but it especially holds true for the small cars.

Today many of New England's remaining 355 diners continue to forge along in the mill towns. Worcester still holds sway with eight operating diners, though this is down from almost a dozen just ten years ago. Boston, the region's largest city and de facto capital, retains surprisingly few diners within its borders proper, but the surrounding communities play host to many of the region's best.

In southwestern Connecticut, the typical diner hardly fits the stereotypical image. The area's proximity to the remaining builders allowed owners to update and upgrade frequently, replacing their worn-out stainless

---

RECOMMENDED READING

No exploration of diner history should begin without at least a casual reading of *American Diner Then and Now*, by Richard J. S. Gutman (Johns Hopkins University Press). Universally recognized as one of the founding fathers of the growing appreciation of this distinctly American architectural form, Gutman has painstakingly chronicled the progress of diner history, from its "invention" by Walter Scott, through its rise, fall, and rise again in the 1980s. His first book, *American Diner*, published in 1979, made many take a second look at something progress had already begun to bulldoze wholesale from the landscape.

If we think of Gutman's meticulous recounting of diner history as a left-brain effort, then John Baeder's *Diners* (Abrams) surely comes from the right side of that collective mind. A painter now well known for his loving use of these gems as his primary subjects, Baeder has elevated the image of the diner since the early 1970s. As an art director working on New York's Madison Avenue, Baeder spent much of his free time roving the countryside, photographing and documenting the diner's decline. The resulting work was depicted in *Diners*, first published in 1978 and updated in 1995. It inspires a wistful ache and a longing for a simpler, slower time.

Robert Williams, author of *Hometown Diners* (Abrams), does with a camera what Baeder does on canvas. A photographer for the *Philadelphia Inquirer*, Williams takes a journalistic approach to this topic. Unlike Baeder, he incorporates the diner's ultimate attraction—its humanity and how it enhances community at large.

Michael Witzel's lavishly produced *American Diner* (Motorbooks International) also contains heaping helpings of nostalgic imagery as it recounts diner history.

Though not specifically about diners, Chester Lieb's *Main Street to Miracle Mile* (Johns Hopkins University Press) puts their progress and decline into a broader cultural and historical context. What hit the diners during the ascent of fast-food chains also hit every mom-and-pop establishment.

diners with newer models styled to reflect the tastes of their mostly immigrant owners.

Sharing the Connecticut River valley, Western Massachusetts and Vermont have a predominantly rural character and a mutual distrust for Boston and New York political power. Most of the diners in this region came from Worcester Lunch Car, but western Massachusetts currently claims one of the region's newest diners, influenced by the recent retro craze.

In New Hampshire and Maine, diners are scattered widely. Sometimes scenic and sometimes just plain rugged, these two states have seen a small resurgence in the numbers of diners in recent years, with several vintage units transplanted from other regions. Included in that group are two brand

---

Though he also includes other roadside attractions, Maine-based Will Anderson's growing library of self-published books have become required reading for anyone with an interest in the topic. The best of the lot, *Where Have You Gone Starlite Cafe?* works the premise of taking a vintage postcard and tracking the history of its subject. Of his others, *Good Old Maine, More Good Old Maine, Lost Diners,* and *Roadside Restaurants* all contain plenty of diner-related information. These books can be ordered directly from the author: Anderson & Sons Publishing, 34 Park St., Bath, ME 04530.

Specific to the towns north of Boston, Gary Thomas's *Diners of the North Shore* (Arcadia Publishing) conducts a visual tour of that region's diner history via a picture-and-caption template. Thomas's assembled images and thoughtful descriptions show a side of our culture too often neglected by mainstream historians: the world of the working class and where they ate. Thomas also gives the reader a good sense of the diner's mobility, as he painstakingly plots the changing locations of many diners past and present.

If you can find them, several out-of-print titles make excellent additions to the broader roadside library. Probably the first literary tour of diners ever published was *Diners of the Northeast* (1979), by Alan Bellink and Donald Kaplan, reissued in 1981 as *Classic Diners of the Northeast.* Amazingly, more than twenty years later, at least half a dozen of the diners in the book are still owned and operated by the same people.

Gerd Kittel's appreciative photographic exploration, *Diners: People and Places,* has little narrative, but it stylishly documents the state of the diners' preservation as of the late 1980s.

If you are a diner aficionado, you may want to consider acquiring Gutman's original *American Diner,* though it's not nearly as comprehensive as the reissue. It also contains three excellent photographic portfolios by Elliot Kaufman. This book usually fetches prices of $100 or more.

new diners built by Starlite Diners of Ormond Beach, Florida, for the Denny's restaurant chain. Its attempt to recast its image using the once shunned diner marks a milestone in the diner's resurrection, indicating in a very real sense that America has readopted the diner as a good place to bring the family.

Rhode Island and southeastern Massachusetts, an area that includes the popular vacation playground of Cape Cod, has also seen growth in diner numbers since 1990. The Cape has only two operating diners now, one of which arrived in 1992. This region also boasts two new Starlites and a new Dinermite design from Atlanta. Route 6, the historic highway that threads through the area, strings together a good dozen must-see places.

Vacation planners often overlook central Massachusetts as a destination, but roadside enthusiasts should not make that mistake. The area may not have the shoreline of the East or South or the mountains of the West and North, but its rich industrial heritage begs further discovery. Diner fans must visit Worcester, where they can see several diners still in operation, as well as the factory that built so many of them.

Navigating the densely populated towns and cities of Boston's North Shore makes for slow going, but it offers some great diners. Much of New England's industrial strength hailed from this area, so at one time it was thick with these eateries. Some of the more notable diners in this region still serve some of the finest meals you'll find anywhere.

DEFINITION OF DINERS
This guide adopts the definition of *diner* from Richard Gutman's seminal book of diner history, *American Diner Then and Now,* which defines the term as "a prefabricated structure with counter service hauled to a remote site." This guide also includes a handful of restaurants built on-site that have both the atmosphere and menu of the typical diner, while providing a quality experience you shouldn't miss. Failure to inform you of these deserving places would only do you a disservice should you travel to that region.

I have made every attempt to list all extant diners, not all of which are still in operation. The information is as current as possible, but keep in mind that the restaurant industry suffers a failure rate of 75 percent within the first two years of operation.

This guide highlights several diners for particular mention. These are diners that have an established history of service and enjoy solid support within their local markets. They also have something that sets them apart from the rest, be it the food, the personality, the degree of preservation, or all three. Additionally, their owners fully appreciate all their unique and special qualities, successfully balancing stewardship of the diner's beauty,

This could be the same Hope Diner now located in Bristol, Rhode Island, or possibly its precursor. Small diners such as these represented a chance at achieving the American dream for hardworking immigrants and other blue-collar workers.

utility, and place in our culture with the unforgiving demands of the marketplace. I regard these individuals as heroes, and I write this book as both a guide for the hungry traveler and a tribute to the owners' efforts.

I invite you, the reader, to share with me your experiences on the road. The landscape changes constantly, and as publisher of *Roadside* and *By the Way*, I've always maintained that our readers were our best resource. So by all means, jump in and share the ride.

RHODE ISLAND and SOUTHEASTERN MASSACHUSETTS

It began in Providence, though if not done by Walter Scott, someone else surely would have fashioned a canteen from a freight wagon and filled it with hot coffee and sandwiches to sell to people walking the streets at night. Indeed, others may have done just that, but Scotty's venture marked the beginning of what would evolve into an entire multimillion-dollar industry that served an estimated 22 billion meals over the course of 130 years.

Today anyone with the desire to return to this cultural mecca can still enjoy the diner experience in much the same way Scotty's patrons did. Every night at four o'clock, the Haven Brothers lunch wagon pulls out onto the streets of Providence, parks next to city hall, and stays there until the next morning at six. Though the current unit was not built by an established diner manufacturer, the original Haven Brothers was a T. H. Buckley White House Café built in 1893. Since then, Providence has unwittingly paid homage to its role in diner history.

The Haven Brothers lunch wagon has survived all the ups and downs of Providence, the restaurant industry, and an attempt by a former mayor to get it evicted. The charm of Haven Brothers lies purely in the experience of going there. The converted semitrailer sports few architectural features in common with its prefab counterparts.

Unfortunately, Rhode Island's capital city shows little other reverence, official or otherwise, for its diners or their history. As of this writing, Providence has only four diners still in operation, two fewer than it had just five years ago. In 2002, the city evicted the famous Silver Top Diner in a highly controversial move to make way for a luxury condominium complex. The Silver Top essentially served as the city's diner ambassador, having appeared in a painting by John Baeder, Donald Kaplan and Alan Bellink's book *Diners of the Northeast,* and just about every photojournalistic document on diners published since 1989—and deservedly so. Run for ten years by Pat Brown, the Silver Top was open only during the late-night hours in a then remote railroad-warehouse district ripe for a revival of some type.

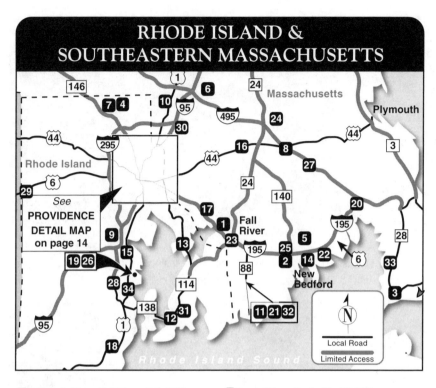

RHODE ISLAND & SOUTHEASTERN MASSACHUSETTS

Massachusetts

Plymouth

Rhode Island

See
PROVIDENCE
DETAIL MAP
on page 14

Fall River

New Bedford

Local Road

Limited Access

Rhode Island Sound

❶ Al Mac's Diner: Fall River, MA (MS)

❷ Angelo's Orchid Diner: New Bedford, MA (MS)

❸ Betsy's Diner: Falmouth, MA (MS)

❹ Blue Onion Diner: Woonsocket, RI (Retro)

❺ Blue Point Restaurant: Acushnet, MA (BR)

❻ Catman Cafe Mansfield, MA (MS)

❼ Champ's Diner: Pawtucket, RI (BR)

❽ Dave's Diner: Middleborough, MA (P)

❾ Denny's Diner: Warwick, RI (P)

❿ Don's Diner: Plainville, MA (MS)

⓫ Eddie's Diner: Westport, MA (MS)

⓬ Fourth Street Diner: Newport, RI (MS)

⓭ Hope Diner: Bristol, RI (BR)

⓮ Jake's Diner: Fairhaven, MA (MS)

⓯ Jigger's Diner: East Greenwich, RI (BR)

⓰ Joe's Diner: Taunton, MA (BR)

⓱ Juke Box Diner: Somerset, MA (P)

⓲ Kiddie Closet: Wakefield, RI (BR)

⓳ Louis Diner: Davisville, RI (BR)

⓴ Mill Pond Diner: Wareham, MA (MS)

㉑ My Tin Man Diner: Westport, MA (MS)

㉒ Nest Diner: Mattapoiset, MA (MS)

㉓ Nite Owl Diner: Fall River, MA (MS)

㉔ Roadside Diner: Middleboro, MA (BR)

㉕ Shawmut Diner: New Bedford, MA (MS)

㉖ Sherwood's Diner: Davisville, RI (BR)

㉗ Sisson's Diner: Middleboro, MA (Trolley)

㉘ Snoopy's Diner: North Kingstown, RI (MS)

㉙ State Line Diner: Foster, RI (MS)

㉚ Tex Barry's Coney Island: Attleboro, MA (BR)

㉛ Tommy's Deluxe Diner: Middletown, RI (MS)

㉜ Travelers Diner: Wesport, MA (MS)

㉝ Wendell's Corner Snack Bar: North Falmouth, MA (BR)

㉞ Wickford Diner: Wickford, RI (BR)

In much the same fashion as Walter Scott operated, Haven Brothers sets up in downtown Providence every night, serving a limited menu of burgers, hot dogs, and drinks.

With the city in the midst of a nationally recognized downtown renaissance, Mayor Buddy Cianci sought to introduce a greater residential component into the city's commercial mix, which now included an enormous upscale shopping mall. Plans to further the development of Providence into a truly world-class city ran into at least one obstacle in the form of a 1939 Kullman diner that stubbornly refused to get out of the way.

For her part, Pat didn't want to hinder the city's progress. Indeed, as with most other businesses downtown, she also benefited from the influx of new people and money coming into the capital, but she reasonably expected fair treatment by the city's development office, and if they wanted her to move, she deserved to get at least as viable a location.

Sadly, negotiations collapsed. In an attempt to stave off the inevitable and acquire additional negotiating leverage, Pat tried to get the diner listed on the National Register of Historic Places. When the historian she retained to research the history produced nothing, the city moved forward, offering her a "fair market value" price of $50,000, and condemned the property. The publicity over the fight attracted development officials in the nearby city of Pawtucket, who offered Pat a site in one of their own struggling mill districts, which they hoped to revive with the diner as its anchor. The plan received support not only from city hall, but also from restaurant architect Morris Nathanson, who kept his own offices nearby. A professed diner enthusiast, Nathanson looked forward to the idea of having a real diner within walking distance of his office's front door and offered his services pro bono.

The diner moved to a vacant lot in Pawtucket in 2002, but little has happened since. Pat's stated intention to continue operating during the overnight hours ran up against neighborhood opposition. Despite Pat's stellar record in this regard, residents of this crime-ridden, decaying neighborhood, bordering one of the busiest interstate highways in the nation, professed their concerns over the additional noise, traffic, and criminal element the diner might attract. A planned one-year project now pushes past two years without as much as a spoonful of dirt overturned.

Not long after the removal of the Silver Top, another Kullman, a 1946 Challenger model, almost left the city limits as well. Originally known as Poirier's Diner, this Atwells Avenue fixture endured enough ownership changes to justify the installation of a revolving door. In its last ten years of operation, the diner was called Arnold's, the Top Hat, John Anthony's, Carlo's Place, Krystal's, and finally El Faro. It closed in 1999 and collected dust until 2002, when a new developer sought to remove it. Ultimately, John Ozbeck, a city employee and a member of its planning board, purchased the diner because, as he put it, he "didn't want to see another diner leave Providence."

Thanks to the work of historian and architectural restorer Kim Smith, the diner now enjoys historic status, with a listing on the National Register as of August 2003. It sits on blocks in a small parking lot in the Westminster Street neighborhood that Ozbeck currently works to revitalize, with restoration of the diner serving as a key component in his plans.

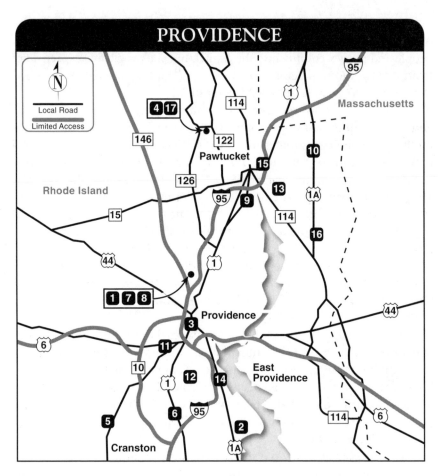

PROVIDENCE

Massachusetts

Rhode Island

Pawtucket

Providence

East Providence

Cranston

❶ Dandy Diner: Providence (BR)
❷ Ever Ready Diner: Providence (BR)
❸ Haven Brothers Diner: Providence (BR)
❹ Hickey's Lunch Wagon: Lincoln (BR)
❺ Johnny B's Diner: Cranston (BR)
❻ La Criolla Restaurant: Providence (BR)
❼ Lemoyne Diner: Providence (MS)
❽ Midway Diner: Providence (BR)
❾ Modern Diner: Pawtucket (MS)

❿ My Kids & Company: Pawtucket (E)
⓫ Pourier's Diner: Providence (MS)
⓬ Prairie Diner: Providence (BR)
⓭ Right Spot: Pawtucket (BR)
⓮ Seaplane Diner: Providence (MS)
⓯ Silver Top Diner: Pawtucket (MS)
⓰ Star Diner: E. Providence (MS)
⓱ Worcester Deluxe 101: Lincoln (MS)

By most measures, the city of Providence has entered a period of renaissance with a magnitude it hasn't seen since the nineteenth century. Unfortunately, like most urban revivals of this type, most of the positive effects remain confined to downtown and a few outlying parts formerly occupied by industrial concerns, but with the exception of Haven Brothers, you will not find any of the diners in the city's core. The city's East Side, long dominated by the presence of Brown University and the Rhode Island School of Design, has always maintained its general prosperity, but the district's blue-blooded heritage precluded the establishment of this blue-collar institution.

Many look at the issue of gentrification as a glass half full–half empty situation, all depending on the thirst of the drinker. Old diners in old neighborhoods in these mill towns typically don't fare well under these conditions. Unless the owners adapt their operations to meet the desires of its new, more upscale market, the value of the land will outstrip the ability of the business to justify the spike in property taxes or the ability of the owner to resist the offer to sell and clear out. In a few areas, such as Brooklyn's Williamsburg section, at least three such diners have made this successful conversion, but in places without the worldly sophistication of a major metropolis, serving fine wine in an old diner becomes a very tough sell.

With this in mind, a diner like the Seaplane would make the next likely target in the advance of the city's progress. The Seaplane is located on a main thoroughfare in the city's underutilized seaport district, where plans to redevelop the tank farms and idle port facilities into condos and upscale shopping have already begun. The diner, a vestige of the city's blue-collar past, continues today to hum along with its humble menu of meat-and-potatoes comfort food and big fresh sandwiches, and with luck will continue to do so for many more years.

The Seaplane Diner's partial exterior restoration raised the restaurant's profile along the Providence waterfront. This O'Mahony enjoys a reputation for hearty breakfasts and generously portioned fresh sandwiches.

Bob Arena and his son Mike have kept the Seaplane flying since the early 1970s. Most recently, they made preservationists happy by removing the T-111 facade to reveal the diner's original stainless steel skin. Further restoration awaits that would also strip away the diner's mansard roof. The Seaplane came from the O'Mahony plant in Elizabeth, New Jersey, in 1949, opening as Girard's Diner in Woonsocket. In 1973, new owners transported it to its current location and ultimately covered over its stainless gleam, then considered hopelessly garish and out of fashion.

Yet another oft-changed diner in another struggling neighborhood sits on Elmwood Street, the city's old gateway boulevard to and from the south. Last called La Criolla Restaurant, the 1947 Worcester car serves up Dominican cuisine. It currently stands closed and for sale. In the previous decade, this diner also saw a number of ownership and menu changes. Its location directly across the street from a city bus terminal has yet to do much to help it stay afloat, but given the changing ethnic makeup, the new wave of immigration may bode well for its future.

Finally, the undaunted diner hunter will find the Prairie Diner at Public and Prairie Streets, buried well within another depressed neighborhood. As one of fewer than ten operating Tierney Diners left in the country, no real diner tour would be complete without a stop here. The Prairie will present few surprises, and most evidence of the diner's original design is seen only on the inside. The structure now presents a boxed-over exterior, but inside you'll still see the original Tierney builder's tag, much of the backbar, and the marble counter.

North of Providence, the city of Pawtucket hosts a real diner landmark. In 1978, the Modern Diner became the first diner listed on the National Register of Historic Places. The distinction brought renewed attention to the cause of preserving these uniquely American constructions and helped stave off the destruction of an extremely rare Sterling Streamliner, a model built by J. B. Judkins between 1939 and 1941 that featured a dramatic architectural profile akin to a speeding locomotive. (See page 26.)

Taking U.S. Route 1 south from Providence, the lucky diner hunter comes across a great diner with an interesting story in the form of Jigger's in East Greenwich. In 1992, Carol Shriner decided to restore the empty shell and thus restore the community spirit to her adopted hometown, and as a result, she created a concept-defining restaurant cited in publications such as *Cuisine* magazine. Currently in the hands of Iva Reynhout, Jigger's still serves freshly prepared meals and local favorites on a now-bustling downtown. (See page 28.)

Until the publishing of Richard Gutman's second book on the history of diners, *American Diner Then and Now,* few people outside the diner-building industry had ever heard the name of Erwin Fedkenheuer. Yet Fedkenheuer was to diners what Les Paul was to the electric guitar. He didn't invent diners, but his specific innovation completely changed the stylistic direction of diner design for the next twenty years. According to Gutman, Fedkenheuer fashioned sheet metal for a Weehawkin manufacturer of restaurant equipment. His suggestion to the owner of Paramount Diners that stainless steel might look nice as trim on a diner then under construction eventually led to his employment there. Pretty soon, stainless steel appeared on just about every diner built, and on as many surfaces as practicable.

In the 1950s, Fedkenheuer and his son Erwin Jr. set out on their own, forming a company they called Erfed, which mostly performed renovations to existing diners. One of those diners operates in North Kingstown, Rhode Island, as Snoopy's Diner. It began as a 1940s vintage Silk City diner, and before Gutman revealed Fedkenheuer's impact on the industry, the renovations of Snoopy's confounded most diner archeologists at the time.

To the seasoned diner hunter, the interior screamed Silk City, with its diamond tile pattern along the wall and counter apron, the vaulted porcelain enamel ceiling, and the simple but streamlined, stainless steel grill hood with menu boards. The exterior looked like nothing that ever left the Paterson Vehicle Company factory, but the quality of the stainless work matched that of any Jersey builder.

Aside from Snoopy's place in diner history, the clean and well maintained little restaurant serves good, basic, hearty meals that will not likely

Snoopy's Diner is another New England anomaly, the only diner in New England renovated by Erwin Fedkenheuer, who started in the business bending stainless steel for Paramount Diners.

leave you hungry. The diner's location close to an exit off the Route 4 express-way to Newport makes it a convenient stop on your trip to the shore.

Nearby, one of the state's older diners still in business reopened in 2003 after yet another renovation. People love to make Wickford a stop on any tour of the Ocean State's shore towns because of its quintessential New England port town character. In the heart of it all, the visitor will find Tucker's Wickford Diner, with its seafood-heavy menu. Little remains of the original features of this 1930s vintage Worcester other than the general shape of the structure.

Across the bay in Newport, the 4th Street Diner, at the rotary just on the other side of the Newport/Pell Bridge, offers a good basic meal in a fairly well-preserved 1952 O'Mahony car. The diner was trucked into Newport from a site on U.S. Route 6 in Swansea, Massachusetts, in 1967, just two years before the opening of the bridge. Though it wasn't built in the factory, the kitchen addition came with it on a second flatbed. Set down at the major traffic circle just before the Newport Bridge to Jamestown, the diner has since benefited from its location at the entry point of the island's east-west connection.

On the other side of the island in Middletown, Tommy's Deluxe Diner keeps the home fries grilling in a diner steeped in local history. Serving originally as the second Al Mac's in Fall River, the diner came to Middle-town when Al McDermott replaced his large 1939 O'Mahony with a new DeRaffele car in 1953. Though the diner remains in very original condi-

The 4th Street Diner sits at the eastern end of the Newport Bridge at the entrance to this seaport community.

The former Al Mac's Diner has changed little since O'Mahony built it in 1939. Tommy's Deluxe is one of the best-preserved diners in the Ocean State.

tion, ownership has allowed time to take its toll on the building. A smoky atmosphere and televisions mounted in the corners do little to foster an atmosphere of conviviality, but the diner has successfully staved off the relentless onslaught of national chain restaurants bearing down with full force on the island.

Back on the mainland in Fall River, Al Mac's Diner stands out as one not to be missed by anyone interested in photographing diners. This diner's sign rates as one of the finest neon diner signs ever. The visual feast continues in and around the diner as well, with little changed from when McDermott purchased this gleaming gem. Run since the 1980s by Bud Bryer, Norm Gauthier, and families, Al Mac's serves well-made home-cooked meals. In 1999, Al Mac's joined fourteen other diners in Massachusetts currently listed on the National Register of Historic Places.

On the other end of town, the Nite Owl Diner closed in 2002 and awaited a new owner as this was written. The small, custom-built 1956 DeRaffele retains the layout of the lunch wagon it replaced, and until recently, its menu centered on hot dogs. The last owners to try their hand in this small space introduced full breakfasts and a broader lunch menu. Fall River's declining population and economic prospects have not boded well for the Owl.

Across the river, along U.S. Route 6 in Somerset, one of the state's newest diners, the Juke Box, arrived in 2000 via Diner-Mite of Atlanta. Diner-Mite,

Another unique DeRaffele creation lingers precariously on this Fall River corner. The Nite Owl Diner, laid out like a large lunch wagon, formerly specialized in hot dogs and deep-fried foods until it closed up shop in 2002.

which designs and markets budget-model retro diners built under contract by various modular construction firms, has built modular food-service structures under various names since 1959. Diner purists take issue with the lower level of craftsmanship in Diner-Mite offerings compared with the Jersey-built structures, and indeed, a typical Diner-Mite diner lacks the stylistic detail seen in the 1950s classics or those currently built by the remaining traditional makers. On the other hand, Diner-Mite will build a unit at one-third the cost of a typical DeRaffele.

This apparently attracted Donald Modesto, who installed his forty-seat Diner-Mite in a strip-mall parking lot on Route 6. The diner's menu mostly conforms to expectations of anyone looking to eat in a shiny retro diner, with heaping portions in a bright, clean atmosphere embellished with lots of ephemera.

Route 6 stretches across the lower half of New England, making for a scenic, diner-rich exploration of the region, and the stretch from Fall River to Cape Cod holds the richest lode of vintage diners per mile.

Continuing east from Fall River, a detour toward Horse Neck Beach eventually stretches to the Handy Hill Ice Cream stand, owned by the Sanford family, which plans a major splash in the diner world. In the lot adjacent to the stand loom two large diners resting on blocks awaiting restoration.

Quentin Sanford and his sister Bethany Sanford-Smith plan to combine the two large O'Mahony units into a single diner restaurant called the Handy Hill Diner.

The first of the two acquired by the Sanfords came from Quincy, Massachusetts. Eddie's Diner closed in 1993 after a fire gutted its interior. The Sanfords eventually purchased the charred hulk and moved it to their parking lot. In the meantime, they sought a second unit and got rather lucky, managing to acquire Eddie's sister diner, formerly known as the Traveler's, which had been sitting in storage since 1991, when a newer model replaced it on its location on Route 46 in Dover, New Jersey. The Traveler's width, bulging over 17 feet, made an overland route next to impossible and prohibited its transport by road across state borders, so the family hired Jan Shipping out of Dover to ship the structure by barge from Newark to a Fall River pier. From there, the movers loaded it onto a flatbed truck for the remaining mileage to Westport. The Sanfords estimate that this project will cost at least $1 million, a substantial sum for a restaurant in this lightly populated area.

Meanwhile, the family already owns another diner in East Providence, Rhode Island, called the Star Diner. It had been closed since 1999, and the Sanfords moved to save the diner after a deal to build a Zoots Dry Cleaners on the site fell through. Previous to that, beginning in the early 1960s, the 1951 DeRaffele served as a Chinese restaurant called the China Star, and

The Star Diner gleams but sits idle in Rumford, Rhode Island. Purchased by the Sanford family in 2001, the resplendent 1951 DeRaffele looks factory fresh thanks to their meticulous restoration, but as of early 2004, it still awaits an opening date.

before that it was Keenan's Diner. The Sanfords have done a remarkable job of refurbishment on the diner and its equally stylish addition, but have repeatedly pushed back planned openings. As of this writing, the Sanfords have owned the diner for more than three years and have yet to pour a single cup of coffee.

Leaving behind Westport, you enter New Bedford, where there is another pair of must-see classics. The Shawmut Diner, just off exit 3 on Route 140, beckons with a recently restored neon Indian head. It came into national focus when its owner, Phil Paleologos, began to broadcast a nationally syndicated talk radio program. If the fine food wasn't enough, early morning customers were treated to the sight of Phil chatting up a storm over the airwaves. (See page 33.)

On Rockdale Street, you will find Angelo's Orchid Diner open for business for breakfast and lunch most days, but only breakfast on weekends. The diner's tight location at a major intersection on Route 6 only enhances the landmark quality of this well-kept gem. The diner generates a busy atmosphere and makes a very popular salmon pie, served only on Fridays.

Though Jake's Diner, at 114 Alden Road, looks like a longtime resident of Fairhaven, it only arrived on its location in 1989. Before that, the early 1950s O'Mahony serviced the old Route 20 post road on the southern corner of Worcester, Massachusetts, as Joe's Diner. Brought to its current location by the late Jake Kalife, who also owned the lumberyard next door, the diner has a unique band of ceramic tile across its facade. Inside, Kalife made

Angelo's Orchid Diner greets travelers to New Bedford coming from the west on U.S. Route 6.

Interior of the Nest Diner. Current operator Randy St. John has brought new life and great meals to this roadside treasure.

a few other minor renovations and ran a popular hangout until his death in 1998. His family kept the grills hot until late 2003, when they sold the diner to Tom Guard. According to early reports, he's done much to further improve the diner's food and service.

The Nest Diner on Route 6 in Mattapoisett, with two previous locations, ranks among the most-moved diners in New England. It left the factory in Signac, New Jersey, in 1951 for a location in East Providence, and then for another in Wareham, Massachusetts. In 1964, the diner came to its current location, its void soon filled by the much larger Mill Pond Diner. Once in Mattapoisett, it took on the name of its new host community. The Mattapoisett saw a succession of operators throughout the 1990s, most leasing it from local real estate developer Ron Talenti. Near perfectly preserved, the diner became the Nest Diner after Dana Barrows purchased it from Talenti in 1998, running it until 2003. Barrows gave the diner its name in homage to a locally well-regarded restaurant located next door. In 2003, its current owners, Randy and Barbara St. John, stepped into breach and have continued to build up the diner's popularity with locals and travelers alike. Some of this popularity comes, no doubt, from their heavenly Grape-Nut custard pudding, a dessert not to be missed.

The Mill Pond Diner sits on a bend in the road on Route 28 just before it merges with U.S. Route 6, less than a mile from the exit off I-195. Current owner Bill "Biffy" Goyette has owned this eighty-seat O'Mahony since the late 1970s and has kept it in mostly original condition, complete with a grand external clock perched on the vestibule, though it does now show its age.

At the town of Bourne, Route 6 and Route 28 split, with Route 28 heading south and Route 6 continuing east toward Cape Cod. South of Bourne, Route 28 passes by the former location of the much-beloved My Tin Man Diner, which burned in 2000 and was removed in 2003. Take the old road to Falmouth to visit Wendell's Corner Snack Bar, arguably one of the oldest operating diners in the country and a relatively well-kept 1920s Tierney. Attached to Wendell's is a stick-built addition incorporating the kitchen and additional seating for those who do not enjoy sitting on stools.

Betsy's Diner in downtown Falmouth came to the region in 1992 as a vintage transplant trucked up from Allentown, Pennsylvania. A successful operation from day one, Betsy's is a prime example of the right way to make a diner a bona fide family restaurant. (See page 34.)

The remainder of southeastern Massachusetts no longer provides much for the diner hunter. Outside of the immediate Boston-Providence corridor, this region consisted mostly of small farming towns that, until recent years, saw little population growth or industry. The few industrial towns, such as Middleborough, Taunton, and Mansfield, all still have diners, but on the roads in between, most have made way for fast-food chains. Cranberry bogs still dot the landscape, but in the past twenty years, rampant sprawl has transformed the region from rural to suburban.

The only Tierney in Massachusetts, Wendell's is hard to find but worth the effort.

This Starlite diner came to Massachusetts in 1998, making it the first for the upstart builder. Since then, Dave's Diner has developed a large following, with its expertly prepared homestyle cooking and cranberry walnut pancakes.

Middleborough, in the heart of this area, has one of the oldest and one of the newest of all the diners listed in this book. Sisson's Diner (see p. 31), which lies on the south side and was built in the 1910s as a trolley car and converted to a diner in 1926, contrasts with Dave's Diner, built and installed in the center of town in 1997. Dave's Diner, near the Route 18, 44, and 28 rotary, came to the area in 1997 from the Starlite factory in Ormond Beach, Florida. Bursting at the seams with 1950s ephemera, the shiny new theme restaurant mostly pays homage to a period when diners served as reputable family restaurants before Howard Johnson's and others ran off with their mantle. Dave's serves pretty good food as well, which has kept customers returning.

This tour ends with Tex Barry's Coney Island in Attleboro. The

The sign says it all. Located near the heart of downtown Attleboro, Tex Barry's Coney Island is one of the oldest diners operating in the country today.

humble little 1926 Worcester car announces itself with little more than a simple neon hot dog hanging over the sidewalk on the outskirts of downtown. Inside, the mostly original gem serves not much more than what its name suggests. Regulars usually order hot dogs in pairs, with the works.

Tex has owned the diner since 1982 and credits much of its success to its secret chili sauce, but the charm of the place by itself would top off the hot dogs quite nicely. Originally called the County Diner, it has changed little since its installation. The structure retains its original marble counter and ceramic tile floor and backbar. Don't go too early, as Tex's opens at 10:00 A.M. every day except Sunday.

MODERN DINER
1940 STERLING #4140
364 East Ave., Pawtucket, RI • (401) 726-8390

With more than thirty diners now listed on the National Register of Historic Places, the distinction has become almost commonplace. Massachusetts likely will claim as many as twenty of those diners by the time you read this. It all began with a very distinctive diner in Pawtucket, Rhode Island, called the Modern. Ironically, in 1978, the rare Sterling Streamliner hardly looked very modern anymore, but its dramatic bullet-nosed end, which flowed back across the length of the structure, exemplified a period in America's history when we looked optimistically toward the future. The striking profile of the Modern installed against a large building on its left end gave it the appearance of a train emerging from a tunnel. Inside, the diner had changed little since J. B. Judkins Company of Merrimac, Massachusetts, built it as one of nineteen Sterling Streamliners constructed between 1939 and 1941.

But in 1978, the future looked pretty bleak for the Modern. The Pawtucket Redevelopment Authority planned to demolish it to make way for new construction. During the darkest days of diner history, when development and obsolescence caused dozens of other classic diner gems to be plowed under, the Rhode Island Historic Preservation Commission decided to take a stand on behalf of the Modern and make it the first diner placed on the National Register. Placing the diner on the register would buy some time for the diner and give efforts to relocate it a fighting chance. One obstacle potentially precluded that listing, however: In 1978, the diner was only thirty-eight years old, twelve years shy of the National Park Service's fifty-year criterion. In the end, the Park Service, which administers the register, made an exception based on the commission's argument that the Modern was "one of two well preserved surviving examples of the Sterling Streamliners, remarkable landmarks in the history of American design and food-service merchandizing and key monuments in the history of that uniquely American melding of the two—the roadside fast-food restaurant, which had its beginnings in Rhode Island." It cited the Salem Diner in Salem, Massachusetts, as the other example.

This proved a watershed event in the history of the diner industry. That same year, Richard Gutman published his first book on diner history, *American Diner,* just after John Baeder's *Diners* hit the shelves.

Unfortunately, the Pawtucket Redevelopment Authority prematurely announced its intent to condemn most of the properties on that block, which had the almost immediate effect of killing the diner's business. Once finally condemned, the diner lay dormant for the next four years while the authority considered its next move. Worried about the effects of vandalism suffered by the newly landmarked building, the authority finally put the diner on the market in 1982, though it had yet to begin any work on the project that had forced the diner's condemnation in the first place. With promises to pay for "reasonable expenses" to move the building, the authority finally found a buyer in the Demou family, who moved it to its current location on East Avenue. The Demous constructed a new kitchen for the business and a small additional dining room with bar.

Currently operated by Nick Demou, a hardworking graduate of the Johnson & Wales Culinary School, the Modern has largely helped redefine what constitutes diner cuisine. Though Nick shuts down after the lunch trade hits the road, his weekend breakfast specials would seem to belong more in a fancy continental bistro. Customers get to feast on such items as challah French toast with apples and brie, a wide variety of fairly exotic omelets, and plate-covering pancakes topped with fresh fruit.

JIGGER'S DINER
1947 WORCESTER #826
145 Main St., East Greenwich, RI • (401) 884-5388

The sleepy town of East Greenwich has enjoyed its own minirenaissance over the past decade. At the heart of it, Jigger's Diner has both propelled it and benefited from it, but as late as 1990, this eventual symbiosis looked extremely unlikely. The 1950 Worcester had fallen on hard times and suffered the indignity of seeing its interior stripped away and its structure used as a storage space for an adjacent paint store. Knowing this can only astound anyone who goes there now to savor the johnnycakes, homemade ice cream, homemade corned beef hash, hearty coffee, and stunningly original Worcester Lunch Car interior design. Or so it seems.

In the late 1980s, Carol Shriner and her then husband had purchased the property, which included the diner with its kitchen and storage converted into an apartment. They rented the empty shell to the paint store and the apartment to tenants. From the turn of the century, four diners operated out of this sliver of space on the town's Main Street. First there was a lunch cart, which then made way for a larger, stationary diner. In 1928, a still larger Worcester dubbed Jigger's came to town and uprooted number two. In 1950, the current Jigger's took its place, sending number three back to the Worcester factory for renovations. That diner subsequently was shipped to a new location in Wareham, becoming the Breaker 19 Diner. It moved again in 1990 to South Carolina, and then again in the mid-1990s to Santa Monica, California, and into the Track 16 Art Gallery.

By 1990, Carol began to take a second look at the diner. Having spent ten years in biochemistry research at Brown University, she seriously considered a transition into the restaurant field. Though she had no previous experience, Carol prepared for the change by taking a job at the nearby Beacon Diner in Greenwich, first washing dishes and then working the grill and doing a little baking.

Undaunted by the work at the Beacon, Carol began the restoration of Jigger's, which had been closed for ten years and was completely devoid of most of its original interior features. She relied upon the help of a carpenter friend, her own hands-on efforts, and the holes left behind by pulled nails and screws to help her figure out what went where. The work began in January 1992 and required Carol to completely reconstruct the diner's entire counter, backbar, and grill hood and replace all the booths, which had been long since removed. Today only an experienced diner historian could discern that much of the diner's interior is brand new and that the hardwood booths came from a different diner, the ultimately demolished Colonial in Brockton, Massachusetts, notable as one of the first Sterling diners ever built.

The woman responsible for reviving the East Greenwich landmark takes a seat at Jigger's Diner's reconstructed counter. Carol Shriner sold Jigger's in 2000 and moved to Vermont, but she leaves behind a lot of happy customers grateful for her efforts.

Six months later, Jigger's finally reopened its doors—to the rave reviews of customers, this author, and the local media. Eventually, even a few national rags chimed in with high praise. Carol noted that some people came to her with tears in their eyes to express their gratitude for bringing back one of their favorite diners.

The revived Jigger's now featured a menu filled with a whole host of homemade items that one might expect from a graduate of a good culinary school, but its new owner came to the grill with a graduate degree in biochemistry, no personal history with diners, and a five-acre organic vegetable farm. Carol attributed her particular style simply to her own personal tastes and her courage to try something different. In a sense, her lack of experience with diners brought her into the field without any preconceived notions and with a willingness to try anything. To Carol, making sausage was easy, as were baking bread and grilling up a special omelet every day.

The progress of Jigger's seemed to parallel that of East Greenwich. Though the town still clings to a few empty storefronts and marginal Main Street businesses, for better or worse, the advance of gentrification has firmly established a foothold, bringing to the town a new sense of prosperity.

In 1997, Carol's hard work and imagination received some gold-plated acknowledgment from a three-page article in *Gourmet* penned by roadside food mavens Jane and Michael Stern, who poured out their praise. The article told the entire country what everyone in and around Narragansett Bay already knew: that the little diner with the curious name had established a welcome new standard in short-order cooking. For a few weeks after the article hit the newsstands, locals noted all the New York license plates on cars parked on Main Street just outside the diner.

By the end of the decade, Carol had decided that running a diner made for too harsh a taskmistress and began quietly searching for a buyer. Today Carol attributes her decision mainly to an inability to stabilize turnover. Because she had no family to rely upon, like many do at this level of the restaurant business, she had a difficult time covering for a slacking waitress or a dishwasher who suddenly quit. Such problems soon sap the joy out of the experience, but Carol remained patiently determined to find a buyer who would change as little as possible.

In 2000, it seemed that Carol had found exactly such a person in Iva Reynhout. Indeed, Iva even bears a subtle resemblance to Carol, but more important, if you didn't know she had sold the place, you'd think Carol still lurked somewhere behind the scenes. The customers continue to turn out in similar numbers. Iva recently began Friday Gourmet Nights, when she treats the customers to a higher level of cuisine.

Meanwhile, Carol has embarked on yet another career, as innkeeper in the Vermont town of Eden, where she operates a bed and breakfast with her new husband. Carol expresses few regrets about leaving the business, and fortunately, because of Iva's near-seamless transition into Carol's place, customers need only regret losing the daily opportunity to chat with the woman responsible for restoring part of this community's very soul. For that, East Greenwich, diner fans, and lovers of good food will always owe Carol a debt of gratitude.

SISSON'S DINER
1910s WASON
561 Wareham St., Middleborough, MA • (508) 946-0359

One of the more notable roadside attractions of New England sits aside Route 28 in South Middleboro in the form of Sisson's Diner, which is the only actual trolley car diner in New England. (In Chepachet, Rhode Island, two former trolleys now serve as the kitchen for a larger restaurant.) Built sometime in the second decade of the twentieth century in Springfield, Massachusetts, by Wason Manufacturing for Brill, this diner essentially shipped itself to its site in 1926. When tracks still ran along Route 28, the trolley rolled down the road under its own power until it reached its current

Sisson's Diner has resisted the ravages of time remarkably well since it rolled down the tracks for the last time in 1926.

location. Workers then picked it up and carried it to the side of the road to prepare it for its conversion by Elmer Sisson.

Before the 1920s, diner owner hopefuls frequently purchased retired trolley cars for quick conversion into food service. Though a less expensive proposition, it also introduced some rather flimsy buildings into the business, ill suited for the demands of the diner trade. Already beaten up from thousands of miles of service, these refugees from the dying trolley and interurban industries did little to enhance the reputation of diners in general. Diner builders responded by improving their own products.

Sisson's somehow endured and has changed little through the years. The trolley's small space makes for cozy dining, but Sisson's does have additional seating in its attached dining room. The charming café serves only breakfast and lunch most days. Its eighty years of service have proven the exception to the historical rule of converted trolleys.

SHAWMUT DINER

1953 O'MAHONY

943 Shawmut Ave., New Bedford, MA • (508) 993-3073

The Shawmut Diner celebrated fifty years of operation in 2004, almost half of which it was run under the management of Phil and Celeste Paleologos. In 1981, Phil segued from a career in radio broadcasting to one behind the counter, taking over a tired old diner with a bad reputation and slowly reestablishing it as a major fixture in the old whaling town of New Bedford. It became a real family affair, with each of the couple's three children doing some time in the bustling place. By the late 1980s, the Shawmut began to pack in the customers with a combination of good food and a generous sense of hospitality.

Phil and Celeste run a very tight ship, and they can justifiably take great pride in having fostered a family-friendly, community-enhancing restaurant that shines as a diner should. The menu reflects the local predominance of Portuguese and French Canadian ethnicities. In most diners in this region, patrons can generally expect linguica sausage, kale soup, French meat pie, and baked beans for breakfast. The Shawmut serves that and more, along with a big smile.

In 1996, Phil returned to the radio business without leaving the diner business when he installed a broadcast booth inside the diner and began to produce a syndicated four-hour talk show for a national audience. Originally carried by the TalkAmerica radio network, the show adhered to a pretty typical talk radio format, with Phil interviewing national political figures, authors of self-help books, and other personalities. Bucking the trend all too prevalent in the talk radio scene these days, Phil's show had a decidedly positive and life-affirming message reflecting his own personal philosophies and background.

In 2001, the show jumped networks but kept the same format and message. Now broadcast via the National Radio Network in more than 250 markets, the show incorporated little of the diner's atmosphere into the structure of the program, but the sight of Phil talking up a storm with guests, both live and over the phone, made for interesting viewing during breakfast.

In early 2004, Phil decided to hang up the microphone once again and turned his full attention back to the diner.

BETSY'S DINER
1957 MOUNTAIN VIEW #498
457 Main St., Falmouth, MA • (508) 540-0060

Cape Cod has come a long way since its slow-paced days as a summer vacation spot and a collection of fishing communities. Today it is the fastest-growing region of Massachusetts and has attracted a large percentage of year-round residents, which include both retirees and professionals willing to make the hour-and-a-half commute to the Boston area.

Just to the east of downtown Falmouth, one of the state's diner new-comers bustles with activity on most days. The idea for the ever-popular Betsy's Diner came from restaurateur Larry Holmes (unrelated to the boxer), who purchased and had the former Peter Pan Diner shipped up from the Allentown, Pennsylvania, area in 1992. The two-sectioned 1957 Mountain View diner landed on the location in June, with Holmes gunning for a September opening. Some had their doubts that he could meet this demanding schedule, but in late September, Holmes had the grills fired up. His schedule also assumed that with the tourist season winding down, the lower traffic volume would allow a relatively easy break-in period. Two weeks after Holmes opened the door, however, curious customers almost had to fight for seats. Holmes had a hit on his hands, and bringing in this stainless steel gem proved exactly what this diner-starved area needed.

A large restaurant already stood on the site when Holmes brought up the diner, but he demolished about two-thirds of the pitched-room building and installed the diner in the empty space. The subsequent incorporation of a spacious dining area attached to the original diner made for an operation capable of serving more than 100 people. Holmes and company met all expectations, with ample portions across all three regular meals, as well as luscious homemade desserts.

A native of Somerville, Massachusetts, Holmes later turned his attentions to repeating his success a little closer to home. In 1994, he sold the operation to Dave Chandler, who changed little of the winning formula. The diner continues to do great business, serving everything from pancakes to fresh salads to big hearty sandwiches to full entrees. The Chandlers beckon customers with the tagline "Pay light, eat heavy," and by most accounts, it delivers.

Betsy's represents a welcome trend that sees many diners in New England successfully shedding any hint of a "greasy spoon" reputation and becoming a full-service family restaurant. In many respects, it exemplifies the possibilities of properly refurbishing vintage diners for contemporary needs.

DINER DIRECTORY

RHODE ISLAND

Champ's Diner
Pawtucket, RI
c. 1929 Worcester
In storage. Originally located in downtown Pawtucket, closed in 1989, and sold and put in storage until another sale in 2000 brought it back to the city. Currently closed. In very good condition.

Dandy Diner
Providence, RI
1933 Worcester 718
In storage. Originally in Attleboro.

Denny's Diner
444 Quaker Lane
Warwick, RI
(401) 826-7613
1998 Starlite
Part of Denny's chain. American food.

Ever Ready Diner
315 Harborside Blvd.
Providence, RI
1926 Worcester 549

Champs served its last meal in 1990, and since then it has sat in storage. Latest plans call for a reopening in its home community of Woonsocket.

Part of diner exhibit at the Johnson & Wales Culinary Archives & Museum. Located at various times in Waterville, Maine; Lawrence, Massachusetts; Peterborough, New Hampshire; Southbridge, Massachusetts; and last operated in Providence, closing in 1989. Diner donated to J&W by noted restaurant architect Morris Nathanson, but it lay exposed to vandals and the elements until 2002. Restoration effort currently under way.

4th Street Diner
184 Admiral Kalbfus Rd.
Newport, RI
(401) 847-2069
1952 O'Mahony
Originally located in Swansea, Massachusetts, and moved to location with its stick-built kitchen in 1960s. In good but weathered condition. American food with seafood specials. Full menu.

Haven Brothers Diner
City Hall Plaza
Providence, RI
Homemade
Defines the primordial diner experience. Lunch wagon is actually a converted semitrailer that rolls up to City Hall every night at 5:00 P.M. for night-owl operation. Very basic grilled fare.

Hickey's Lunch Wagon
Lincoln, RI
1947 Worcester 798
In storage. Rare lunch wagon mounted on six-wheeler flatbed. Originally operated in Taunton, Massachusetts, by John Hickey from 1947 until 1986. Currently threatened.

Hope Diner
742 Hope St./Rte. 114
Bristol, RI
(401) 253-1759
Worcester?
"Don't be a dope. Eat at the Hope!" is
the slogan on the menu. Prewar vintage,
with considerable renovations. Basic
grilled diner fare. Big breakfasts. Fresh
soups. Breakfast and lunch only.

Jigger's Diner
145 Main St./Rte. 1
East Greenwich, RI
(401) 884-5388
1947 Worcester 826
Restored by Carol Shriner in 1990
and reopened with highly innovative
menu featuring many local specialties
and homemade items. Restorative
work includes new hood and counter
expertly crafted in the style of the original. Featured in *Gourmet* magazine
in 1997. New ownership largely continuing the tradition. Breakfast and
lunch only.

Johnny B's Diner
1388 Cranston St.
Cranston, RI
(401) 944-4650
1920s Unknown
Severely remodeled. Basic grilled diner
fare. Breakfast and lunch only.

Kiddie Closet
329 Main St.
Wakefield, RI
c. 1936 O'Mahony
Converted into a retail store. Retains
original structural outlines.

La Criolla Restaurant
777 Elmwood Ave.
Providence, RI
1947 Worcester 806

Hickey's operated on the square in Taunton,
Massachusetts, from 1947 until Jack Hickey's
retirement in 1986. It then became the property
of the city of Taunton, rolled out for special
occasions. Today the hobbled lunch wagon sits
idle in Lincoln, Rhode Island.

Small Worcester car with porcelain
enamel ceiling panels. Serves Hispanic
fare. Full menu.

Lemoyne Diner
Providence, RI
c. 1939 O'Mahony 1104
In storage. Formerly located in Pennsylvania and moved to Baltimore in
1980s for proposed but unrealized
restoration project. Moved to Providence in 2002 by Dick Shappy, who
continues restoration and plans to
reopen as the Cadillac Diner.

Louis' Diner
Marine Rd.
Davisville, RI
1933 Worcester 708
Removed from longtime location
in Concord, New Hampshire, in 2001
and placed in storage. Originally served
as the "annex" half of Rich's Diner in
Newburyport, Massachusetts. Currently
threatened by exposure to the elements.
Closed.

Midway Diner
Providence, RI
1930 Worcester 659
In storage. Formerly located in Dedham
on Route 1.

Mike's Diner
East Providence, RI
1966 Mobile DeRaffele
One of a kind DeRaffele lunch wagon
built in mid-1960s. Until 1993, it operated in or near downtown Providence.

Modern Diner
364 East Ave.
Pawtucket, RI
(401) 726-8390
1941 Sterling 4140
First diner ever listed on the National
Register of Historic Places. Originally
located in downtown and moved in

In 1966, DeRaffele built this unique lunch
wagon, which operated in Providence for much
of its existence. Unlike traditional lunch wagons,
Mike's layout featured a counter that ran the
length of the trailer. The city eventually shut
it down, citing health code issues. Today it's
idle and in storage in East Providence.

1980s to avoid demolition. Generally
excellent neo-diner fare and lunch
menu, reasonably priced. Creative
weekend brunch specials. Breakfast
and lunch only.

My Kids & Company
855 Newport Ave.
Pawtucket, RI
1970s DeRaffele
Converted for use as child-care business.

Poirier's Diner
Westminster St.
Providence, RI
1946 Kullman
"Challenger" design. Listed on the
National Register of Historic Places.
Closed in 2002 but saved by local busi-
nessman for restoration and revival.

Prairie Diner
416 Public St.
Providence, RI
(401) 785-1658
1924 Tierney
Original diner enveloped in boxlike
building. Retains many original interior
features. Basic grilled diner food. Breakfast and lunch only.

Right Spot
200 South Bend
Pawtucket, RI
1930s Worcester
Remodeled and altered layout for use
as concession.

Scrambler's
65 Founders Dr./Rte. 122
Woonsocket, RI
(401) 769-4646
2002 Diner-Mite
State's newest diner, and its only from
Diner-Mite of Atlanta. Retro-style exterior with odd mix of streamline and Vic-
torian interior ornamentation. American
food with daily specials. Full menu.

Seaplane Diner
307 Allens Ave.
Providence, RI
(401) 941-9547
1950s O'Mahony
Originally operating as Girard's Diner in Woonsocket. Moved to current location in 1973 and mansarded and covered with plywood T-111. Roof remains, but the stainless exterior uncovered in late 1990s. Basic grilled diner fare. Good sandwiches. Breakfast and lunch only.

Sherwood's Diner
Marine Rd.
Davisville, RI
1940 Worcester 755
Originally placed in Medford but was repossessed by the Worcester company in 1941. Diner resold and placed on Foster Street in downtown Worcester, where it remained until the 1970s. Diner removed to make way for the civic arena and reopened as an ice cream stand in Auburn, Massachusetts. Moved to Rhode Island and put in storage at Quonset Point in 1999.

Silver Top Diner
Middle St.
Pawtucket, RI
1938 Kullman
In storage. Formerly located in Providence and cleared to make way for newer development in 2002. Rare Kullman for this vintage and well preserved.

Snoopy's Diner
4001 Quaker Lane
North Kingstown, RI
(401) 295-1533
c. 1950 Silk City/Erfed
Silk City diner updated by notable diner remodelers Erfed of Rutherford, New Jersey. In very good condition. American food. Grilled diner fare with daily specials. Breakfast and lunch only.

A rare narrow "Jersey-style" Worcester car, the State Line Diner sits less than 200 yards from the Connecticut border in Rhode Island.

Star Diner
140 Newport Ave.
E. Providence, RI
(401) 438-5559
1951 DeRaffele
Originally Keenan's Diner. Fully restored but curiously closed iconic 1950s diner that last operated as a Chinese restaurant. In immaculate condition.

State Line Diner
195 Danielson Pike, Rte. 6
Foster, RI
(401) 647-9951
1955 Worcester 846
Originally located in Southbridge, Massachusetts. Rare Jersey-style, narrow car. In very good condition. Basic diner fare. Breakfast and lunch only.

Tommy's Deluxe Diner
159 East Main St.
Middletown, RI
(401) 847-9834
1939 O'Mahony
Rare prewar car in very original, though weathered, condition. Originally the second Al Mac's Diner and located in Fall River until its replacement by newer DeRaffele in 1953. Basic diner fare. Full menu; Sundays breakfast and lunch only.

Wickford Diner
Brown St./Rte. 1A
Wickford, RI
(401) 295-5477
1920s Worcester?
Small and significantly renovated. Now more of a sit-down restaurant than actual diner. Serves lunch and dinner.

Worcester Deluxe 101
Industrial Way
Lincoln, RI
1961 Worcester Deluxe 101
Unfinished framed diner started as a speculative venture by Francis Van Slett of Worcester, who purchased the assets of the Worcester Lunch Car Company at auction. In dry storage from 1962 to 1999, when it was moved to Fall River storage. Moved to present location in 2002 and left exposed to elements. Currently threatened.

SOUTHEASTERN MASSACHUSETTS

Al Mac's Diner
135 President Ave.
Fall River, MA
(508) 679-5851

The Blue Point Diner now specializes in fresh seafood dinners.

1953 DeRaffele
Listed on the National Register of Historic Places. Almost demolished in the 1980s, but saved by local community support. Adorned with spectacular neon sign. Serves full menu of American food with daily specials.

Angelo's Orchid Diner
805 Rockdale Ave. & Rte. 6
New Bedford, MA
(508) 993-3172
1953 O'Mahony
Well-preserved classic, serving breakfast and lunch. American food with Portuguese specialties. Salmon pie.

Betsy's Diner
457 Main St.
Falmouth, MA
(508) 540-0060
1957 Mountain View 498
Formerly operating as Peter Pan Diner near Allentown, Pennsylvania. Moved to Falmouth in 1992. Very popular family-style restaurant features excellent hot platters and homemade desserts. Full menu, seven days.

Blue Point Restaurant
6 Dayton St.
Acushnet, MA
(508) 995-9600
1939 Worcester 748
Originally The Diner Deluxe and installed in New Bedford. Remodeled and now part of a restaurant. Seafood specialties. Lunch and dinner.

Catman Cafe
16 Old Colony Way
Mansfield, MA
(508) 339-0038
1940 Sterling Dinette 4020
Rare Sterling dinette model, but severely remodeled.

Dave's Diner
390 West Grove St./Rte. 28
Middleborough, MA
(508) 923-4755
1997 Starlite
First diner to come to Massachusetts
since 1971. Popular and friendly. Serves
very good American diner-style meals
and desserts. Full menu.

Don's Diner
121 South St./Rte. 1A
Plainville, MA
(508) 695-7036
c. 1950 Mountain View
Remodeled exterior obscures original
1950s stainless diner, with mostly
original interior. American food. Good
homemade corned beef hash. Breakfast
and lunch weekdays; breakfast only
weekends.

Eddie's Diner
55 Hix Bridge Rd.
Westport, MA
1952 O'Mahony 2215
Formerly operating as Eddie's Diner in
Quincy, Massachusetts. Suffered a fire in
1993. Purchased by Westport family, with
plans to combine this diner with the former Travelers Diner for larger restaurant.

Jake's Diner
114 Alden Rd.
Fairhaven, MA
(508) 990-7786
c. 1951 O'Mahony
Formerly operating as Joe's on Route 20
in Worcester. Ceramic tile sided and in
very good condition. Handicapped acces-
sible. American food with daily specials.

Joe's Diner
51 Broadway/Rte. 138
Taunton, MA
(508) 823-2193

1940 Sterling 408
Formerly located in Everett, Massachusetts. American food. Breakfast
and lunch only, with weekend late-
night hours.

Juke Box Diner
1155 GAR Hwy., Rte. 6
Somerset, MA
(508) 677-1907
2000 Diner-Mite
State's newest diner, and its only
from Diner-Mite of Atlanta. Full
menu, full bar. Comfort food.
Daily specials.

Mill Pond Diner
2571 Cranberry Hwy.
Wareham, MA
(508) 295-9688
1950 O'Mahony
Large O'Mahony, originally operating
in Fall River as Earnshaw's. In very good
condition. Standard grilled diner food.
French meat pie. Breakfast and lunch.

My Tin Man Diner
Westport, MA
1940 Sterling Streamliner 4012
Originally operating in New Bedford
as the Jimmy Evans Flyer. Suffered catastrophic fire in 2000. Only surviving
"double-ended" Sterling Streamliner,
but barely extant. Moved to storage
in 2003.

Nest Diner
81 Fairhaven Rd./Rte. 6
Mattapoiset, MA
(508) 758-9555
1950 Mountain View 309
Splendid, well-preserved stainless
steel diner. Breakfast and lunch,
seven days. Well-made American
food with an outstanding Grape-Nut
pudding.

The Nest Diner shows Mountain View styling at its peak.

Nite Owl Diner
1680 Pleasant St. & Rte. 6
Fall River, MA
1956 DeRaffele
Unique lunch-wagon layout for a diner of this vintage, but much like the lunch wagon it replaced. Closed in 2002. Subject of John Baeder painting.

Roadside Diner
Rte. 28
Middleboro, MA
1928 Worcester 612
Suffered catastrophic fire in 1989, and amazing that it's still standing. Originally operating as Holt's Diner in Salem, Massachusetts.

Shawmut Diner
943 Shawmut Ave.
New Bedford, MA
(508) 993-3073
1953 O'Mahony
Listed on the National Register of Historic Places. Large stainless steel diner in excellent condition. Until January 2004, also served as the studio for the owners' nationally syndicated talk radio program. Clean, friendly atmosphere.

Breakfast and lunch most days. American food with Portugese and Greek specialties.

Sisson's Diner
561 Wareham St./Rte. 28
Middleboro, MA
(508) 946-0359
1910s Wason Mfg.
Only known trolley car diner in New England, placed on site in 1926 and converted for food service. Basic grilled diner fare. Breakfast and lunch.

Tex Barry's Coney Island
31 County St.
Attleboro, MA
(508) 222-9787
1926 Worcester 542
One of the oldest extant operating diners in the country. Originally called the County Diner, and still very original. Now serves mostly hot dogs and other grilled sandwiches. Lunch and dinner only.

Traveler's Diner
Westport, MA
1951 O'Mahony
In storage. Originally located in Dover, New Jersey. Brought to Massachusetts in 2003 for use in ambitious restaurant project to combine this with Eddie's Diner. Shipped by barge.

Wendell's Corner Snack Bar
Old Main St.
North Falmouth, MA
1920s Tierney
Only Tierney in Massachusetts. In fairly original, albeit well-worn condition. Basic diner fare with seafood specialties. Breakfast and lunch only.

BOSTON
METRO

A sad but inevitable aspect of modern urban gentrification is that it almost makes inevitable the obsolescence of the neighborhood diner. Ironically, the new, upscale neighborhoods that spring forth desperately need a good, community-enhancing touchstone such as that embodied in a real, homespun diner. Today's version of such a place more typically comes in the form of yet another Starbucks coffee shop. The economics of restaurants in the new millennium make it nearly impossible for anyone to set up shop in a high-traffic, prosperous neighborhood and serve home-cooked meals without some ironic spin and high prices. As a consequence, a city the size of Boston, with a population of more than half a million, currently has the fewest number of actual diners per capita of any city in the Northeast with a population of at least 100,000. Progress and urban renaissance, while a boon for our aging metropolitan centers, generally mean doom for the vintage diner.

Long referred to as "the Hub of the Universe," Boston's claim to that distinction arguably diminished in the postwar period. With its port shrinking, industries shuttering, population declining, and overall economic power entering into the shadow of the emerging South and West, the city verged on becoming a quaint, historic anachronism by the 1970s. About the only thing the city had going for it was its world-class universities, which would prove instrumental in its rebirth.

Cities at this stage of their development cycle frustrate planners and ambitious mayors eager to stick some kind of development feather in their caps, but it typically represents the last gasp of the vintage neighborhood diner. Before Boston's economic "miracle" took hold in the early 1980s, the city and its immediate suburbs boasted a number of diners easily double what we find today. In the Fenway section, near the famous ball park, stood the Fenway Flyer, a striking Sterling Streamliner, as did the diminutive Tom Thumb Diner. Until the 1970s, the spectacular Garden Diner awaited Bruins and Celtics fans pouring out of the legendary Boston Garden arena. Other diners scraped from the landscape during this period include the Englewood in Dorchester; Jimmy's Diner in Mattapan; the F&T and the short-lived Kendall Diner in Kendall Square, Cambridge; the Monarch in Waltham; and many others.

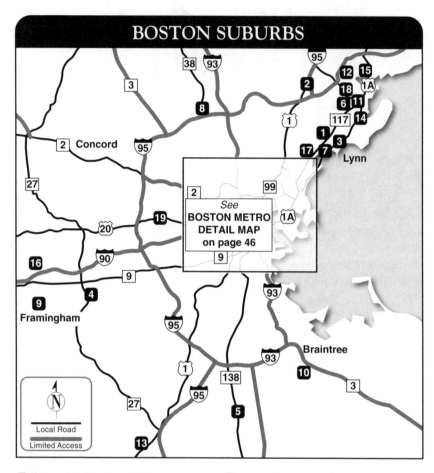

BOSTON SUBURBS

1. Balloon Boutique: Lynn (BR)
2. Bel Aire Diner: Peabody (MS)
3. Capitol Diner: Lynn (BR)
4. Casey's Diner: Natick (BR)
5. Corkery Tractor Trailer Canton (MS)
6. Driftwood II Restaurant Peabody (BR)
7. Full Moon Restaurant Lynn (MS)
8. Lanna Thai Diner: Woburn (MS)
9. Lloyd's Diner: Framingham (BR)
10. Olympian Diner: Braintree (E)
11. Pilgrim Diner: Salem (MS)
12. Portside Cape Ann Diner: Danvers (BR)
13. Red Wing Diner: Walpole (BR)
14. Salem Diner: Salem (MS)
15. Subway: Beverly (R)
16. Timmy's Diner: Framingham (BR)
17. Vree's Sterling Diner: Saugus (BR)
18. Whistlestop Diner: Peabody (BR)
19. Wilson's Diner: Waltham (BR)

Today Boston itself has only three operating diners out of six extant structures: the Victoria Diner, the Breakfast Club, and the South Street Diner. The Pig & Whistle, though currently closed, stands a fighting chance of reopening. The newest diner, the Newmarket, came to the city in 1971, lasting a short while as a steakhouse restaurant. Stripped of any hint of its

The Pig & Whistle, named for the long-gone Brighton rail and stockyards here when it came to town, closed up in 2002.

food-service past save for the stainless steel trim around the windows, it now serves as the offices for Beckwith Elevator. The latest diner to cross city limits, the Big Dig Diner, closed in 2003.

Owned and operated by an organization called the Federated Dorchester Neighborhood Houses, the Big Dig Diner was the brainchild of Joe Carpenito, the director of the Log School in Boston, now a unit of the FDNH. Carpenito wanted to set up a program similar to that in operation in Baltimore, where another nonprofit operates the Hollywood Diner, better known as the star of Barry Levinson's movie *Diner*. The Hollywood employs and trains young people convicted of nonviolent crimes for work in the food-service industry.

In 1995, Carpenito got his diner, a 1946 Silk City restored by Steve Harwin of Cleveland. The Big Dig originally sat on Route 22 in the little town of Ono, Pennsylvania, until 1994, when Harwin bought the diner and moved it to Cleveland for refurbishing. Carpenito proposed a location for the diner on the vast City Hall Plaza in Boston and hoped public and private sources would endow the program with substantial donations and grants.

Eventually the city found a lot on Drydock Street in the city's South Boston waterfront district, and Carpenito dubbed the new diner the Big Dig, after the nickname for the $15 billion highway project then snaking its way through downtown Boston. Though the school completed installing and outfitting the diner by 1999, it took another two years before the Big

BOSTON METRO

1 Apple Tree Diner (BR)
2 Beachmont Roast Beef: Revere (BR)
3 Beckwith Elevator: Boston (R)
4 Big Dig Diner: Boston (MS)
5 Breakfast Club: Allston (MS)
6 Buddy's Truck Stop: Somerville (BR)
7 Deluxe Town Diner: Watertown (MS)
8 Jonquille's Diner: Revere (BR)
9 Kelly's Diner: Somerville (MS)
10 Liberty Diner: Roxbury (BR)

11 Maplewood Tavern: Malden (BR)
12 Phyllis's Diner: Everett (BR)
13 Pig & Whistle Diner: Brighton (MS)
14 Rosebud Diner: Somerville (MS)
15 South Street Diner: Boston (MS)
16 T & D Trucking: E. Boston (MS)
17 Tantawan Thai Cuisine: Watertown (R)
18 Lulu's Diner: Malden (BR)
19 Victoria Diner: Boston (E)

Dig opened for regular, though very limited, hours. It also occasionally hosted special events.

But with local and state government facing severe financial crises, programs such as the Big Dig Diner faced elimination. As this goes to press, the diner remains closed, with its future in doubt.

In January 2004, Victoria Dining became the Victoria Diner, more in keeping with the true heritage of its special architecture, but it also heralds the end of an era in Boston's diner history. When Mike Hajj took owner-ship, it meant that the Georgenes family would finally leave the scene after nearly eighty years of service, which began with the purchase of a Worcester Lunch Car in 1926 by James Georgenes.

The Victoria is the only diner north of the Connecticut border built by the Swingle company of Middlesex, New Jersey. Joe Swingle ended a career selling diners for Fodero and O'Mahony to strike out on his own in 1957. Swingle became one of the first to introduce Early American styling to the interiors of diners, and the company splashed this motif all over the Victo-ria. At this time, the Georgenes family, much like every other diner operator in the mid-1960s, fought for survival by attempting to appeal more to the family dining market. Though the diner sits in the middle of an industrial zone, the owners sought to expand its appeal to families by eventually adding a more formal pub they called the Café George in 1975, but they appeased workers by leaving the diner section untouched.

With Nick and Charles Georgenes both in their seventies, they sought and found a buyer in Hajj, after resisting offers to turn the property into a fast-food outlet or a bank. Hajj already runs Mike's City Diner in Boston's South End neighborhood. At only thirty-three, this diner aficionado already has twenty years in the business. And befitting the structure's classic her-itage, he plans to introduce a more retro feel into the colonial building.

Closed and facing an uncertain future, the Big Dig Diner came to town in 1995 as part of a nonprofit program to rehabilitate troubled teenagers. The restored Silk City closed in 2003 after only a few months in operation.

Massachusetts and northern New England have only one colonial style diner still in operation. In late 2003, the Victoria Diner on Massachusetts Avenue got a new owner who promises to introduce a more retro feel to this 1965 Swingle diner. The transition also marked the end of more than eighty years in the business by the Georgenes family.

Throughout Boston's reemergence in the 1980s, its Allston and Brighton districts, on the city's western side, endured as two of its few remaining healthy blue-collar enclaves. As the twentieth century closed, prosperity and the increasing economic power of the city's universities brought the encroachment of more gentrification. One of the diners in this district managed to adapt, but the other closed up shop.

The Worcester Lunch Car now called the Breakfast Club began as Fahey's Diner in 1954. At #841, Fahey's was Worcester's second of a short-lived product line that made a futile attempt to play catch-up with the Jersey-based competition. Though classically 1950s in appearance, even this attempt by the company still retains many baroque vestiges of the company's lunch-wagon past. Despite the widespread use of terrazzo flooring by diner builders during this period, Worcester continued to tile the floors. Though trimmed in stainless, the shapes still adhered to older Romanesque patterns. The company continued to build solid, durable buildings, but their design did little to capture the attention of a market constantly hungering for the next new advance in style and technology.

Even Worcester's traditional New England customer base seemed to slip away, and after Fahey's came only nine more diners in the next three years. Nonetheless, C. J. Fahey remained extremely loyal to the company, owning three Worcester cars starting in 1928, trading up in 1936 and again in 1954 for #841. Fahey retired in the early 1960s and sold his diner, which then became Ted's Diner. In a bit of trend bucking, Ted had altered the diner's counter layout to bring the grill out from the kitchen. Today's fire codes usually will not allow this in new construction, and some owners prefer to keep their cook away from the customers in order to avoid confusion. In a smaller place, particularly if the owner also works the grill, putting it in the diner itself affords the opportunity to mingle with customers and keep a close eye on the scene.

In the early 1970s, Ted's Diner became Henry's, which operated until the late 1980s. Henry's typified the romantic ideal of the diner as that most democratic of restaurants. Its location in an industrial zone just around the corner from the world's most prestigious university meant that at any given time of the day, one might find a UPS driver sharing the counter with a Harvard professor, exchanging their views on the state of the nation.

Kenny O'Connell took over the diner in 1990. In 1993, he made a drastic move by first truncating and then completely removing the counter on the diner's left side to allow for more seating. This alteration also removed the grill to the kitchen. In such a small space, the temptation to squeeze a few more seats in a restaurant with no room for expansion frequently overrides any concern for the diner's preservation. In this case, the sloppy manner in which O'Connell hacked his renovations damaged the diner's classic,

The Breakfast Club recently appeared in a McDonald's commercial. Its latest owners have done great things with the 1954 Worcester, not the least of which includes restoring the diner's recently removed counter.

time-tested atmosphere. Booths under a hood just don't look right, and whether they know much about diner history or not, customers will notice something amiss. A year later, O'Connell and crew left the diner, and with them went chef Richie Daniel's excellent corn chowder recipe and amazing roast turkey sandwiches.

The diner struggled through the rest of the 1990s, until new owners took up the spatula in 2002. Renaming it the Breakfast Club, the diner's new young owner, George Athanasopoulos, restored the counter to its Ted's days, brought in new booths, gave it a thorough cleaning, and introduced a new semitrendy menu. This club has grown membership ever since.

The South Street Diner in downtown Boston technically would not merit inclusion in this guide, except that the stick-built structure looks and feels completely authentic to the untrained eye, and omitting it would be a disservice to anyone seeking good diners or a good place to eat. The structure occupies a corner lot in a section of downtown still known as the Leather District, a name bestowed because of the predominance of leather merchants from the late nineteenth century until World War II. The cur-

---

WHAT HAPPENED TO THE TWENTY-FOUR-HOUR DINER?

To some people, only those diners open twenty-four hours qualify as "true" diners. The very word *diner* conjures up romantic images of glowing roadside beacons awaiting the lonely, late-night traveler wandering up a country road, ready and able to pour a fresh cup of coffee or make a hot turkey sandwich at any hour of the day. Sadly, in most of New England, this practice ended about the same time Ted Williams took his last turn at bat.

For better or worse, the realities of the industry have forced this change. Competition, the labor market, and changing habits of the dining public have converted most smaller, vintage diners into mere luncheonettes.

In Massachusetts, only three diners currently maintain a twenty-four-hour, seven-day operation (the Boulevard in Worcester closes Sunday afternoons). New Hampshire has only one. Vermont, Maine, and Rhode Island have none. Connecticut, with its many larger, Greek-style diners, keeps the lights on in the tradition, but the trend of late has more operations closing by 11:00 P.M.

Though Vermont has only twenty-one diners listed here, sixteen, or 75 percent of them, regularly serve dinners. Forty-four percent of New Hampshire's diners serve the dinner hour, as do at least 55 percent of Maine's. In contrast, only about 20 percent of the Bay State's diners invite customers in after 3:00 P.M. Most serve only breakfast and lunch, but in no way should anyone question their authenticity as real diners.

rent diner replaced an authentic diner in 1947, and it likely drew most of its business from those who worked in the leather shops and on the vast rail yards that once spread across blocks of real estate immediately south of the diner.

The diner declined along with the surrounding neighborhood until 1986, when a textile merchant named Don Levy took a chance in the remote downtown location and introduced the concept of the upscale diner to Boston. This anomaly had already been made famous by the establishment of the Empire Diner in New York, but the idea of $7 burgers served with bleu cheese on fresh-baked rolls in a greasy-spoon diner was new to the Boston area. The updated spin on classic comfort food became a hit, and before long, the Blue Diner came to anchor a rebounding district that saw art galleries filling spaces long since abandoned by leather merchants.

Though more expensive than the average diner, the Blue Diner did typically offer a great meal for the money. Few items on the menu came from a package or a can. Customers could expect fresh-ground coffee, homemade soups, and innovative menu items rarely found in such a place, enjoying their food in a vibrant, eclectic atmosphere with the sounds of classic jazz or swing music wafting through the air. Open twenty-four hours, the diner was one of the few places in a city this size where you could get pancakes, huge and fluffy, at two in the morning.

Levy opened a second restaurant around the corner called the Loading Zone, an eclectic, highly creative interpretation of a Cajun-barbecue joint. When it failed, it hung like an albatross on Levy's finances and put the Blue Diner in jeopardy as well. In the end, Levy sold both businesses to a group who then created some confusion for diner patrons. The group abandoned the Blue Diner property but applied the name to the former Loading Zone space.

Peter Kalymeres became the new operator in 1994, renaming the former Blue Diner the Boston Diner, but he failed to attract a new customer base. The diner had reverted back to its no-frills, blue-collar menu, without any hint of the charm or attraction found there during the Levy days. The Big Dig Central Artery Project's construction was now in full swing, casting some doubt on the diner's prospects as well. Though thousands of construction workers now crawled all over the area, accessing it by car became much more difficult.

In 1997, Sol Fidell took over, changed the name to the South Street Diner, and has managed to turn the place around. Though not quite pushing the culinary envelope in the way Levy did, Fidell has successfully reinvigorated the space by sticking to a basic diner formula of good meals at good prices. The Leather District's renaissance stumbled when the early 1990s recession hit, forcing a retreat of most of the art galleries and other upscale retail businesses. Since then, Boston's red-hot real estate market has seen the neighborhood regain and probably surpass the previous demand for commercial and residential space.

Don Levy slipped away from the scene after the demise of his Blue Diner, but he has since returned with a vengeance. Levy's second act in food service would appear to disprove the adage of lightning not striking twice. Since occupying the old Town Diner in Watertown's east end, he has finally realized the full potential of this landmark structure. (See page 65.)

With the Cambridge real estate market overheating and pushing out more and more of the city's homespun businesses, the town of Somerville has received much of the outflow. For years, pundits lamented the demise of Harvard Square as the region's hip epicenter, as chain stores gradually but relentlessly pushed out the small, local proprietors of everything from stationery stores to sandwich shops, but much of this element didn't necessarily disappear. Some of it merely moved to Davis Square in Somerville.

While the historians have yet to uncover any photos showing a diner or lunch wagon in Harvard Square, the city at large did once have its share during the industry's heyday. Today Cambridge has its share of restaurants of just about every type imaginable, but none operating out of a real diner.

Somerville, on the other hand, has three, with the latest added to the collection in 1995. The man responsible for the hyper-successful Betsy's Diner in Falmouth, Massachusetts (see page 34), applied the golden touch

Don Levy discusses the day's specials with a tireless employee.

to a corner of Ball Square. Larry Holmes took advantage of a fire-sale price to purchase a large, seventy-seat O'Mahony located on U.S. Route 13 near Wilmington, Delaware, to bring to Somerville. Frank's Diner had closed in the late 1980s, and when Holmes closed the deal, the owner was using the diner as part of a garden center, so the diner sold for only $8,000.

Moving it was another matter. The diner was 54 feet in length and more than 16 sixteen feet wide, requiring several slow detours on the 500-mile trek to Massachusetts. But by 1995, Holmes had pulled it off, and any casual observer new to the area would assume that Kelly's Diner had operated on that site for decades. It occupies a traditional spot, right up the sidewalk in a densely populated, easily walkable neighborhood. Holmes leaves the diner's operation in the able hands of his son Jay and daughter Kelly, who keep the place hopping during the breakfast and lunchtime hours.

The 1948 diner features the usual menu staples, with few frills, but it does them with quality and care. The crew runs a tight ship and maintains a family-friendly atmosphere that is well received by the locals. As of early 2004, it looks like Larry Holmes has begun a search for his third diner, and with his track record, some Boston-area neighborhood might get lucky.

The fortunes of Davis Square in Somerville have been reflected closely in the operation and reputation of the Rosebud Diner. Installed in 1941, this Worcester car came to town during the square's last years as a hub for this prosperous blue-collar community as it emerged from the Depression. As the square declined into an urban horror story, the little diner suffered as well. In recent years, however, the Nichols family has rejuvenated the business just in time for the square's renaissance. (See page 68.)

As a breakfast staple, nothing beats homemade hash. Everyone makes it differently, and this area has some of the best renditions. Many of the smaller short-order luncheonettes will often forgo the effort and expense of making their own, even though the history of the dish originates from the grillman's attempts to make extra money from his leftover meat, potatoes, and other tasty grilled remnants. Not willing to leave a good thing alone, the food processing industry began to package corned-beef "red flannel" hash, and no matter the brand or price, it all comes out of the can with that same mushy, overly consistent texture and dubiously reminiscent aroma. Anyone the least bit familiar with the canned version can spot it a mile away. Even fully equipped and well-staffed kitchens resort to using it and frequently charge more than for homemade.

So imagine the pleasant surprise for the hash aficionado upon entering Buddy's Truck Stop on Washington Street in Somerville. The 1929 Worcester car, complete with pocket door entrance, immediately tips off customers to the unique experience that waits inside. And it won't disappoint.

Buddy's Truck Stop typifies the disappearing primordial diner experience. The twenty-stool diner serves up the basics, fast, hot, and without a speck of pretense.

Buddy Barrett bought the diner in 1965, but the 1929 Worcester originally opened in Leominster, Massachusetts, coming to the Somerville location in 1951, where it replaced an older diner. John Barrett joined his father in the late 1960s and eventually filled his shoes in a seamless transition upon Buddy's retirement in the 1980s.

No, John Barrett won't likely host his own show on the Food Network, and no, don't expect to see Martha Stewart drop in anytime soon. And thank God for that. Buddy's Truck Stop splendidly represents that aspect of dinerdom at its most primordial and true. The tiny twenty-stooler provides a refreshing, no-frills, unpretentious experience where customers can watch John prepare meals before their eyes, chat up the latest news, and, yes, get an ample portion of homemade corned-beef hash with their fresh eggs. In fact, newcomers just might get the following warning, as I once did: "It's homemade, you know. It's not that dog food you get in a can!" Apparently some customers actually winced at the unexpected taste of fresh ingredients, such as onions and peppers and the added spices not typically found in the unappetizing canned version.

Before the construction of the interstate highways, Route 99 tracking north out of Boston was once designated as Route 1, and along the old route, one would expect to find old diners. Time and progress have scraped the vast majority from the road, but between Boston's city limits and Route 128, you will still find three left: Phyllis's Diner, Lulu's, and the Bel Aire Diner.

In Everett, another precious experience awaits at the counter of Phyllis's Diner. Sadly, the woman responsible for this lively diner, Phillis D'Amore, died in 2000, but she left the business in the experienced hands of her grill cook, Haj Gamale. Gamale's years in the diner business stretch back to the 1940s, and his life story seems to include a stint in almost every diner that operated during that time in the Boston area.

A well-seasoned veteran of the diner scene, Haj Gamale (below, right) is a treasure trove of diner lore.

Befitting a seasoned journeyman in this field, Gamale orchestrates the flow of his little diner with great ability. Now in his seventies, Gamale is one of the last of the old-time dinermen, a guy who cut his teeth behind the counter of so many diners and has likely seen and heard just about everything. In diners like this, the only thing better than the food is the tales told by guys like Gamale.

In 2003, Gamale made one major change to the operation. Because the diner's length occupied almost the entire frontage of the property, only on-street parking was available, which in this era almost means no parking at all. If people can't park right at the front door, they're just as likely to keep driving and park a quarter mile away in a mall parking lot. Gamale took the somewhat drastic step of turning the diner 90 degrees to orient it perpendicularly to the street. This allowed for the construction of a driveway and access to the rear of the property, where Gamale now provides about four spaces. Additional construction put a vestibule at the street end and gave the diner a new kitchen and restrooms at the other end.

The menu at Phyllis's is as basic as they come, with each item listed on a paper plate taped to the hood and backbar behind the counter. It's a place for regulars, but Haj makes sure newcomers get a warm welcome, and no one leaves a stranger.

Farther north on Route 99, the drive grinds through some heavy traffic, many stoplights, and old traditional neighborhoods. When Route 99 intersects with Route 60 in Malden, a left turn brings you soon to Lulu's, a 1932 Worcester car whose layout is more typical of a much smaller lunch wagon, with the kitchen at one end, a wall counter wrapped around the perimeter, and a few tables in the middle. Judging by the markings on the diner's floor, it likely underwent remodeling many years ago.

This diner appeared in a Baeder painting and in his first book, *Diners*, which depicted it as Viv's. Through much of the 1990s, Judy Valleire ran the business but didn't own the diner. Today the diner soldiers on much as it ever did, although it stands out nicely with its new bright red paint job.

Route 99 soon rejoins the current U.S. Route 1 for the state's most classic strip of miracle mile. In his book on Route 1, entitled *The Great American Road Trip*, author Peter Genovese describes the highway like this: "Five miles south of Topsfield begins one of the more amazing stretches of U.S. 1. This section, from I-95 to the Tobin Bridge in Boston, is not for the faint-hearted, lead-footed, or aesthetically sensitive."

In 1988, the *Boston Globe* further characterized the highway as "an enduring monument to wretched excess. It's an unmoveable (and to some, preferably removable) feast of tackiness, tawdriness, weirdness, and exuberant tastelessness." Sadly for roadside architecture enthusiasts, this descrip-

Lulu's Diner makes a good breakfast and lunch for the Malden area locals.

tion becomes less accurate every year. The highway still features many of its ultratacky landmarks, such as a giant forty-foot cactus, a palatial tiki hut, and a restaurant in a clipper ship replica. But every year sees the forces of homogenization chipping away at the road's dubious but celebrated distinctions.

The state first paved this stretch of Route 1 in 1922, and then rebuilt it nearly to interstate standards in 1953. Perhaps not coincidentally, the first crop of stainless steel diners appeared about the same time. The Danvers Diner got an early jump on the trend in 1950. The Suntaug Diner came in 1954, as did the Agawam Diner No. 3. In 1955, the last Monarch Diner, a Fodero, opened, as did the new and spacious Hyland Diner, a ninety-six-seat Mountain View.

The Galanis family installed Agawam Diner No. 3 just north of the Saugus-Peabody border on this road (see page 93), selling it in 1960 to another operator, who moved it south to a site across the road from the famous Hilltop Steakhouse. Rechristened the Thunderbird Diner, it lasted only until 1967, when a fire consumed it and a McDonald's then replaced it. The Hyland Diner in Danvers put in a good twenty years of service until its owner, John Keohane, lost his lease in the late 1970s. Attempts to find a buyer for the building failed, and its date with demolition came in 1979. The Monarch closed and a buyer trucked it up to Coventry, Vermont, where it now operates as Martha's Coventry Diner. The Suntaug moved to Stoneham, Massachusetts, in 1960 and burned in 1980.

The Danvers Diner eventually became something called the Flash in the Pan, a reservations-only restaurant serving haute cuisine. Its proprietor and chef, Patrick Belanger, claims to have enjoyed great success with his counterintuitive concept, but in 1993, he decided to leave the business for greener pastures. The Honda dealership next door purchased the property and sought to dispose of the building. In 1994, a Spanish restaurant developer purchased it and shipped it to Madrid. Its fate remains unknown.

The sole remaining diner along this highway looks, feels, and acts every bit like a classic truck-stop diner so long romanticized in books, songs, and movies. The Bel Aire Diner came to the highway in 1953, thanks to the Kallas family, and aside from everything around it, little has changed since then.

Diner fans got a bit of a scare in 2000 when current owner Harry Kallas announced his plans to sell the property to the Hooters restaurant chain, and he mollified no one with assurances of his plans to move the diner to the lot next door. Fortunately for us, though less so for the Kallases, the town of Peabody shot the plan down, and there the diner stays. (See page 70.)

The tourists and transients that rocket up and down Route 1 could almost be forgiven if they never associate the names Danvers, Saugus, and Peabody with places with real neighborhoods and downtowns. The breakneck speeds at which cars whiz past give drivers little opportunity to soak in any of the local color. As mere names on a map, the towns more likely invoke images of vast parking moats surrounding big-box stores than real communities.

As much as the state's highway department has attempted to Jersey-fy the landscape, this trio of towns does merit further exploration. Danvers also hosts the Portside Cape Ann Diner on Route 35, a well-preserved 1948 Worcester car that retains the "Cape Ann" porcelain panels because of its original installation in downtown Gloucester. Today the Portside Diner fills its plates with healthy portions of home-cooked meals in a quaint neighborhood setting.

The Portside Diner retains its original features, including the front panels that reveal its first location. The cozy Worcester car serves a full menu in the quaint Danvers neighborhood.

Peabody, once the center of the area's leather tanning industry, calls itself "the leather city." Its downtown currently enjoys many of the fruits of the region's general prosperity, and though this historical thick and thin, what is now known as the Whistlestop Diner chugs along astride the dormant railroad tracks that course through the city. A most energetic and determined Barbara Henry now runs the little diner with a big heart, having assumed ownership and operation from the late Marianna Cox, who died in 1999. Mrs. Cox had developed quite a reputation for her Teutonic, no-nonsense attitude and her amazing German apple pancakes.

In 1950, Mort Kurland brought the 1929 Worcester car to Peabody from Lynn, Massachusetts, where it operated as Harry's Diner. Kurland and his wife, Inez, gave it the name Kurley's and kept the diner in extremely original condition right through the 1970s, when it almost faced demolition for the sake of a few parking spaces. Kurland successfully rallied the local community around his enterprise and ultimately saved it for at least another twenty-five years of operation in Peabody.

Sadly, sometime in the early 1980s, the diner suffered some severe renovations that saw the trashing of all the original equipment. Today the diner still has a cozy atmosphere, but it remains devoid of the classic Worcester backbar, countertops, and interior trim. Though currently covered with T-111 plywood, its original steel paneled skin remains underneath. Henry hopes one day to restore the diner to at least some of its former glory but has to wait until her finances improve.

Yet another of the Bay State's twenty-one registered historic diners, the Salem Diner soldiers on as one of only two operating Sterling streamliners left. It opened on July 3, 1941, to wildly enthusiastic crowds, presumably as eager to see the diner's dramatic styling as to eat its fine foods. In *Diners of the Northeast*, Kaplan and Bellink interviewed one of the diner's original employees, Napoleon "Nappy" LeBlanc. According to Nappy:

> I worked here three days, three nights, without going home, with two other men washing dishes—the three of us. That's how busy it was. It never let up, day or night, because we were open twenty-four hours a day then. It never let up for three days or three nights because it was a holiday, like a weekend, you know. You opened up around three o'clock in the afternoon the day before the Fourth. And it was a holiday the next day, and that place kept jammin' and jumpin' all the way through, day and night. We'd take turns at taking snoozes down in the cellar.

Kaplan and Bellink's account of the diner's state of preservation in the late 1970s would apply today as well. The Salem's atmosphere still benefits

Lanna Thai Diner is the latest name applied to this custom-built Worcester car, listed as Jack's Diner on the National Register of Historic Places.

greatly from the swooping lines and original Sterling equipment still in service. The current owner, Stella Georgiakakos, heads up a family operation that hopes to make similar history.

Lynn's two other diners will disappoint purists but still merit inclusion in their photo collections. One, the Balloon Boutique, a Sterling, now sells balloons and flowers, and the other, the Full Moon Restaurant, sits tucked away on a side street. This large 1952 Worcester car began its life as the Lynway Diner, named for the stretch of "miracle mile" commercial highway that coursed south toward Revere and Boston. In the 1970s, the sale of the diner resulted in its removal and reinstallation around the block on Bennett Street, a comparative backroad. Today, though the diner remains in largely original condition, it now serves Thai cuisine.

A happier development has evolved a little farther south in Revere, just outside the entrance to the Suffolk Downs racetrack. There, Jonquille's Diner shines with a Portuguese flair, thanks to new ownership. The diner augments the staples with Iberian specialties such as chourico and linguica sausages, and new customers might get a sample of the traditional quick-bread. John Ribeird Jr., the owner, hails from the Portuguese island of Madeira. He took over the diner in 2002, reopening only after giving the place a thorough scrubbing.

The stick-built diner would easily fool even the trained eye. Indeed, it almost appears as if the builder stole the plans for a 1920s or 1930s Worcester car. The quilted stainless panels came later, but the diner's interior has all the same charm of its vintage prefab cousins.

West and south of Boston, the diner count spreads out rather thinly. Most of these suburbs, particularly to the south, have transitioned into quiet bedroom communities, with all Cape Cod and other southbound tourist traffic relegated to the superhighways. With the closing of the Olympian Diner in Braintree in 1998, the South Shore area lost its last operating full-service diner.

The town of Walpole can claim one notable holdout. There, along busy U.S. Route 1, the Red Wing Restaurant incorporates a 1933 Worcester into its operation, using it as a small lounge area. The popular Red Wing features large portions of fresh fried seafood dinners and provides a good value. The diner lies ensconced in a covering of shake shingles painted red.

Venturing west of Beantown, the diner fan has a little more luck. Waltham offers the much-photographed Wilson's Diner, a stately, intact Worcester car with azure blue panels, right on the city's main drag. The breakfast-and-lunch-only affair serves a popular weekend breakfast, and it also enjoys the distinction of a listing on the National Register of Historic Places, as do the last two diners in this chapter.

About the only thing more American than the diner might just be the hot dog. From this, we could describe Casey's Diner customers as the ultimate patriots. The 1922 Worcester car serves, by owner Fred Casey's account, more than 600 hot dogs a day, to the people who file in and out of this ten-stooler and to the long lines that form at the take-out window. Few diner

Jonquille's Diner, recently refurbished but still full of charm, now features Portuguese specialties.

Lloyd's Diner became a Framingham favorite thanks to Richard Lloyd's generous portions of his fine home cooking.

experiences provide the enthusiast with a more authentic experience than the fifteen minutes spent on the oak-topped stool at Casey's. If you don't appreciate what the diner represents after a visit here, then it's time to leave the country. (See page 63.)

Lloyd's Diner came to Framingham in 1990, thanks to Richard Lloyd, who purchased the former Whit's Diner from where it sat idle in the little town of Orange, Massachusetts. With the help of Richard Gutman, Lloyd restored the transplanted Worcester car and gave it new red exterior panels with his own name emblazoned in the porcelain enamel. The diner's small size makes its restoration a rare event in the last twenty years of diner history.

By modern standards, any food-service facility with so little floor space rarely serves much more than hot dogs and hamburgers. The Lloyds built a dining room, kitchen, and restrooms on the back but expanded the total capacity to barely fifty seats. Nevertheless, since 1991, Lloyd has provided hearty breakfasts and lunches to a grateful market. As is typical for diners like this, the specialty is breakfast. Lloyd piles the home fries high on the plate and slaps down plate-size pancakes. Rare is the appetite that doesn't get beaten into submission here.

CASEY'S DINER
1922 WORCESTER
36 South Ave., Natick, MA • (508) 655-3761

Casey's Diner usually ranks in the top ten in just about every diner fan's must-visit list, and for all the right reasons. The diner is very old. Built in 1922, it probably holds the title of the oldest operating Worcester car, if not the oldest operating diner—at least for the moment—in the world. The diner is unusually small. It seats exactly ten, on stools, at a wooden counter-top, and in a setting with only minor alterations. The diner still retains the intricate ceramic tile floor, the oak panels and countertop, Monel metal hood, and sliding front pocket door. The spindly wooden-topped stools with cast-iron bases would otherwise belong in a museum or in a movie from the gilded age.

The meal of the day at Casey's, as it is every day, is hot dogs. According to Fred Casey, grandson of the founder of this historic little enterprise, the diner serves more than 600 per day, at the counter and through the take-out window installed to handle the extra business. By this measure, Casey's has served nearly 17 million hot dogs since 1927.

Easily the best way to order a Casey hot dog is "all around," with mustard, relish, onions, and a side dish of another hot dog. Maybe two. Don't come looking for fries, soups, or mac and cheese. For eighty years, this splendid cart has served mostly the same things—dogs, burgers, drinks, maybe a slice of (store-bought) pie—with little room or reason to change. Casey's boils its hot dogs and places them in buns conspicuously steamed in a shiny, custom-made copper kettle. Two dogs, a drink, a bag of chips, and maybe a slice of pie will set you back about $5.

Richard Gutman's *American Diner Then and Now* best tells the diner's history. In 1927, after operating a wagon for someone else, Fred Casey purchased his own secondhand Worcester cart and dropped it on a downtown Natick location. In the early years, Casey's served lunch, dinner, and the night-owl business. Fred ran the cart until 1952, passing the business down to his son, Joe Casey. Joe changed very little in the diner, with the exception of having Worcester Lunch Car install a new grill, sandwich board, and icebox in 1958. In 1977, Joe sold the property the diner occupied to a local bank and moved to the current location on South Avenue. Joe's son, Fred, took over from his father in the 1980s, and like his father and grandfather before him, he plans to keep things much the same.

The business has certainly endured because of its charm and the quality of its product, but hot dog joints tend to do well because of the simplicity of the concept and because people choose to remain blissfully ignorant of the ingredients. These meals require minimal prep work, and as even the most gourmet hot dogs can cost as little as 50 cents each in volume, they provide good margins. Casey's customers don't linger over their meals, so the diner turns over seats in fifteen minutes. Anyone willing and able to handle the high volume of such a place stands to profit handsomely—at least in comparison to a more full-service diner or restaurant. Additions to the menu only muck up the works.

That said, don't expect anyone to duplicate the Casey's formula anytime soon. The diner's longevity alone contributes much to its mystique, a fact recognized by fans of diners and hot dogs the world over. Taking a seat at Casey's provides an experience unique for many reasons, not the least of which is the taste of the food. Corporations spend billions of dollars trying to convince potential customers of the unique qualities of their product through brute persuasion. These expensive marketing campaigns work to craft a fiction for people to draw some kind of personal association.

By contrast, Casey's and places like it thrive because they've done the same good thing day in and day out. The efficient preparation and service of dogs, burgers, and drinks without a speck of pretense, and with a not-broke-so-don't-fix-it regard for the operation, create their own value and integrity. Customers have and always will recognize and respect this and will gladly line up at the window to contribute to Casey's success.

DELUXE TOWN DINER
1947 ON-SITE/WORCESTER
Mt. Auburn St., Watertown, MA • (617) 926-8400

Before Don Levy added the word "Deluxe," the Town Diner had a nagging reputation as a middling breakfast-and-lunch-only affair and served a basic and predictable menu. Its former owners underutilized this splendid streamlined product of postwar optimism, apparently unaware of or incapable of recognizing the changing demographics of its host community. Over the past twenty years, Watertown had evolved from a blue-collar Greek and Armenian enclave into a yuppified bedroom community, housing a good share of the area's influx of high-tech workers. Able to seat about 100, the diner had ample capacity and the capability to serve dinners to patrons too busy or too tired to prepare their own at home.

The news of Levy's new venture immediately impressed those who fondly remembered the best days of the Blue Diner in downtown Boston. The Town Diner sorely needed someone with his appreciation for and ability to create a higher standard of diner meals, and who would market them properly to a changed community. After years of falling behind the times, the diner would finally catch up with its market.

Levy calls his concept "fine dinering," which certainly appeals to the new locals. "There are a lot of video production studios in this area, and those people come here all the time," he says. "I see one place having meetings here almost daily." On any given weekend morning, a long line extends out the door, but Levy and crew will take your cell phone number and call you when your table is ready.

For anyone nostalgic for the Blue Diner, the Deluxe Town Diner's menu should induce déjà vu. The new diner marked the return of some of Levy's trademark contributions to diner cuisine, such as ploye (Acadian buckwheat pancakes), "wets" (french fries with gravy), and traditional daily specials such as mac and cheese, roast turkey, or meat loaf, prepared with the Levy flair.

As befitting any truly great diner, the Deluxe Town serves a superlative breakfast, featuring homemade corned-beef hash, large fluffy pancakes with real maple syrup, and perfect omelets, and augments this with still more greatness in its specials and other unique items. The lunch menu might offer lentil vegetable soup and a fine chowder in the land of fine chowders. Hearty sandwiches served with side salads of fresh greens (the menu boards promise "no iceberg here") compel repeat visits to sample the whole menu. And the coffee is superb as well; you'll try none better.

Preservationists will appreciate the restoration of the diner's interior. Though it is a stick-built structure, the building's designer had an obvious appreciation for architectural form. Rich in detail, the streamlined structure

Anchoring the east Watertown neighborhood, the Deluxe Town Diner has adapted to the changing local demographics. Today few diners—indeed, few restaurants—display the level of quality and creativity found here. Owner Don Levy revived a tired but underused streamlined gem and now sets the standard for diner cuisine.

sports all the best features of a "real" diner with some added girth that allows for wider booths not typically found in diners of this vintage. The Deluxe also features banquettes in the rounded corners, a rarity in much of New England.

This structure replaced an older, monitor roof Worcester car, which was converted into the new diner's kitchen. Hints of this structure can be seen in the hallway ceiling leading to the restrooms. Over the years, owners covered up the exuberant azure blue porcelain tiles with faux-wood paneling and installed lighting completely out of character with the diner's original style.

Before he opened the diner, Don immediately worked to restore that character. He removed the paneling that covered the tiles and, in a bit of inspired remodeling, replaced the ceiling laminate panels with brushed aluminum. He also restored the exterior neon, dimmed for years, and hung new lighting more in keeping with the streamlined decor.

The Deluxe Town Diner scores hits with almost everything it does, and Levy currently plans to add a retail component to the operation, selling Deluxe Town Diner branded dry goods and other retro-inspired products. Levy's multifaceted experience in fashion retail, publishing, and now food service creates many potential tangents for a high-profile operation. He hopes to build a small store attached to the diner where a tattered storage shed now stands. Watertown is already a highly attractive place to live and work, and Levy's new venture has made it all the better.

ROSEBUD DINER

1941 WORCESTER #773

381 Summer St., Davis Square, Somerville, MA • (617) 666-6015

In 2002, the *Boston Globe* voted the Rosebud Diner the area's best diner. This marked the culmination of a major effort by the Nichols family to restore not only the diner itself, but its long-suffering image as well. The diner stands on the fringe of Davis Square, and its fortunes and reputation have closely followed those of its surrounding neighborhood. When the Worcester Lunch Car Company built this diner for the Nichols family in 1941, Davis Square was the hub of a bustling, prosperous blue-collar community. But by the end of the 1980s, the square had come to typify the decline of traditional neighborhoods, and it had become the butt of jokes and a place to avoid. By then the diner had devolved as well into a dive bar that fronted a strip joint.

When the Massachusetts Bay Transit Authority extended its Red Line subway branch via a tunnel under the square in the 1980s, it marked the beginning of an amazing turnaround for both diner and square. The Nichols family saw the writing on the subway wall and decided that the time had come to reinvest in the property. Though tired and run-down, the diner still retained much of its originality and had great potential. The Rosebud featured the talents of Worcester's craftsmen at their peak, but the years had seen the removal of the diner's marble top, booths, and backbar and the grafting of a mansard roof. Yet the cobalt blue tile that wrapped around the diner's perimeter and counter base and the black porcelain enamel skin on its streamlined exterior remained wonders to behold.

The Nichols family closed down the back restaurant while they made some significant improvements to the diner that largely restored its original feel and flavor. The new replica booths fit in nicely with the rest of the decor, and the lighting and other fixtures adapted perfectly into the diner's streamlined stylings. The exterior restoration has stalled and remains a source of frustration for the Nicholses as they fight with the contractor, but the diner's interior now provides a warm, friendly setting for customers to enjoy some excellent meals.

By most measures, the Rosebud's menu today would fall into the upscale category, but not so much to alienate anyone seeking the classic experience. Big, hearty breakfasts feature fruit-filled pancakes, fluffy omelets, and homemade corned-beef hash. Lunchtime brings forth fresh homemade soups and the usual sandwiches and hot plates. Dinner gives the kitchen a true chance to shine, producing meals one would expect in more expensive bistros. The Rosebud also features a full bar with a selection of microbrewed beers. Indeed, counter seating seems more loungelike than dinerlike, thanks to the mirror that has replaced the stainless steel and the display of liquor bottles, but the Rosebud in every other way looks and feels perfectly family-oriented as well. Its rough-and-tumble days have long since passed into history.

BEL AIRE DINER

1953 MOUNTAIN VIEW #359

U.S. Route 1, Peabody, MA • (978) 535-3555

Among the diner's many romantic images, one of the most pervasive has it as a stainless steel, middle-of-nowhere truck stop, where the coffee is strong, the waitresses sassy, and the food portions big. The Bel Aire Diner would fit well within that image. When Mountain View installed the Bel Aire in 1953, it likely stood alone, well outside the boundaries of any traditional commercial district. U.S. Route 1 served as a tourist road in the early days of auto tourism, and places like the Bel Aire established themselves as pioneers in their locations.

The diner got its name thanks to swanky connotations associated with the car and the fashionable California neighborhood, but everything about it proclaims working-class, truck-stop diner, and all the good things that go with that distinction. Low prices, long hours, and good food in what has become, thanks to local ordinance, a smoke-free atmosphere make the diner great for families on a budget.

Because of its location, the Bel Aire does not classify as a neighborhood diner per se. Southbound travelers jumping off I-95 or returning from a trip to the big-box store farther north will find access difficult at best, but the diner provides a perfect jumping-off point for any trek north. The classic, towering sign that beckons travelers has grown a little tattered around the edges, much like the diner itself, but the friendly staff and broad menu selections will certainly meet, if not exceed, expectations.

Favorites here include blueberry pancakes, chowders, and of course, meat loaf. The Bel Aire operates without a shred of pretense. The seasoned servers will always greet you warmly and serve you with efficiency and a smile.

The diner's appeal to truckers comes from the close proximity of the family's diesel station next door, the phones at the tables, and the large-screen television Harry Kallas installed in one of the diner's windows in the mid-1990s. For all travelers, a handy mileage chart on the menu board measures the distance to major cities in the area. For this part of New England, the Bel Aire represents one of the largest diners in operation, with eighty-plus seats, and it's one of the few today with a full liquor license, a relatively common feature in these sizable hash houses in their heyday.

Today Harry and family continue a well-trod but highly valued tradition of serving good, basic comfort foods in a setting unchanged in fifty years. This increasingly rare experience serves as a civilizing touchstone for all levels of our society. The Bel Aire doesn't just nourish the hungry, it also anchors our culture to the common values of pride, quality, and community.

CAPITOL DINER
1928 BRILL
431 Union St., Lynn, MA • (781) 595-9314

One of the nation's first diner enthusiasts, Larry Cultrera, once described an experience at the Capitol Diner in these terms: "If you walk out of the Capitol without a smile on your face, there's something wrong with you." You could write volumes more about this splendid place, its history, food, and people, but it would all come back to Cultrera's rock-solid assertion.

Anyone who attempts to describe the truly great diner might as well just drop the name of this rare 1928 Brill diner. Stepping into the Capitol transports you back in time, and you immediately get a sense of having entered a kind of oasis from the modern world and all of its troubles. During a busy Friday lunchtime, the frenetic activity behind and in front of the counter might intimidate the uninitiated, but only for a moment. As hard as the folks at Capitol work, they still smile and extend hearty welcomes to all.

The Capitol Diner came to Lynn just as the country began its long descent into the Depression, and yet for most of its seventy-plus years, it has managed to thrive, even when it looked like the city of Lynn might never emerge from its own doldrums. A former site of boot manufacturing and home to a General Electric jet engine plant, the city today has only begun to benefit from its nearness to the shore as well as the general economic prosperity that has mostly returned to eastern Massachusetts, thanks to a boom in high-tech and financial services industries.

In the thick of it, this little diner carved out a tiny haven on a city block around the corner from the train station. The diner sits perpendicular to the street, but it maintains a small courtyard where the late Buddy Fennell kept his pet chickens and, in later years, built a koi pond. Buddy died in 2000, but not before his son Bobby established his own indelible mark on the family business. Bobby stood at his father's side in the late 1960s and learned well. Just the sight of Bobby today, wearing a white shirt and tie while flipping an omelet, looks like a scene from a dusty old photograph pulled from someone's archive.

Short-order cook and elected state representative Bobby Fennell helps foster community at the State House and behind the counter of his Capitol Diner in Lynn.

The Capitol's fare won't likely surprise anyone who visits for the first time, but the overall quality just might. The small diner actually turns out a surprisingly varied number of items for an operation of this scale. Home-made desserts finish off homemade stews, soups, hot plates, and the diner's signature broiled haddock sandwich. It hardly gets simpler, but somehow, the Capitol makes it sublime.

Until 2003, lucky customers had the great pleasure of having longtime waitress Marie LeFrancois serve them all this wonderful food. That year, Marie ended twenty-four years behind the diner's glass counter to take a "quiet" job in an office. During that time, Marie executed her duties with great care, taking orders by memory, orchestrating the flow of food with precision, and remarkably remembering the names of even the most sporadic regulars. Her energy, ability, and concern for her customers caused them to value her very highly in what tends to be an underappreciated profession. She will be missed.

But she leaves behind a diner in very good hands, to be sure. The Capitol makes one wonder how different the roadside might look if every diner could maintain this level of quality in both service and food. Ray Krok might never have stood a chance.

If the story of the Capitol wasn't interesting enough, it became more so in 1994 with the election of Bobby Fennell to the Massachusetts legislature. Now in his third term, he represents the tenth legislative district in the state's House of Representatives. Fennell's main issues, as one might expect, concern the challenges of urban development and the revitalization of aging industrial centers. Unlike many who have jumped on that bandwagon, Bobby, his family, and the loyal crew at the diner work at the front line of that battle, exemplifying a winning strategy and how a good diner can play a role in that effort.

In a 1995 article in *Roadside*, Bobby described one advantage his background brings to his new job: "I've always been proud of my diner and what my father's done, so I'm not embarrassed to tell people about the way I make my living. So when someone calls to complain about something, they'll often say, 'What are you? A lawyer like the rest of them up there?' And I'll tell them, 'No. I'm a short order cook!' That switches them right around."

DINER DIRECTORY

BOSTON METRO

Apple Tree Diner
North of Boston, MA
1929 Worcester 641
In private storage. Fabled diner formerly located in Dedham, Massachusetts, until late 1980s. Restored.

Balloon Boutique
41 Boston St.
Lynn, MA
(781) 595-0112
1941 Sterling 4105
Converted to florist and balloon vendor.

Beachmont Roast Beef
619 Winthrop Ave.
Revere, MA
1948 Worcester 811
Originally a barrel roof diner. Complete exterior remodeling, but barrel ceiling

This photo shows O. B. Hill Rigging shoehorning the Apple Tree Diner into Dave Waller's converted fire station home in 1994.

still discernible. Features roast beef sandwiches.

Beckwith Elevator
Southampton St.
Boston, MA
(508) 676-1616
1971 Fodero
Massachusetts' newest diner until 1996, but only briefly served food. Currently used as an office.

Bel Aire Diner
131 Newbury St./Rte. 1
Peabody, MA
(978) 535-3555
1953 Mountain View 359
Classic stainless steel truck-stop diner, located on Route 1 North, just before I-95 on-ramp. Currently features big-screen TV in the window. Full-service menu on weekdays. American food. Open during dinner hours.

Big Dig Diner
Drydock & Channel
Boston, MA
1946 Silk City 46101
Operated or sat on Route 22 in Ono, Union Township, Pennsylvania, across from the Ono Truck Center. Last operated in Ono as the Windmill Diner, which closed in 1985. Bought in June 1994 by Steve Harwin and Diversified Diners, who shipped it to Cleveland and restored it. Shipped to Boston in August 1995 as part of a nonprofit youth training program, finally opening for a short time in 2000. Closed in 2003 with uncertain future.

Breakfast Club
270 Western Ave.
Allston, MA
(617) 783-5844
1953 Worcester 841
One of the last examples of Worcester Lunch Car's attempts to keep up with Jersey competition. Originally Fahey's Diner, which had two other diners on this location. Also formerly Ted's Diner and Henry's Diner. Clean and sympathetically renovated in 2002. Serves well-regarded breakfast and lunch.

Buddy's Truck Stop
113 Washington St.
Somerville, MA
(617) 623-9725
1929 Worcester 624
Originally installed in Leominster, Massachusetts, and moved to Somerville in 1951. Twenty-stooler featuring homemade hash. Stainless side panels added recently, but features original sliding door. Fine and friendly diner experience. Breakfast and lunch.

Capitol Diner
431 Union St.
Lynn, MA
(781) 595-9314
1928 Brill
Without a doubt one of the best diners in the country. Serves full menu and well known for fresh fish sandwiches, chowders, and hearty breakfasts. A true community landmark and not to be missed. Listed on the National Register of Historic Places.

Casey's Diner
36 South Ave.
Natick, MA
(508) 655-3761
1922 Worcester

They replaced the sign (for one much taller), but otherwise the Bel Aire has barely changed since this post card was issued.

Listed on the National Register of Historic Places. Claims to serve more than 600 hot dogs a day. Tiny ten-stooler near downtown Natick in beautiful condition. Arguably one of the oldest diners in continuous operation in the country. Closes for the month of August for vacation.

Chick's Roast Beef
218 Main St./Rte. 127N
Gloucester, MA
(508) 283-1405
1949 O'Mahony
Formerly Michel's Cape Ann Diner, but now a sub shop and partially stripped of many of its original interior features. Exterior very intact. Sandwich-based menu. Lunch and dinner.

Corkery Tractor Trailer
868 Turnpike St./Rte. 138
Canton, MA
(617) 828-5617
1957 Fodero
Formerly Jimmy's Diner of Boston's Mattapan neighborhood. Used as office for construction company and bricked over. Still shows much of its stainless exterior and therefore picture worthy.

One of the largest Worcester cars ever built, the Full Moon Restaurant, tucked away in an industrial neighborhood of Lynn, now specializes in Thai cuisine.

Deluxe Town Diner
627 Mt. Auburn St.
Watertown, MA
(617) 924-9789
1947 on-site/Worcester
Built on-site but looks like a true classic diner. Listed on the National Register of Historic Places. Sets the standard for all diners to follow. Stylish, funky, but family-friendly setting. Unsurpassed food quality, and an essential stop on any diner tour that comes within 50 miles of Watertown. Kitchen is an actual diner but you have to go inside to see. Well-rounded menu of freshly prepared neo diner cuisine. Homemade desserts, soups, corned beef hash, and some of the best coffee anywhere.

Driftwood II Restaurant
94 Foster St.
Peabody, MA
1928 Worcester
Remodeled and now more of a restaurant.

Full Moon Restaurant
38 Bennett St.
Lynn, MA
(781) 596-3860
1952 Worcester 833

Former Lynway Diner, located on Route 1A, called "the Lynway," in Lynn, Massachusetts. In 1996, converted to Asian cuisine. Still in very original condition.

Jonquille's Diner
275 Lee Burbank Hwy.
Revere, MA
(617) 284-9885
c. 1940 on-site
Built on-site but looks exactly like a vintage Worcester barrel roof diner. American food with Portuguese specialties.

Kelly's Diner
674 Broadway
Somerville, MA
(617) 623-8102
1948 O'Mahony
Brought to Somerville from Wilmington, Delaware, in 1995. Formerly known as Frank's Diner. Large, well-preserved stainless steel diner. American food. Daily specials. Breakfast and lunch only.

Lanna Thai Diner
901 Main St./Rte. 38
Woburn, MA
(781) 935-5682
1952 Worcester 834
Listed on the National Register of Historic Places. Unique and beautiful custom-made car. Seats only twenty-five, unusual for a diner of this vintage. Originally known as Jack's Diner. Subject of painting by John Baeder when it was known as Stella's.

Liberty Diner
1003 Massachusetts Ave.
Roxbury, MA
(617) 442-9262
1930s Worcester
Monitor roof car, extensively remodeled.

Lloyd's Diner
184 Fountain St.
Framingham, MA
(508) 879-8750
1942 Worcester 783
Listed on the National Register of Historic Places. Originally operating as Whit's Diner in Orange, Massachusetts. Moved to current location in 1990 and restored with the help of Richard Gutman. American food, served in large portions. Breakfast and lunch only.

Maplewood Tavern
25 Lebanon St.
Malden, MA
1920s Worcester
Dilapidated condition. Last used as tavern. Shoehorned between buildings and enveloped in exterior remodelings.

Olympian Diner
Salisbury, MA
1962 Fodero
In storage. One of the newer diners in the state, operating in Braintree until 2001, when it was closed and removed from original location.

Phyllis's Diner
183 Broadway
Everett, MA
1930s on-site
Built on-site but closely conforms to classic 1930s vintage Worcester car. In 2003, owner turned diner 90 degrees to provide access to back parking lot. Classic comfort food. Reasonable prices. Breakfast and lunch only.

Pig & Whistle Diner
226 North Beacon St.
Brighton, MA
(617) 254-8058
1952 Mountain View 320

Closed in 2002. Stainless steel car originally located in Watertown Square, where Pat's Diner (not a true diner) and the funeral home are now located. Name comes from the stockyard and rail yards once located nearby. In very good condition.

Pilgrim Diner
4 Boston St./Rte. 114
Salem, MA
(978) 745-2348
1936 Worcester 725
Serves breakfast and lunch only. In good condition except for the absence of much of the original furnishings and equipment.

Portside Cape Ann Diner
2 River St.
Danvers, MA
(978) 777-1437
1948 Worcester 813
Formerly in Gloucester, hence the Cape Ann portion of the name. Barrel roof car. American food with Greek specialties. Full menu.

In 2003, Haj Gamale took the diner that had belonged to his former employer and turned it 90 degrees, giving customers access to a small back parking lot. Here, Phyllis is waving in the window.

Red Wing Diner
Rte. 1 South
Walpole, MA
(508) 668-0453
1933 Worcester 709
Used as bar and lounge for seafood restaurant. Exterior of this barrel roof diner is concealed by red shingles. Lunch and dinner.

Rosebud Diner
381 Summer St./Davis Square
Somerville, MA
(617) 666-6015
1941 Worcester 773
Listed on the National Register of Historic Places. Rare streamliner model, largely restored to original condition in mid-1990s. Local "best diner" award winner. Full menu with full bar. Daily specials, homemade corned beef hash, and well-prepared hot platters. Late nights.

Salem Diner
326 Canal St./Rte. 1A
Salem, MA
(978) 744-9776

The Whistlestop retains precious little of its original Worcester features and fixtures, but its new owner, Barbara Henry, has hopes and plans to bring some of those back. In the meantime, she feeds and entertains a growing group of happy customers near the heart of downtown Peabody.

1941 Sterling Streamliner 4106
Listed on the National Register of Historic Places. One of only two remaining Sterling Streamliners still in operation. Breakfast and lunch only. American food with Greek specialties.

South Street Diner
178 Kneeland St.
Boston, MA
(617) 350-0028
1947 on-site
Most famously known as the Blue Diner until 1992, serving upscale, neo diner cuisine. Twenty-four-hour operation now serves standard diner fare with daily specials. Homemade soups and hot plates.

Subway
Rte. 1A
Beverly, MA
1950 Worcester 828
Originally the Miss Beverly Diner. Part of the Subway chain outlet as of early 2004.

T&D Trucking
580 Chelsea St.
E. Boston, MA
(617) 561-4600
1949 O'Mahony
Originally operated by the Georgenes family as the Victoria Diner in Dorchester. Moved in 1965 to make way for Swingle replacement. Dilapidated. Last used as office for T&D Trucking. Now abandoned.

Tantawan Thai Cuisine
356 Arsenal St.
Watertown, MA
(617) 926-8371
1930 Worcester
Very little remains of what was once the Arsenal Diner, named for its proximity to the Watertown Arsenal. Thai cuisine.

Timmy's Diner
Framingham, MA
1933 Worcester 717
In private storage. Purchased and
restored in late 1980s by Hanna family,
who struggled unsuccessfully to establish it in a new location in Framingham.
Last reports have the diner in very poor
condition again.

Lulu's Diner
906 Eastern Ave.
Malden, MA
(781) 321-0257
1933 Worcester 690
Laid out in a lunch-wagon configuration. Basic grilled diner fare. Breakfast
and lunch only.

Victoria Diner
1024 Massachusetts Ave.
Boston, MA
(617) 442-5965
1965 Swingle
The state's only Swingle, this one of
Colonial design and one of the newer
models to come to the Bay State. When
the Georgenes family sold the Victoria
in January 2004, it ended an era span-
ning seventy-five years of their diner
operation in Boston. American food
with Greek specialties. Full menu.

Whistlestop Diner
1 Railroad Ave.
Peabody, MA
1929 Worcester 650

The splendid classic Worcester car on Waltham's
Main Street should not be missed by anyone
traveling through the area. The graceful beauty
of Wilson's Diner has made it the subject of
paintings, countless photographs, and the set
of at least one movie.

Formerly Kurley's Diner and the Railroad Diner. Renovations stripped original furnishings and equipment, but
diner retains vintage charm. Basic grilled
diner fare. Breakfast and lunch.

Wilson's Diner
507 Main St./Rte. 20
Waltham, MA
(781) 899-0760
1949 Worcester 819
Listed on the National Register of Historic Places. Extremely well-maintained
barrel roof diner just east of Waltham's
downtown. American food with Greek
specialties. Breakfast and lunch only.

THE MERRIMACK VALLEY

As one might expect, the heavily industrialized and populated region of Massachusetts north of Boston had dozens of diners over the course of the last century. It also had three companies that built them, the most famous being the J. B. Judkins Coach Builders of Merrimac. Though Judkins enjoyed a relatively brief six-year period of building diners, its history stretched back to 1857 as a builder of horse-drawn carriages. The advent of the automobile forced the company to adapt to the new technology, so it began to build coaches for this new industry. As the industry consolidated, the major companies no longer contracted for their car bodies. Judkins had to adapt yet again, so in 1936, it entered the diner business.

The Depression saw several established firms making similar moves, though most of them came from a background of building railcars of various types. For a company like J. G. Brill, a major manufacturer of trolleys and railroad coaches, the similar proportions and construction techniques of diners made for a relatively easy retooling when rail orders dropped off. During the Depression, the diner industry was one of the few that actually saw growth, easing the decision even further.

Judkins acquired the patent of Maine boatbuilder Bertram Harley which described the construction of a multisectioned diner sliced in 4-foot sections akin to a loaf of bread. This made for the easy transport of diners as lengthy as the owner wanted or could afford. Though a patented process, the Bixler Manufacturing Company in Norwalk, Ohio, apparently anticipated Harley and built diners to very similar specifications from 1931 to 1936.

Though short-lived, the company constructed some of the most beloved and rare diner designs the industry ever produced. Its Sterling Streamliners capitalized on the then-current rage in industrial design that streamlined everything from locomotives to saltshakers. One savvy operator pushed this design to its natural extreme, building a faux tunnel from which the diner appeared to emerge.

Judkins built seventeen of these, of which only two currently remain in operation and one more is seriously threatened. A fourth, My Tin Man, still stands as a burnt-out hulk, and yet another is broken apart and lies in storage. Of Judkins's other style diners, which struck a more conventional pro-

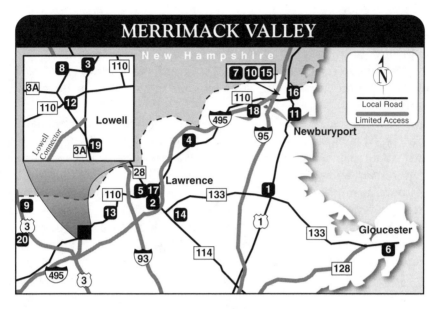

1 Agawam Diner: Rowley (MS)
2 Al's Diner: Lawrence (BR)
3 Arthur's Paradise Diner: Lowell (BR)
4 B&M Diner: Groveland (BR)
5 Carro Rojo: Lawrence (BR)
6 Chick's Roast Beef: Gloucester (MS)
7 Chubby's Diner: Salisbury (MS)
8 Club Diner: Lowell (BR)
9 Dream Diner: Tyngsboro (OS)
10 Englewood Diner: Salisbury (BR)

11 Fish Tale Diner: Salisbury (BR)
12 Four Sisters Owl Diner: Lowell (MS)
13 Lin Garden Dracut (BR)
14 Midway Diner: Andover (BR)
15 Miss Newport Diner: Salisbury (BR)
16 Pat's Diner: Salisbury (BR)
17 Sam's Steak Out: Lawrence (BR)
18 Trader Allan's Truck Stop: Amesbury (BR)
19 Trolley Stop Diner: Lowell (BR)
20 Tyngsboro Diner: Tyngsboro (BR)

file akin to a standard railroad coach, not many remain extant either. Intrepid roadside archeologists will take note that Judkins seemed to enjoy some success selling these diners in upstate New York. This region could count at least six still in operation as late as 1990. In contrast, only one Worcester diner operated in New York State throughout the 1980s and 1990s—the former Service Diner, which came to Bolton Landing from Attleboro, Massachusetts, in 1989. No records show any Worcester cars in New York before that.

In New England, surprisingly few Judkins-built diners have lasted into the twenty-first century. Aside from the three Streamliners, only five Sterlings still operate with any degree of structural preservation. Of these, only the basic frame of the Miss Lyndonville in Vermont remains, and Catman Cafe in Mansfield, Massachusetts, is just a shell of its former Sterling self. Two more

Sterlings stand intact and in storage, one rots in a storage lot in Worcester, an additional two serve other retail uses, and three exist in pieces in a warehouse in Fall River. Outside New England, only four are still in operation.

The other company, Pollard, based in Lowell, has only two extant examples of their products on the landscape, one in New Hampshire and the other in Maine.

And strictly speaking, Donald Evans merits inclusion in this list, having constructed one car in 1952 for the use of his nephew Bill Evans, who also owned Ann's Diner in Salisbury. Evans built a diner nearly indistinguishable from a real Sterling Streamliner, using interior parts likely fashioned by Worcester Lunch Car. The diner took Don Evans nearly seven years to complete, and it didn't stay in its intended location for very long. After a four-year run at Salisbury Beach, Evans sold the diner to Edward G. Bryer, who moved it to a location in Lowell. Here you will still find it, now called the Trolley Stop, and thoroughly and ironically remodeled to look like a trolley car.

Our tour of this area begins at one of New England's most popular diners, the Agawam. This small, unspoiled Fodero car has become a living legend in the local restaurant scene, bringing with it over fifty years of history that involved four diners in five locations. You'll likely find it busy just about any time of the day, with a healthy proportion of customers not leaving without a piece of the diner's famous banana or coconut cream pie. Though most meals here are essentially utilitarian takes on the diner classics, the desserts reign surpreme. Don't miss out. (See page 93.)

While two of the four Agawam Diners have gone to the great roadside in the sky, the original still stands and operates in one of the most scenic locations of any diner in New England. The mouth of the Merrimack River separates the towns of Salisbury and Newburyport, and on the northern bank in Salisbury sits the Fish Tale Diner, overlooking the marina, the U.S. Route 1 bridge, and the town of Newburyport. In the summer, few things beat a good diner meal on the Fish Tale's front deck overlooking the water. No other diner in all of New England enjoys such a vista.

Worcester Lunch Car refaced this diner twice for the Galanis family, refitting it with new porcelain signature panels in 1949. These gave way to shake shingles, which in this setting look almost natural. Inside, the bustling, hard-pounding activity endured by this diner during the Galanis years hardly shows its effects. The Fish Tale retains most of its original interior features, and today Michelle and David Freeman treat both the diner and their customers with great care. As expected in such a setting, the menu features a variety of fried seafood dishes to savor along with the view.

Besides the beaches, Salisbury's position on the map makes it a crossroads of sorts. With the advent of automobile travel, traffic plying the Route

The Fish Tale started out as Agawam #1. In 1979, it "retired" to this piece of waterfront on the banks of the Merrimack River. Ownership recently added the front deck, giving customers one of the most scenic views of any diner in New England.

110 corridor up from Worcester and Lowell would join the flow moving between Boston and Portland, Maine. This confluence of commerce made the town an ideal place for a diner, upon which Jim and Ann Evans eventually capitalized. Their son Bill now remembers a time when Route 110's popularity with the truckers largely meant finding a diner in just about every significant town along its length. A significant number still can be found on or near the route.

In 1948, the Evanses purchased a used unit, the former Arlington Diner, previously located in Haverill, Massachusetts. They traded up after only two years of brisk business. In 1950, they purchased Worcester #824, a large custom car with a dining area partitioned with a pocket door. This diner still stands there today, albeit with some modifications and signs of age.

The Evanses did well with their enterprise until the construction of I-95 and I-495, which sent the diner into a slow decline under a series of operators through the 1980s and 1990s. In 1992, one operator apparently ran off with the diner's original Worcester-fashioned clock. The town and general area have rebounded in the years since, with an influx of new residents and the rebounding Massachusetts economy.

In 1999, when Pat Archambault became the diner's new owner, she gave it a new name, hers, and subsequently replaced the elegantly lettered porcelain enamel panels with ones made of plywood. Though preservationists winced at the affront to diner aesthetics, Pat claimed to have retained the original panels, and the diner's interior has changed little. Unfortunately, the diner suffers from a more serious structural problem, as indicated by the

The original sky blue porcelain panels were replaced with T-111 plywood.

The interior of the former Ann's Diner has changed little since Worcester trucked it to Salisbury, save for the missing clock, but the sagging roof will soon need some work.

slumping roof. The building housing the kitchen has sunk into the ground and pulled back the diner's rear wall, weakening the roof supports. Shoring up the outbuilding's foundation will be costly, and indeed, it may exceed the ability of any operator to pay. These issues aside, Pat can take the credit for giving the diner its longest run under a single owner in a decade.

In 1996, Salisbury gained its third diner with the arrival of Chubby's, a rare iconic 1940 O'Mahony, refurbished by Ralph Musi Diners in Carteret, New Jersey. The diner had a former life as the Village Diner in Armonk, New York, and it had a moment of fame as the subject of a painting by John Baeder, who depicted it rotting in a field as the Blue Moon Diner.

Musi's work hardly qualified as museum quality, but he did restore the structure's usability and some of its original luster. Unable to fashion proper corner pieces for its stainless steel cornice, Musi affixed square pieces. Booths, stools, and the diner's countertop did not survive the refurbishment. In fact, Musi removed and disposed of the diner's original black marble countertop and opted not to restore its booths.

Freddy Shaheen and Ron Cipullo reopened Chubby's, but this partnership ended rather quickly. Shaheen described himself as the marketer for the diner, while Cipullo assumed the kitchen duties, saying that he intended to provide first-rate meals using fresh ingredients in a smoke-free atmosphere. But Cipullo left less than six months after opening, and soon after that, Sha-

Ralph Musi performed renovations on this classic O'Mahony in 1996, but the folks responsible for bringing it to Salisbury lasted only a couple years after they opened. John Baeder depicted this diner in an Armonk, New York, junkyard as the "Blue Moon Diner," though it originally opened as the Village Diner in that town.

heen left the diner to his mother-in-law, Liz Dizazzo, who immediately lifted the ban on smoking. Despite a very high-profile location near the entrance to I-495, the diner failed to attract a strong following.

In 1998, truck dealer Dave Pritchard entered the diner business by purchasing Chubby's. Pritchard mainly sought to secure an adjacent parcel, but the bonus of also getting Chubby's led to a deepening interest in diners in general. Pritchard mostly keeps his hands out of the operation, having hired a manager to keep tabs on the business.

Pritchard's interest in these roadside artifacts grew, leading to his purchase in 2003 of the nomadic Englewood Diner, becoming another in a long line of owners in a relatively short time. Pritchard indicates that he may finally finish the diner's restoration and set it up locally, but in the meantime, he added to his collection with the purchase of the striking Miss Newport Diner from its longtime location in Newport, Vermont. This fire-engine red Worcester car spent its entire productive existence in the far northern Vermont town (see "Western Massachusetts and Vermont," page 134). The diner's near perfect condition was only slightly marred by a grill fire in the mid-1990s. Its pink vaulted ceiling, cozy hardwood finish, marble counter, and original oak booths always made it a required addition to any diner aficionado's photo archive.

Pritchard doesn't reveal any definite plans for the Miss Newport, except for a half-serious proposal to sell it to someone living in one of the nation's twenty-four other Newports. He probably has a better chance of winning the lottery. Today both diners sit together in Pritchard's lot, surrounded by semitrailers.

As is typical for a northeastern industrial region, most of the diners that ever operated here have given up the ghost. According to Gary Thomas's thoroughly researched book, *Diners of the North Shore,* perhaps dozens of diners once may have served this market at any given time between 1900 and 1950. On the old roads that connect the major towns, a few of those ghosts still stand in testament to that age.

In North Andover, Doug Johnson slowly restores Worcester #666 on his property. The diner was once half of a double diner operation in Shrewsbury, Massachusetts, separated in the late 1980s, with the other half eventually ending up in Hanover, New Hampshire. Both owners permanently took the diners out of service for private use.

Trader Alan's Truck Stop might not survive the publishing of this book, but its wreck teeters on Route 150 near I-495 in Amesbury. This Worcester car started in 1947 as Russell's Diner in Quincy, Massachusetts.

In Haverhill, the structure last known as the B&M Diner awaits either a buyer or a bulldozer. This diner appeared in a John Baeder painting as Alley Oops, but it began its life as Baldwin's Diner in Roxbury, Massachusetts, in 1928. After service in Charlestown, Massachusetts, it made its way to Haverhill. In 1946, Kenny Kichu purchased the diner at auction and attached it to his cafeteria-style restaurant, stylishly clad in black Vitrolite panels. Kichu

B&M Diner

put the same paneling on the diner as well, but the decline of Haverhill likely meant the decline of Kenny's Restaurant and Diner as well. Today the diner sits empty, its windows boarded with curtains painted on the plywood.

The once proud city of Lawrence has become something of an economic basket case, made more glaringly obvious by the prosperity of the surrounding region. The city's huge red brick mills still stand as testaments to the city's former economic prowess in the days of the nineteenth century, when the Merrimack Valley produced textiles for a young nation. A city such as Lawrence could likely claim diners in every neighborhood. Today Lawrence has only three left, with one converted to a Hispanic restaurant and buried under several renovations.

Perhaps Lawrence will eventually see the same rebirth as its own Al's Diner. The fire that hit the 1934 Worcester in 1999 might have finished it off but for the determination of its current owner, Kenneth Field, and the devotion of its customers. Field restored the diner to almost better condition than before the fire. Previous ownership had encased much of the interior in Formica-like surfaces and had removed the original booths and stools. Field rebuilt the booths in much the same fashion as the originals and re-created the diner's original monitor-style wood-paneled ceiling.

The diner began as O'Neil's Diner after its purchase by Charles O'Neil, who was apparently the only customer Worcester Lunch Car had for a new

FLOOD SCENE, LAWRENCE DAM, MARCH 20, 1936

SAUNDERS STUDIO

COLLECTION OF JONATHAN YONAN

Today, Sam's Steak Out sits on the location of the diner in this view, taken at the time of the flood that followed the Great Hurricane of 1936.

diner that year. He placed it just down the road from where Al's Diner now sits. Al Demuth purchased the diner in 1953 and gave it his name, which remains associated with the business today.

The diner serves its customers well, with good basic comfort food with a French Canadian twist. Al's serves a French pork pie, baked beans with breakfast, and homemade salmon pie on Fridays. On the Route 110 river road between Lawrence and Lowell sits the former Old Colony Diner. At 60 feet in length, the Old Colony was the largest ever built by Worcester, which built it for the Georgenes family in 1937 as the flagship of their five-diner Boston area chain. The Old Colony served the Dorchester section of Boston until the family sold off all their locations except the Victoria Diner and Restaurant, now located on Massachusetts Avenue in South Boston (see pages 33–34).

Rarely does a fire actually help bring a diner back, but owner Ken Field made it happen after his own 1999 tragedy. Today Al's Diner looks closer to original condition than it had in a good twenty years. Before the fire, laminate panels covered all the splendid Worcester woodwork, which has since been restored to its original luster.

The structure stands shrouded in plywood and stripped of all but a few of its original decorative features. It now provides storage for the Lin Garden restaurant. The 1980 guidebook *Diners of the Northeast*, by Alan Bellink and Donald Kaplan, described the Old Colony as "practically a mint condition" 60-foot diner with bright red enamel panels. Inside, "the green stools have squared off white porcelain bases and a brass footrest runs the length of the counter. The floor is completely tiled in green." Looking at before and after views of this structure makes you wince.

In contrast to the economic doldrums that hover over Lawrence, Lowell shows every sign of a city on the verge of renaissance. Lowell was another mill town growing from the burgeoning industrial revolution, and its textile mills saw their decline by the turn of the nineteenth century. By the latter half of the twentieth century, Lowell's bleak prospects gave little cause for hope. But in the late 1970s, thanks to the efforts of its congressional repre-

Lowell's general recognition of its history in America's industrial revolution led to the exterior restoration of the Paradise. When its neighborhood became a historic district, the old Worcester car got a fresh coat of paint.

sentative and then U.S. senator, the late Paul Tsongas, Lowell's industrial heart became a national heritage park, sparking renewed interest in its tired, dormant mill buildings. Lowell also played a role in the Massachusetts economic miracle of that period when the Wang computer company built its towering headquarters there. Through the 1980s, Wang's success in the rapidly growing mini-computer sector of the industry put the city back on the economic map. The company's demise in the 1990s might otherwise have sent the city back into a tailspin, except that the national park designation began to bear fruit and attract new investment.

The city has since seen significant progress, and though many of the typical problems associated with old industrial towns persist, the city seems on the brink of a whole new era. Lowell proudly promotes its new single-A minor league baseball team, its reviving downtown, its Bread and Roses Folk Festival, and its collection of world-class textile and history museums. Serving all these visitors and many of its longtime residents, the city's three remaining diners have battled successfully against obsolescence and thrived. A fourth diner, the Trolley Stop, now serves as a pizza joint, and previous operators have stripped the structure of all the features identifying it as the only diner built by Donald Evans.

When Arthur's Paradise Diner became part of this historic district, its owners restored the exterior, expertly repainting the diner's name on its steel panels. The 1937 Worcester car sits on a site created by the leveling of a slope down to the adjacent canal. By the 1980s, the original paint had decayed so badly that only the faint ghost of the diner's name remained evident. Though the diner now presents a much prettier exterior, its interior retains all the charms of its original fixtures and decor, albeit severely worn and tired. Reportedly, Lowell's native son Jack Kerouac warmed a stool here on more than a few occasions.

The Paradise's claim to fame is its Boot Mill Sandwich, named for the boot-manufacturing mill next door. Not for anyone with a cardiac condition, this breakfast sandwich consists of a grilled roll with eggs and cheese, bacon, sausage, or ham, and a fistful of home fries.

The Club Diner, on Dutton Street, sports a sympathetically refurbished facade concealing a Worcester monitor roof diner. Much of the original interior also remains in this classic, and train buffs get treated to the sight of an old Boston & Maine Railroad steam engine sitting across the street, as well as the restored trolley car that shuttles visitors between museums.

David Lavesseur keeps the lights on in this Lowell institution and prepares all the usual suspects, along with the popular French Canadian favorites typically found in this region. The Club Diner generally keeps night-owl hours, opening at 11:00 P.M. and running until 2:00 the following

Time has brought charm to this diner's extensive 1960s-era renovations, and the Lowell Heritage National Park has brought it new business.

afternoon, depending on the time of the year and the availability of help. It always maintains regular breakfast and lunch hours, but call first to be sure.

The Four Sisters Owl Diner first served customers in 1940 as the Monarch Diner, located on Main Street in Waltham, Massachusetts. When its O'Mahony replacement arrived in 1951, the Worcester streamliner eventually moved to its present Lowell location, complete with new front panels replacing the word "Monarch" with "The Owl." It has since become a Lowell breakfast institution. (See page 96.)

Honorable mention for inclusion here must go to the Dream Diner in Tyngsboro. The building itself shares none of the heritage of its prefab counterparts, but the woman responsible for its success leaves little doubt where she got her chops. Marybeth Shanahan honed her skills working at her uncle and aunt's diner, the demanding Four Sisters. Hard-working, attractive, and sharp as a knife, Marybeth has made the best of a bland structure, creating a restaurant that has all the best elements of a great diner, by applying her experience gained by working in one of the best diners in existence.

In some ways, the Dream Diner is indistinguishable from the Four Sisters. Both serve big meals for little money, including big slabs of ham. Both have sincere, attentive waitresses. And both offer at least a couple dozen styles of omelets, although the Dream omelets are named for diner builders, past and present. In the words of Doug and Polly Smith, fellow roadside mavens from the Niagara region and authors of *The Cheap Gourmet's Dining Guide to the Niagara Frontier*, the Dream Diner would qualify as a "NAD-BOB": Not A Diner, But Ought to Be. No argument here, and if Marybeth ever does finally realize her dream, she will get that "real" diner eventually. It's only a matter of time.

This journey ends at KJ's Airport Diner in Shirley, just off the Route 2 expressway. The 1933 Worcester car now comes clad in all stainless, a feature likely added to this monitor roof diner in the 1960s or 1970s. It arrived from Clinton, Massachusetts, where locals remember it as the White Elephant Diner, and was set down by the owner of the small, single-runway airport. Unfortunately, the diner does not face the runway, so aviation buffs can't watch take-offs and landings while they dine.

AGAWAM DINER
1954 FODERO
U.S. Route 1 & Route 133, Rowley, MA • (978) 948-7780

Mention the Agawam Diner to just about anyone who lives within twenty miles of it, and you will likely invoke the same response: "Mmm . . . Great pie!" Since the Galanis family opened their first Agawam Diner in Ipswich, Massachusetts, naming it for the river running through the town, little has changed except the personnel, the prices, the locations, and the diners themselves. For the past sixty years, the Agawam has served a tried and true menu of basic comfort foods, fried clams, and fresh-baked desserts. Look up the words *consistency* or *reliability* in the dictionary and you just might find a picture of this diner.

The Galanis family purchased four diners total, moving and shuffling them around the North Shore. The first Agawam was a small Worcester diner, purchased in 1940 with a $750 deposit (against a total price of $9,750) and brought to its location in Ipswich. In 1947, the family purchased a second, larger Worcester, displacing Agawam number one, which the family moved to a new location in Rowley. In November 1954, the family decided to upgrade their Ipswich location with a new Fodero diner from Bloomfield, New Jersey. This new stainless model replaced Agawam number two in Ipswich, which the Galanises sold to a buyer in Salem, Massachusetts. According to Louis "Junior" Galanis, son of the original owner, the family went with Fodero because of its more modern qualities. "Worcester stayed with the same old class," he said. "They never moved up. Fodero built the best diner in the world."

In fact, they liked their new Fodero so much that they bought another for a new location in Peabody on U.S. Route 1. For almost seven years through the 1950s, the Galanis family operated a chain of three diners, in three towns, as well as a bowling alley and motel. Growing tired of the demands of multiple locations, the family sold the Peabody location in 1960, and ten years later, they sold Agawam number one, the Worcester, replacing it with Agawam number three, and concentrated all their efforts in Rowley.

Declining business as a result of declining activity at the Ipswich Sylvania plant contributed to the family's decision to consolidate. The decision seemed counterintuitive at the time, because the interstate already bypassed Route 1, and Rowley's rural setting could not provide the sizable customer base they enjoyed in Ipswich or in Saugus. Still, the old route saw plenty of tourist traffic traveling to and from the popular vacation areas of New Hampshire and Maine. As it happens, the diner serves as a well-placed respite for the start of and end to vacations in these two states. Yet the family endured a few months of nail biting in the beginning. As Junior tells it, after about three months, "It was like the heavens opened up. All of a sudden, Route 1 was lined with cars. It hasn't stopped since."

COLLECTION OF ARTHUR GOODY

The Agawam Diner number three in its original location in Ipswich, Massachusetts.

And the business kept coming, because the Agawam could write the book on how to run a small diner. While too many other diners overemphasize glitz and theme, Bubba Galanis, third-generation chef, credits consistency as the key to his family's success. When Bubba finds a reliable supplier, he sticks with it. In return, the supplier gets a loyal and valuable customer. The philosophy applies on the other side of the counter as well. The hot turkey sandwich you loved so much this week will be available next week, and the week after, and it will be just as good as the last time you had one.

One potential downside of this degree of operational efficiency is the toll it might take on a diner's personality. But with so many family members involved, the Agawam successfully manages the delicate balance of efficiency and hospitality. In fact, family members make up a third of the staff. These include two brothers, Junior and Andy Galanis, and a brother-in-law, "Uncle Smiley" Pappas. Junior, though retired, still comes in to help out. Uncle Smiley assumes early morning chef duties, and Andy supervises the dining area. Bubba, Junior's son, is the afternoon chef. Smiley's two sons, Jim and John, also work as chefs. And Andy's two daughters, Ethel and Angela, cordially waitress this busy place. One can always find a family member present, but not being a Galanis or a Pappas doesn't mean that employees aren't treated as part of the family. In fact, Bubba credits this attitude for low turn-over rates, and people do seem to enjoy working there, always a sign of a good diner.

Since 1970, the area has changed dramatically, its rural character gradually transformed into a bedroom community. Once in a remote, middle-of-nowhere location, the Agawam now shares the intersection with a couple of strip malls, a McDonald's, a Dunkin' Donuts, and many other businesses. So valuable has the location become that the Galanises now find themselves fending off large offers from developers itching to get their hands on the prime corner location.

Bubba assures that the end of an era will not come soon. The diner continues to thrive and make a good living for the family. The desserts taste as heavenly as ever. And the diner still looks nearly brand new.

FOUR SISTERS OWL DINER

1940 WORCESTER #759

244 Appleton St., Lowell, MA • (978) 453-8321

FEATURED DINER

The Four Sisters Owl Diner on Appleton Street might serve as a template for all the diner-themed restaurants that have come and gone since the Shanahans took over the place in 1981. At the Four Sisters, waitresses call you "hon," orders get barked across the diner, cups never empty, and the food always fills the plate. Unlike those at many of the pretentious diner wanna-bes that began to dot the landscape throughout the 1980s and 1990s, the staff of the Four Sisters doesn't follow a script, doesn't dance on the counter, and doesn't sass you back. All diners should be this friendly, lively, and honest.

As one of the most popular breakfast spots in this region, the Four Sisters belongs to that class of diners that simply exemplify the genre. Although the diner does offer lunch, the Four Sisters enjoys a deservedly stellar reputation for serving one of the best breakfasts anywhere. The menu features twenty-eight different styles of omelets, all named after Lowell streets. Pancakes come plain or with chocolate chips, blueberries, or bananas, and a short stack will usually satisfy all but the most ravenous appetites, especially if you get a side order of the diner's famous ham. The diner provides a slab of fresh baked ham cut right from the bone.

Tom and Marybeth Shanahan have operated the diner since 1981. That year, the family took over a tired, dirty business in a bad neighborhood, planted stakes, and hoped for the best. They had previously operated, but didn't own, the city's famous Peerless Diner, hoping all the while to persuade the owner to sell. This prospect continued to look unlikely when the Owl Diner hit the market, so the Shanahans, along with Marybeth's three sisters, Rose, Martha, and Bridget, seized the moment and began to work at cleaning up the old girl.

The Owl Diner started out as the Monarch Diner (one of the local chain) on Main Street in Waltham, Massachusetts. In 1951, the Worcester streamliner made way for a newer O'Mahony diner and may have returned to Worcester for refitting. The two different styles of lettering on the Owl's facade indicate the diner's split heritage, and at some point, the company likely removed the panels displaying the word "Monarch" with new panels etched with the words "The Owl." The second Monarch went on to eventu-

ally become the Lafayette Diner in Salisbury and then the Tilt'n Diner in Tilton, New Hampshire.

To the Shanahans' dismay, a few years after they vacated the Peerless, the landlord did finally sell it. The new owner was Ralph Moberly, who hoped to install it in the Florida Keys. For years afterward, the family wondered what had become of it, only to learn that Moberly had cut the structure down the middle in order to fit it across a bridge. After leaving the sections unsecured beside the road for a few days, Moberly returned to find the diner stripped of its panels and fixtures. Parts of the Peerless soon popped up at Gary Neil's Timber Village antique shops right after the reopening of the Ross Diner.

Today the Four Sisters continues on without Martha, who since moved on to the Dream Diner, and then to even greener pastures. The business maintains its solid tradi-

Tom Shanahan takes orders at the grill in his justly popular diner. Since the 1970s, Tom, his wife, and her three sisters wake up Lowell, Massachusetts, every day with large slices of fresh ham, plate-sized pancakes, fresh hot coffee, and the finest service anywhere.

tions with the help of the extensive Shanahan tribe. On any given day, a niece, nephew, grandchild, or cousin greets grateful customers and guides them to seats, either in the well-kept diner or in the spacious and comfortable dining room.

THE NOMADIC ENGLEWOOD DINER

1941 STERLING #4113
In storage at 74 Main Street, Salisbury, MA

FEATURED DINER

The whole unique concept of the diner defines itself through the ability to change locations at the whims of their owners with relative ease. Indeed, most diners you visit that date before 1960 likely operated in another location at some point in their history. Then there's the Englewood Diner, a 1941 Sterling diner that has become a veritable nomad over the last twenty years.

The Englewood began service as a link in the Boston-based chain of Englewood Diners, operating in Dorchester. It likely stayed at the location of its original installation until 1980, when its owners sold it at auction for a mere $8,800 to David Keller of Charlestown, who moved the diner to Cambridge and kept it in storage. In 1986, it was put back on the auction block, selling it to Brian Burke for $26,000. Burke brought it back to Dorchester, setting it up in the parking lot of a Bradlees department store on Victory Boulevard. Burke leased the diner to the well-seasoned dinerman Haj Gamale, a talent behind the grill who seems to have had some involvement with dozens of diners throughout Boston's South Shore and beyond. (You can now find Gamale at Phyllis's Diner in Everett.)

Burke's venture would prove short-lived, but it was the only one in the past twenty years that put the diner in actual service. In 1992, Bradlees' corporate parent wanted to expand the store right into the lot occupied by the Englewood, forcing Burke to close the Englewood and again sell it at auction. For $20,000, real estate developer Paul Downey became the new owner. Downey had put his hands into the diner trade in the early 1990s, seeking to profit from the expanding popularity of diners by "flipping" them. He and a handful of others would purchase closed units for eventual resale to an increasing number of people who had recently read the books by Gutman or Baeder or saw the movie *Diner,* and wanted to get, restore, and operate one of their own. Downey indeed profited handsomely. After keeping it in storage for several months, he sold the Englewood for $33,000 to Dennis "Skip" Scipione, owner of the Blue Moon Diner in Gardner, Massachusetts.

Though Skip had experience in this field, having already moved and restored one diner, he would not find similar fortune with this second enterprise. Skip originally intended to restore the diner while in storage in the north-central Massachusetts town of Ashburnham, and then move it to a planned new location on U.S. Route 1 in York, Maine, a popular vacation area.

The diner's charms make themselves immediately evident once inside. The seafoam green and creamy yellow porcelain panels and subtle art deco touches instantly convey a warm, cozy feeling to anyone who steps inside. But the Englewood's small size made its future use as a working diner something of a problem. Skip planned to connect the structure to a larger dining area, with the diner serving as the lure to customers driving by.

Ultimately, however, Skip found that the projected costs of the diner's restoration, transport, and installation on an expensive location would not justify the investment. With nearly $60,000 already sunk in the project, Skip reluctantly put the Englewood back on the market, with an asking price of $65,000. Having so much already invested in such a small diner, the prospects for recovering his money looked pretty bleak. As the weeks and months passed by, he found few takers. In what would later become an ironic twist to this saga, a movie production studio had approached him in 1993, seeking to rent and temporarily move his diner to Beacon, New York, to appear in the movie *Nobody's Fool,* starring Paul Newman. Skip offered to rent the diner for three months for only $10,000, but the studio turned it down, instead renting a local diner for the interior shots and the Columbia Diner in nearby Hudson for the exterior.

The Englewood sat in a field for another four years when his friend Bill Saladini proposed that the two set up the diner at Saladini's convenience store in nearby Fitchburg. Skip agreed and paid to transport the diner to the new location. But the city delayed operating permits, citing, among other things, the diner's lack of handicapped access. About the same time, Skip sold the Blue Moon Diner to Ralph Brown and prepared for his Florida retirement, leaving behind his life in the diner world and leaving Saladini to complete the installation of the Englewood on his own.

Brown's inability to fill Skip's shoes at the Blue Moon forced Skip to abruptly end his retirement plans. At about the same time, Saladini realized he couldn't afford to open the Englewood, and Skip ended up taking back possession of both diners. The Englewood subsequently returned to Ashburnham on Skip's dime.

With his losses mounting, Skip must have seen the Englewood as his own albatross. To make matters worse, he lost the use of his Ashburnham storage site in 1998 and had to move it once again, this time to a yard owned by O. B. Hill Rigging in Framingham, Massachusetts.

Skip's asking price dropped to $45,000, and by the time he sold in 2000, he let the diner go for only $20,000. The buyer, Dan Johnston of Holden, Massachusetts, picked up Skip's mobile money pit and moved it to storage in Holden. Johnston spoke of vague plans to reopen the Englewood, but he soon had it listed on eBay, which failed to attract a buyer. This would eventually prove fortuitous, because it allowed Johnston to pull off one of the more amazing deals in the history of modern diner flipping.

In 2001, the new Hollywood powerhouse Dreamworks called, looking for a diner to use in a scene in the movie *The Road to Perdition*, which also starred Paul Newman. The diner grapevine reported that Johnston sold the Englewood to Dreamworks for almost $40,000, with the first option to purchase it back. It was then transported to the Chicago area. Diner purists note that the 1941-vintage Englewood appears in a movie set in 1931, but the studio allowed this and several other anachronisms.

In preparation for shooting, the crew repainted the facade with a matte finish to cut down on the glare from the porcelain, replaced the steel on the door, and removed an entire exterior section to accommodate the choreography and filming of a gunfight. After filming was completed, with the section restored to the diner, Johnston exercised his option and purchased the diner back for less than half his original sale price.

In 2002, a few months after accepting its return, Johnston flipped the Englewood yet again, this time to Matt Letellier of Elliot, Maine. By this time, the diner had been closed a decade and had passed through the hands of six owners while serving only a single "customer"—Tom Hanks. Letellier reportedly had definite plans to reopen the Englewood, but the premiere of *Perdition* came and went, as did the Academy Awards presentation the following year. Letellier missed both opportunities to capitalize on the potential publicity.

Ultimately, Letellier, who already owned the stick-built Downeast Diner, opted not to put the Englewood into service. In 2003, he sold it to Dave Pritchard, a truck dealer in Salisbury, for $50,000. In the end, the estimated net profit generated by the diner over the previous fifteen years hovers around $26,000, with Skip Scipione the biggest loser during the period, having sunk at least $40,000 into the project.

The Englewood serves as a cautionary tale for anyone looking to buy a vintage diner for his or her own enterprise. Essentially, the lesson here is not to buy a diner unless you have secured your location. The recent history of diners has far too many examples of dreamers who have failed to do their homework, and who tragically believe that everyone will see the same beauty and charm in an antique diner as they do. In fact, many people still see diners as noisy "greasy spoons" and don't relish the idea of having one in their communities. Add this to the fact that most diners constructed before World War II no longer comply with modern building codes.

With luck, Pritchard will find a good home for the Englewood and maybe even get it back into service. Until then, we can rest assured that it sits safe and sound on his property.

DINER DIRECTORY

THE MERRIMACK VALLEY

Agawam Diner
Rte. 1 & Rte. 133
Rowley, MA
(978) 948-7780
1954 Fodero
Listed on the National Register of Historic Places. Third of a four-store chain of Agawam Diners, but the last remaining. In beautiful condition and always busy. Open every day of the year except Christmas. Full menu of basic American food. Well known in the area for its cream pies. Late nights on weekends. Smoke-free.

Al's Diner
297 S. Broadway
Lawrence, MA
(781) 687-9678
1934 Worcester 720
Monitor roof car with brick facade. Interior restored after fire in 1999. Originally O'Neil's Diner until its sale

Al Demuth has left the building, but his name remains on this popular diner located on the busy southern entrance into Lawrence.

to Albert Demuth in 1953. Good, basic grilled diner fare. Daily specials. Breakfast and lunch only.

Arthur's Paradise Diner
112 Bridge St.
Lowell, MA
(978) 452-8647
1937 Worcester 727
Original condition, though weathered. Known for its signature Boot Mill Sandwich. Breakfast and lunch only.

B&M Diner
246B Winter St.
Haverhill, MA
1928 Worcester 608
Originally Baldwin's Diner in Roxbury, Massachusetts. Came to Haverill by way of Charlestown in 1946, becoming Kenny's Diner and part of a larger restaurant. Subject of John Baeder painting as Alley Oops. Currently closed and dilapidated.

Carro Rojo
596 Essex St.
Lawrence, MA
(508) 687-0998
1930 Worcester 669
Originally Dempsey's Diner. Sits perpendicular to street and well hidden by updated facade. Name translated means Red Car, similar to former name, Red Caboose. Hispanic cuisine.

Chubby's Diner
72 Main St.
Salisbury, MA
(978) 462-3332
1940 O'Mahony/Musi 1116

Originally operating as the Village Diner in Armonk, New York. Iconic early 1940s design renovated by Ralph Musi in 1996 and brought to Salisbury. Subject of painting by John Baeder, depicted as the Blue Moon Diner. American food, grilled diner fare. Breakfast and lunch.

Club Diner
145 Dutton St.
Lowell, MA
(978) 452-1679
1933 Worcester 703
Diner features framed newspaper articles covering its opening in the 1930s. Remodeled interior and exterior. American food. Open twenty-four hours on weekends, depending on availability of help.

Dream Diner
384 Middlesex Rd./Rte. 3A
Tyngsboro, MA
(978) 649-7097
www.dreamdiner.com
1997 on-site
Extremely popular diner-style restaurant, patterned much after Four Sisters Diner in Lowell, whose owner is from same family. Many omelet varieties, all named after diner builders. Fresh baked ham. Breakfast and lunch.

Englewood Diner
Salisbury, MA
1941 Sterling 4113
In storage. Likely one of the most nomadic diners in the country. Originally located in Boston's Dorchester neighborhood and part of a chain of Englewood diners.

Fish Tale Diner
Rte. 1
Salisbury, MA
(978) 465-1674

1940 Worcester 762
On the banks of the Merrimack River, overlooking its mouth and Newburyport on the opposite side. First of four Agawam Diners, formerly located in Rowley. Features a deck near the water. Serves standard diner fare with homemade chowders and fish specials. Breakfast and lunch only.

Four Sisters Owl Diner
244 Appleton St./Rte. 110
Lowell, MA
(978) 453-8321
1940 Worcester 759
Listed on the National Register of Historic Places. A real Lowell institution, known for big, well-made breakfasts featuring fresh ham and many different omelet varieties. A true gem, not to be missed. Originally part of the Monarch Diner chain and located on Main Street in Waltham. Removed from that location and brought to Lowell in the early 1950s. Breakfast and lunch, seven days.

KJ's Airport Diner
Lancaster Rd.
Shirley, MA
(978) 425-0290
1933 Worcester
Formerly operating as the White Elephant Diner in Clinton. Moved to Shirley in the late 1980s.

Lin Garden
511 Merrimack Ave./Rte. 110
Dracut, MA
(508) 458-8113
1937 Worcester 726
Originally operated by the Georgenes family as the Old Colony Diner in Dorchester. One of the largest Worcester cars for this vintage ever built. Stripped of most interior and exterior features and currently used for storage.

To stay viable, sometimes old diners have to learn new tricks. This diner now specializes in steak sandwiches and other lunch items.

Midway Diner
Andover, MA
1936 Worcester 666
In private storage. Originally half of the double diner in Shrewsbury, of which its twin now sits in Hanover, New Hampshire. Under restoration.

Miss Newport Diner
Salisbury, MA
1950 Worcester 823
In storage. Pristine car, originally located in Newport, Vermont. Moved in 2003.

Pat's Diner
11 Bridge St./Rte. 1
Salisbury, MA
(978) 465-3060
1950 Worcester 824
Listed on the National Register of Historic Places. Custom-made, with a partitioned dining area. Slightly larger than most Worcesters of this vintage. Formerly known as Ann's Diner. Current

owner replaced original porcelain panels with plywood T-111; otherwise the diner is in very good condition. Serves standard diner fare with daily specials. Breakfast and lunch.

Sam's Steak Out
135 Broadway
Lawrence, MA
(508) 685-1633
1939 Worcester 750
Remodeled inside and out, but retains barrel roof, and picture window over river is a nice touch. Steak subs are the featured item on the menu.

Trader Alan's Truck Stop
Rte. 150 & Rte. 495
Amesbury, MA
(508) 388-3300
1947 Worcester 801
Extremely dilapidated. Not long for this world.

Trolley Stop Diner
984 Gorham St. 3A
Lowell, MA
(978) 937-8626
1950 Evans
Built in Salisbury by Don Evans over a five-year period in the style of a Sterling Streamliner, using many Worcester interior parts. Currently shows little of original design. Remodeled to the style of a trolley car. Serves pizza and other Italian specialties.

Tyngsboro Diner
Tyngsboro, MA
Worcester
In private use.

CENTRAL
MASSACHUSETTS

Worcester County conveniently delineates the central Massachusetts region for the purposes of this guide, and within it, diner fans find their mecca. Though some have designated the city of Worcester as the birthplace of the diner, they only got it partially right. Worcester more accurately lays claim to being the birthplace of the diner-building industry, where canny entrepreneurs took hold of Walter Scott's concept, perfected it, and marketed it. It was in Worcester that people first set up shop building lunch wagons and then diners for others to operate, and thanks to the Worcester Lunch Car Company, it did so until 1961.

Befitting its role in diner history, Worcester still retains a relative abundance of diners, though just a fraction of what you might have found in the 1950s and 1960s. Sadly, over the last ten years, the city has seen its bounty decline even more. As this is written, one of its most famous, Charlie's, and one of its most beleaguered, Muggsy's, sit in storage inside city limits—Muggsy's up in Worcester's remote airport and Charlie's in a lot on Shrewsbury Street. Charlie's likely will find a future at a new location in town, but Muggsy's probably will have collapsed from decay by the time this book rolls off the presses.

Though you can't get a meal there, you can watch Mike O'Connor slowly restore Worcester #705 in his yard off West Boylston Street, and a drive down Stafford Street brings you to the former LaPrade's Diner, possibly built by Wilfred Barriere, now a private residence.

Historically, Worcester's economic classes divided along an east-west axis separated by Park Avenue, with workers on the east and management on the west. Expectedly, the city's diners and taverns kept to the east, so for the most part, our exploration stays on the east side.

Of the city's operating diners, two now share the distinction of a listing on the National Register of Historic Places and probably represent the best preserved in the city. These two, the Boulevard Diner and the Corner Lunch, differ markedly in appearance and style of operation.

The Boulevard stands out both as a shining example of a Worcester diner from the Depression period and as the city's most iconic and best-remembered diner by current and past residents. Situated right on the side-

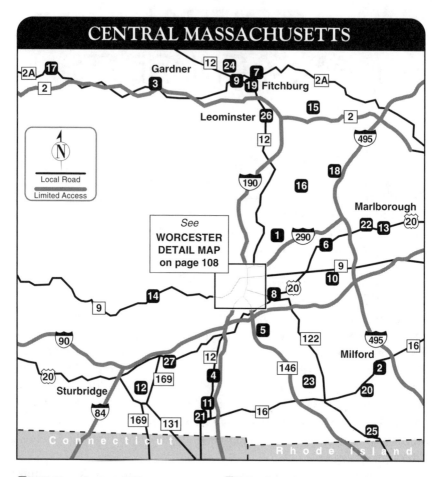

CENTRAL MASSACHUSETTS

1. 1921 Diner: Boylston (BR)
2. Blue Belle Diner: Millis (BR)
3. Blue Moon Diner: Gardner (BR)
4. Carl's Oxford Diner: Oxford (BR)
5. Central Diner: Millbury (BR)
6. Chet's Diner: Northborough (BR)
7. East Side Diner: Fitchburg (BR)
8. Edgemere Diner: Shrewsbury (MS)
9. Fifty-Fifty Diner: Fitchburg (R)
10. Home Plate: Westboro (R)
11. House: Webster (BR)
12. Jim's Flyin' Diner: Southbridge (MS)
13. Joy Asia Restaurant: Marlborough (MS)
14. Kenwood Diner: Spencer (BR)
15. KJ's Airport Diner: Shirley (BR)
16. Lou's Diner: Clinton (BR)
17. Main Street Diner: Athol (BR)
18. Mindy's Diner: Bolton (BR)
19. Moran Square Diner: Fitchburg (BR)
20. Myriad Ballroom: Mendon (MS)
21. Nap's Diner: Webster (BR)
22. Nelly's Diner: Marlborough (BR)
23. Peg's Diner: Whitinsville (BR)
24. Ray's Diner: Fitchburg (MS)
25. Stewart's Diner: Blackstone (BR)
26. Tim's Diner: Leominster (MS)
27. Yankee Diner: Charlton (BR)

walk in the city's bustling restaurant district, the Boulevard has endured thanks to the determined stewardship of the George family for the past five decades. Purchased and hauled to its site by John "Johnny Ringo" George, the diner became well known for its red-sauced Italian specialties. Indeed, on one visit, when I quietly remarked how much I liked the lasagna to a friend, the grillman turned around and bellowed out for the entire crowd, "It's da behhhhst!"

When Johnny Ringo died in 1992, he nearly left the diner in a state of limbo. Though his wife kept the diner going, she did consider selling the structure off the site, which they rented on a month-to-month basis. Then, in stepped prodigal son Jim George, who embarked on an ambitious and welcome plan to restore the diner's original luster. His work and dedication to his father's legacy paid off, and the tradition continues. Jim rechromed and refinished every surface in the place and has since restored all the neon. He keeps the diner open twenty-four-seven, an extreme rarity in this state. Only the Fillin' Station in Whately keeps similar hours (see pages 139–41).

The Corner Lunch, on the other hand, came to the city relatively late. Hauled into town in 1968 by the Ganais brothers, it was set up on a triangular lot in what was then the city's industrial heart. The pair bought the diner from a former Kullman Industries employee named Ralph Musi, who had set off on his own to build and remodel diners. Musi acquired the diner

In 1998, Jim George gave his departed father's diner a thorough makeover, restoring it to mint condition. Here you'll find great meatballs and other Italian specialties.

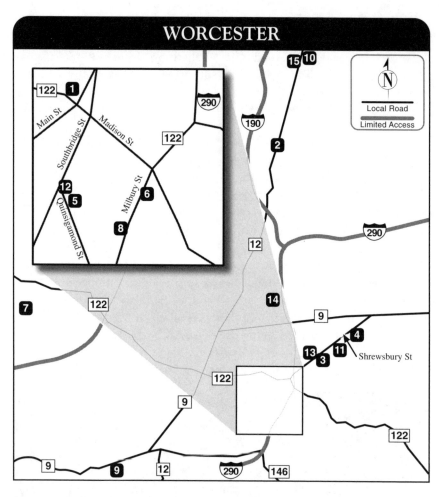

WORCESTER

1 Alice & the Hat Diner: Worcester (BR)
2 Art's Diner: Worcester (R)
3 Boulevard Diner: Worcester (BR)
4 Charlie's Diner: Worcester (BR)
5 Corner Lunch: Worcester (MS)
6 Emerald Isle: Worcester (MS)
7 Finely Fran's: Worcester (BR)
8 George's Green Island Diner: Worcester (BR)
9 LaPrade's Diner (residence): Worcester (BR)
10 Lou-Roc's Diner: Worcester (R)
11 Mac's Diner: Worcester (R)
12 Miss Worcester Diner: Worcester (BR)
13 Parkway Diner: Worcester (BR)
14 Ralph's Chadwick Square Diner: Worcester (BR)
15 Tony's Diner: Worcester (BR)

to sell to the brothers, and to make it fit into the tight triangular lot on Lamartine Street, he lopped off roughly a third of the diner's dining area and converted it into a kitchen. You'll get a sense of the diner's former size if you keep in mind that the front entrance originally stood in the center of the overall length.

The story of Charlie's since April 2003 has made no one happy, least of all its owner, Steve Turner, grandson of the original Charlie. Evicted from its location of almost forty years to make room for about six parking spaces, the diner once embodied everything good about Worcester. As this is written, the diner sits on blocks in the city waiting for a new location.

After the Ganais brothers sold off the business, the Corner Lunch saw a succession of struggling owners, including local legend Ralph Moberly, who already owned the Chadwick Square Diner, followed by Paul Pourier, who kept it going for much of the 1990s. After Pourier, the diner changed hands almost annually, which did little to attract and maintain new business. One hapless operator failed to last longer than a month in 2002.

Toward the end of that year, the diner finally seemed to fall into capable hands. Stefan Chios signed a lease in fall 2002 and promptly scrubbed the place up and down. Though Chios introduced a more updated and creative menu to the solidly blue-collar district, including such diner rarities as French press coffee and sushi, he barely lasted a full year before handing the diner over to Elaine and Charles Boukalis. Both Elaine and Charles have extensive restaurant experience and seem to understand the challenges of diner operation, and they've revamped the menu to follow more traditional lines. Elaine promises to stay put and rebuild the business. Keep your fingers crossed.

Until April 2003, visitors to the city also could have paid a visit to Charlie's Diner, a fixture on Plantation Street owned by the Turner family since the late 1950s. Sadly, the diner and its latest owner, Steve Turner, found themselves evicted that month, resulting in the diner's removal and storage in a nearby lot. As this is written, Steve hopes to finalize a deal that will allow him to move his 1948 Worcester to a new location in the town of Spencer. For more about the plight of the diner, visit its website, www.charliesdiner.com, which is maintained by loyal customer Bill Caloccia.

For those looking to add to their photo collections, Worcester provides two rare opportunities to get two competing diners in the same frame, albeit with some effort. Almost directly across from the Boulevard, the Parkway has served almost as a culinary counterpoint to its iconic competitor. Though the Evangelista family remodeled the exterior in the 1960s, its diminutive interior largely retains its prewar charms. It also retains Johnny Evangelista, who currently reigns as the city's longest-running dinerman. Johnny, with his three brothers, purchased the diner in the 1930s and ran it as a twenty-four-hour operation for years afterward. The operation also features a larger dining and lounge area built off the back, but the diner is where the action happens, and typically people will stand around waiting for a stool before they resort to taking a booth in the dining room.

True diner fanatics will appreciate the de facto historic landmark at the corners of Southbridge and Quinsigamond. On one corner sits the Miss Worcester Diner, another classic postwar Worcester car, and on the other corner, you'll find the factory that built it. The proximity might suggest that the company built the diner as a showroom model, but the mere expense would

Here's one apple that didn't fall too far from the tree. The Miss Worcester Diner faces the home of the company that built it. Across the street, the Worcester Lunch Car Company turned out this and another 650 diners and lunch wagons between 1910 and 1957. The diner served a once-bustling industrial district that included the New Haven Railroad Worcester yards, Wyman-Gordon, and an assortment of other manufacturers.

have made the idea prohibitive. The simple fact that the Miss Worcester sits on what was once a high-profile site in the heart of Worcester's largest industrial district was ample reason for its location. Also, WLCC owner Philip Duprey owned the land and would not renew the lease unless another diner was put on it. The diner's location less than 200 yards from the Corner Lunch provides photographers with the other opportunity to capture two diners in one shot—provided they use a wide-angle lens and stand in the middle of a busy intersection.

As of this writing, the Miss Worcester stands closed because of a legal dispute over who actually owns the structure. In the factory building, you can still walk through both the work areas and the company's office, which now house a thrift store and a tattoo parlor. In the tattoo parlor, the same craftsmanship the company carpenters built into its diners went into this space as well, as demonstrated by the resplendent oak paneling and ceramic tile floor.

Lou-Roc's Diner has regained a following in recent years. The diner was drastically remodeled by former owners, who purchased the well-preserved Silk City in 1989 and encased the structure in a brick box and quasi-gambrel roof. The effort hardly paid off, as business only declined further. After a two-year dormancy, Peter Prodromidis came forth in 2001 to reenergize the business. Though he hasn't changed any of the previous owners' remodeling, he spruced up the interior and updated and improved the menu. The diner is now a popular weekend breakfast spot for the locals, who don't care about the structure's low degree of preservation. The proof is in the pudding, as they say, and the pudding tastes pretty good.

Worcester is a midpoint of sorts for the best of New England's diner drives along Route 12. Anyone driving south along this corridor from Worcester should do so with an empty stomach, because the first diner you'll encounter enjoys a widespread and justifiable reputation for its portion sizes. The Oxford Diner virtually shovels it on the plate, and if you actually manage to clear the decks and ask for more, the owners happily oblige. On one visit, I quietly asked the man at the grill how the diner can stay in business while serving such huge portions. Without skipping a beat, he declared for all to hear, "We are a nonprofit organization!"

Truth be told, while the portion sizes would choke a hog, the prices typically reflect the extra tonnage. Legions of loyal regulars obviously feel they get their money's worth. The man responsible for establishing this reputation has long since retired, but Carl Thomas still takes an occasional turn at the grill and hangs out with appreciative customers. In 1990, Thomas sold the business to Paul Bremmer, who picked up exactly where Thomas left off.

Worcester County has two diners converted into residences. This diner, in use as a rental property and likely a Worcester, sits on Route 12 in Webster.

Thomas took over the venerable diner in 1975 after a layoff left him looking for a new line of work. Though he had no experience whatsoever in the restaurant field, apparently Thomas possessed the requisite intelligence, drive, and sense of hospitality to compensate. He found himself having to ask his new customers how to make some of the meals they requested. The portion sizes that have since become the diner's hallmark began as a way to cut down on spoilage. As Thomas explains it, limited storage capacity necessitated the policy. "Instead of throwing it away, I put it on their plates."

On my first visit, a request for two eggs, home fries, bacon, and toast generated a bounty of three eggs, a separate plate for the pile of home fries, six strips of bacon, and four slices of toast. Every quantity seemed to multiply by a factor of at least 1.5. When I managed to clear my plate of eggs, another appeared as I looked away. Though it might defy the laws of restaurant physics, Thomas and Bremmer seem to make it work.

Farther down the road, you'll drive past another diner-as-residence just before crossing into Webster, and still farther along Route 12, Nap's Diner and Restaurant awaits. Basically an entry-level-model Worcester car that seats fifteen on stools only, Nap's displays few frills other than its inherent historic charms. Preservationists will also appreciate the adjacent restaurant, which serves mostly the same menu and has a full bar.

From this point, we begin a counterclockwise loop around the rest of Worcester County. On this circular diner route, we first come to the Yankee Diner in Charlton on U.S. Route 20. The Yankee enjoys a location on a historic post road and one-time premier diner highway. This east-west route across the Bay State played host to perhaps a couple dozen diners at any given moment from the 1930s through 1950s. The Yankee rolled onto this location well after the highway's prime in 1969.

Current owners Chris and Deb Downey came from careers in the restaurant field, last working for a regional chain outfit known as the 99 Restaurants. In late 2002, they learned that the Yankee's owner, Rich Garon, wanted to change careers, and they took over the following January. They reopened their newly immaculate diner by March, and six months later, they have no regrets.

Turning south on to Route 169, we come to the Southbridge Airport and Jim's Flyin' Diner, one of the region's handful of generally rare Master diners. The Master Company had a short-lived existence in Pequannock, New Jersey. Only thirteen of its diners are still in operation, of which New England claims four. Jim's unlikely location atop a mountain at a small municipal airport for pleasure craft would initially seem an unwise disregard of the old adage about location, location, location, but the restaurant has many fans among aviation enthusiasts. Here pilots and passengers can sit on the deck during the warmer months and watch the planes come and go.

Our diner loop now turns north on to Route 131 and stops in Spencer at the Kenwood Diner. The 1933 Worcester had a rebirth of sorts in recent years. David Eckleberry once owned a lot of property in town, including one of its premier restaurants, the Spencer Inn. Eckleberry, a colorful individual with illustrious careers in the air force and civilian airlines, also had a fondness for

Few things warm the heart of a diner fan more than a real diner—here, the Kenwood—right on Main Street.

collecting, and in 1995, he added the Kenwood Diner to his menagerie. In a circumstance almost unique to diners, he owned the land but not the structure. So when the state seized the diner and closed the business for tax default, placing it up for auction, Eckleberry made his move to consolidate, purchasing the diner and its contents for $15,000. Eckleberry immediately began restoring the diner and extended its hours to include dinners, a rare thing for diners of this size. With Eckleberry's considerable local clout and resources, the Kenmore soon regained a reputation as a family restaurant. This remained the status quo until Eckleberry's death in 1997.

In 1998, Helen Ryant, who had owned a deli business around the corner, moved into the diner upon the invitation of Eckleberry's widow, who had no desire to run the diner herself. Since then, Ryant has contracted the hours to a more typical breakfast-and-lunch affair, but she still does the diner tradition justice.

Heading north, we come to Athol, one of a string of mill towns once tied together by the construction of the Fitchburg Railroad. Here you'll find the Main Street Diner. This small Worcester car keeps breakfast and lunch hours in a very cozy setting too small for table seating.

Turning east, the chair city awaits, as does your seat at the Blue Moon Diner. The Blue Moon formerly sported a name that ranks among my all-time

The Kenwood Diner, in the heart of Spencer, was restored by the late David Eckleberry in 1997. Today it offers hearty breakfasts and lunches to a grateful community that almost lost this gem at a 1995 auction.

Burger King slayer? Not exactly, but in New England, you don't often see a thriving diner next door to a closed fast-food giant. The Main Street Diner in Athol underwent some restoration thanks to its former owner, Woody Blanchard, who showed how to do great things in a little diner. Woody sold the diner in 1999.

favorites—the Miss Toy Town, so dubbed because of its original location in Winchendon, Massachusetts, a.k.a. Toy Town, thanks to its toy manufacturing history. The current Blue Moon, another Worcester, sits on the same location as the first Blue Moon, an earlier Worcester. In 1988, it attracted a new owner, Dennis "Skip" Scipione. Skip had recently retired from the Fitchburg police force and sought a change of career. As Skip explained it, "I hung out in so many doughnut shops, I figured I could run a diner."

Until 2000, he did just that, doing an excellent job until he grew weary of the long hours and hard work. In that time, however, Skip turned the diner into a community focal point, often greeting customers with coffeepot in one hand and the other outstretched to shake theirs. In 1992, the diner served as the setting for a scene in the movie *School Ties,* which starred a young Brendan Fraser and Matt Damon.

In 2000, Skip sold the business to Jamie Brouillard, a local former waitress, who has managed to keep the grills hot and the customers happy. The diner's extensive menu features three kinds of hash: corned beef, roast beef, and turkey. Though she had large shoes to fill with Skip's departure, in the three years since she's taken ownership, the Blue Moon shines again.

A little farther east, we come to Fitchburg and Leominster, twin cities that were a once-bustling manufacturing center. Leominster still makes the iconic plastic pink flamingo lawn ornaments, but both cities continue to struggle in the postindustrial economy. That industrial heritage has left behind one of the most beautiful examples of an early 1940s Worcester car

The late 1940s Worcester cars fell far behind their New Jersey competitors in terms of style, but today they glow with charm. The Blue Moon's new panels replaced those emblazoned with its former name, the Miss Toy Town, the nickname of its former home of Winchendon, Massachusetts.

The interior of the Blue Moon Diner looks much the same as it did when it left the factory in 1949. See it in its full glory in the movie *School Ties*, with Brendan Frasier.

in or out of any museum. The Moran Square Diner in Fitchburg had a long run under its second owner, the late Louis Vitelli, who also kept the diner in impeccable condition. It faces south, with an unobstructed view from the street corner, so it's nearly impossible to take a bad picture of the place. Photos of the diner with its fire engine red panels against a clear blue sky are requisite for any true diner fanatic's collection.

In Leominster, Tim's Diner sparkles in its own way, both in terms of the care given to it by Tim Kamataris Jr. and because of its physical dimensions, which are unusual for a Silk City diner. The Paterson Vehicle Company typically built most of its diners in any given year with few variations. Most of its diners came in the same size and shape, varying only in color and layout. If you wanted a larger Silk City diner, you bought a second one and attached it to the first. Paterson built Tim's Diner roughly half the size of its standard models, and if any others like it were made, they no longer exist. Tim's became notable for its broth-based clam chowder, made from Tim Sr.'s own secret recipe. The diner usually closes most weekdays by 1:00 in the afternoon, and even earlier on Saturdays.

Clinton is the smallest town in Massachusetts in terms of geography, and appropriately, one of the state's smallest diners is located here. The sight of "Ladies Welcome" painted on the exterior of Lou's Diner should

Worcester Lunch Car regularly took in old diners and gave them new shine. This 1929 car received a fresh 1950s vintage facelift, complete with new grill hood and deuce booths. Food at Lou's is basic and good.

This long-struggling O'Mahony went from a package store to a real diner again, only to become recently an Asian restaurant. Find this grand gem in Marlboro on U.S. Route 20.

inspire a pang of nostalgia. This vestige of the industry's formative years originated from the realization that catering to the softer sex would prove good for business. Such invitations, as well as the introduction of booth service in the 1920s and 1930s, did their part to attract more women. The idea caught on further as some men associated female patrons with better food. Lou's Diner also represents a fairly common practice of the Worcester Company for updating old diners. Originally built in 1929, the current Lou's features a grill hood and exterior skin more typical of its early 1950s models. Don't expect too many fancy dishes here. The diner's size precludes extensive prep work, but it serves a good basic breakfast and lunch, as well as warm welcome in abundance.

Our diner loop next takes us through Marlborough, where two diners struggle to emerge from years of marginalization. The White City in downtown Marlborough was named for its former location in the "White City," the nickname given to Shrewsbury and the once-famous amusement park that lined the shores of Lake Quinsigamond. Farther east on U.S. Route 20, the Boston Trolley Diner near the Sudbury line returned to food service from use as a liquor store in 1995 and has succeeded in developing a loyal clientele.

Our loop now jogs east along U.S. Route 20. In Northborough, Nancy Pantesa, now in her eighties, still serves up breakfast at Chet's Diner for her loyal regulars. According to Nancy, Worcester Lunch Car built Chet's, but did so on location. Ask and she'll show you the bill of sale she has framed and mounted behind the counter. If you want to eat here, go early: Chet's now closes at 11:00 in the morning.

We next pass into Shrewsbury, where the troubled Edgemere Diner awaits and, until recently, revealed itself in all its original, though dilapidated, splendor. The town's practice of auctioning biannual leases to prospective operators has virtually ensured the slow disintegration of one of the most beautiful diners ever built. A legal fight with one former operator left the diner without its original, ultraclassic winged clock, and the newest

According to its longtime owner, Nancy Pantesa, the Worcester Lunch Car Company actually built this diner on-site. Nancy keeps very short hours, closing up at 11:00 A.M.

Time has had little effect on this diner's interior.

operator removed the diner's original icebox. The short leases have the effect of stripping away any incentive for these operators to perform much-needed improvements or restorative work. Worse, such terms won't likely attract people with real experience in the industry, leaving the Edgemere to limp along at a location where it should thrive.

From Shrewsbury, we reenter the Blackstone River Valley and turn south into Millbury, home of the much-beloved Central Diner, run until recently by Richard and Brigid Gore. Richard, an ex-marine and Massachusetts state trooper, and Brigid, a former executive with Starbucks coffee, returned to their home base after living on the West Coast for several years. Hearing that the tiny twenty-two-seat Central Diner needed new owners, they made

ZIPPY THE PINHEAD VISITS NEW ENGLAND DINERS

You either get Zippy or you don't. This microcephalic comic strip character has served as a skewed lens on our often conflicting realities and as a muse for his creator, Bill Griffith. When you hear the question "Are we having fun yet?" you can credit Zippy as its source.

Since 1970, Zippy the Pinhead has roamed the real and surreal landscape with a cast of characters that has included Griffith himself. In 1998, Zippy began to make his first appearances in diners, and unlike so many other cartoon depictions, those appearing in the strip were the real deals. Griffith draws his diners with great detail, with an obvious appreciation for their form and function. When a local diner appears in one of the daily Zippy strips, it often results in some welcome publicity. Appearances of the Miss Worcester and the Tumble Inn Diners both generated stories in their towns' local papers, despite the fact that neither carried Zippy. Only about 150 newspapers do.

Also in 1998, Griffith completed a move back to the Northeast from his longtime home in San Francisco, settling in Hadlyme, Connecticut, just down the river from O'Rourke's Diner. Since then, Griffith has added dozens to the

their move. Tiny diners that serve a full menu have largely become a dying breed, and Richard soon reassessed his original intention to serve dinners as well. Few things inspire more romantic thought among diner enthusiasts than the sight of a lighted diner in a sleepy New England town during the dinner hours, where inside one finds a good, hot meal and a friendly face. Unfortunately, the extra work and limited capacity of the diner pretty much disabused the Gores of that notion, and they settled on providing a good, honest breakfast and lunch.

The first Central Diner, also a Worcester car, arrived on that location in 1910. It made way for its replacement in 1930. Except for a few interior modifications, the diner has changed little since those years.

parade of diners. Zippy has also paid visits to other roadside attractions, including the large fiberglass statues that dot the countryside, where he frequently engages in existential discourses.

You can find complete collections of Zippy, in and around diners and beyond, gathered together in the Zippy annuals. Order them from Griffith's website at www.zippythepinhead.com, or look for them at a big bookstore or comics store.

We end this loop in Whitinsville at the counter of Peg's Diner, a 1930s vintage Worcester car run by Peg Gagner and her son Jim. The precious eatery anchors this mill town founded by Whitin family, who built a sprawling machine shop and factory. Technically a village of Northbridge, Whitinsville still retains a small-town character made all the more vital by the presence of this little diner. Peg makes great soups and friendly conversation, and all in all this is a worthwhile detour off Route 146.

PEG'S DINER
1937 WORCESTER #723
87 Church St., Whitinsville, MA • (508) 234-0170

I've long retained a soft spot in my heart for Peg's Diner. Shoehorned in a tiny lot on the sleepy main street of Whitinsville, this humble operation never calls much attention to itself. Whitinsville, a village of Northbridge, doesn't really lie on the road to anywhere. To get there, you need to turn off the Route 146 expressway or the slower Route 122 post road.

Peg's seats fewer than thirty people and serves only breakfast and lunch, offering a simple array of sandwiches and hot plates. But one cup of Peg Gagner's homemade soup or one bite of her chocolate cream pie will reverse the sourest of attitudes. Peg herself has kept this diner going through the thick and thin of Whitinsville's fortunes, and while too many nearby storefronts have gone dark, the community still turns out for a good, hearty lunch at their local diner. I most love this place for the fact that it shines as an example of an informal town hall—a community gathering place where neighbors can get out to meet each other.

Peg became the owner of the little diner in 1996, purchasing the business from her former boss and friend, Barbara Chouinard, who ran the diner with Peg's help starting in 1966. Peg originally came aboard to help out for just a week while Barbara got the place up and running. Many things about the community have changed since those years. Factory closings have meant a decline in business from blue-collar workers tied to the clock, but business from the new wave of professionals keeps the place humming without the rigid pace.

Life in the diner seems to have treated Peg well. She still greets her customers with a smile, exchanges local gossip, and gladly bakes her own pies for dessert. On a recent visit, a fresh-baked apple pie made a grand effort to influence my decision away from chocolate cream.

Peg's presents the diner experience at its purest and therefore its most rare. For those reasons alone, it deserves the extra time and effort to seek it out, as places such as hers provide us with gentle reminders of the simple pleasures in life.

CENTRAL DINER
1930 WORCESTER #673
90 Elm St., Millbury, MA • (508) 865-0705

Richard and Brigid Gore seem to go at each other likes cats and dogs, but the lucky customers in the front row of this verbal boxing match take it all in stride and frequently join the fray. The Gores obviously love each other a great deal, and despite the banter, they have taken great care with this 1930 Worcester car, whose degree of preservation and charming and lavish interior construction are sure to impress. The Gores represent the latest in a line of proprietors who have kept a diner on this location since 1910. Until 1986, the Central Diner has had only two owners. The O'Connor family brought the original diner to the spot. They sold it in 1924 to the Gillert family, who replaced the original car with a newer, slightly larger Central in 1930. The Gillerts served the community until 1986, when they sold the diner to a Rhode Island woman, who leased the diner to a succession of owners. These included Paul Pourier, who went on to run the Corner Lunch in 1991, and then his mother, Lorraine Augusto, who finally exited the scene in the late 1990s.

The Central struggled until the Gores stepped up to the challenge in 2000. Since then, they've made this diner an extremely popular local attraction once again. One of the best-selling items on the menu originates from Richard's stint in the military. The S.O.S. describes a kind of sausage gravy on toast, served with home fries. Placing it on the menu sparked a bitter debate between the Gores, but in the end, Richard's intuition proved correct.

Besides the breakfast, the Gores delight customers with a tidy selection of hot plates that include meat loaf, fresh fried haddock, and hearty sandwiches. The small quarters do not allow for extensive prep work, so the menu sticks to the basics, with a couple of daily specials.

MORAN SQUARE DINER
1940 WORCESTER #765
6 Myrtle Ave., Route 2A, Fitchburg, MA • (978) 343-9549

I had the good fortune to meet the diner's long-time owner, Louis Vitelli, in 1991. He had just celebrated the diner's fiftieth anniversary the previous year, and I immediately took a liking to the man, with his soft-spoken, gentle, but confident nature. Louis regaled me with stories of the diner's operation over five decades, wistfully describing Fitchburg's final years of industrial prowess, when the Moran Square never closed. Louis's words filled a diner barely changed since leaving the factory fifty-one years before. This diner's interior almost outshone its bright red porcelain exterior. Indeed, here one finds Worcester Lunch Car at its best—intricate ceramic-tiled floor, richly veined

Chris Gianetti is only the second owner of the fabulously well-maintained Moran Square Diner. In 1994, he took over from the revered and legendary Louis Vitelli, who retired the year before because of health problems. Chris and crew have since stayed true to the traditions, making the diner a well-loved local landmark.

brown marble countertop, elegant black tile backbar, and hardwood booths and wall panels.

Health problems forced Louis to retire in 1993, and he died in 2002. A year after he retired, he sold the diner to a couple of fresh faces, Chris and Mary Gianetti. The reopening of the Moran Square Diner in 1994 brought a collective sigh of relief, not just from diner fanatics, but from Fitchburg itself. Struggling, with some success, to redefine itself in the high-tech age, the old mill town could scarcely afford to lose this institution. And indeed, the city has shown its gratitude to Chris and Mary for their efforts. Eager to see the diner reopen, customers swamped the place on its first day, and it remains popular ten years later.

Although she is not a full-timer at the Moran Square, Mary's training as a dietitian shows its influence on the diner's menu. Here one sees the struggle between Mary's nutritional sense and Chris's desire to maintain the classic traditions of diner cuisine for the diner's longtime regulars, who expect him to keep everything the same as Louis left it.

"In the beginning, we used to put ham in the macaroni and cheese, and there would be a guy sitting at the counter watching me make all this stuff. He'd say, 'Louis would never put ham in the macaroni and cheese!' and walk out. At the end of the day, you'd get five or six of those. I'd go home and ask Mary, 'Are we doing the right thing here?'"

I've visited the Moran Square many times since that first occasion, and I've enjoyed a wide variety of fine meals during Chris's tenure. I'm grateful for several items on the menu, notably the homemade corned beef hash, served only on Sundays. Fresh-roasted turkey, also a staple, makes each Tuesday visit memorable, as does an apple crisp that's too good to share. The diner serves another extremely pleasant surprise with the fish fry: hand-cut, fresh-made cole slaw, not the turbo-sliced mush doled out with an ice-cream scoop that I usually find.

Chris has adjusted well to his new role at the grill, still standing right behind the counter, where you can watch your food being prepared. After eight years at this work, he looks every bit as comfortable behind the counter as his predecessor. This comfort extends to all parts of the business—the atmosphere, the food, and the people who bring the place to life.

RALPH'S CHADWICK SQUARE

1930 WORCESTER #660
Prescott St., Worcester, MA

A little-known part of Worcester's history was its role in the development of punk and garage music in the late 1960s and 1970s. Toward the end of the 1970s and into the 1980s, Worcester may have developed a music scene to rival the punk scenes in New York and London. Starting in 1979, one of the best places to become part of that scene had a diner attached to it.

Ralph Moberly's affection for twentieth-century Americana had reached its zenith with the purchase of the Chadwick Square that year. Until then, the diner had seen years of service in its namesake location, and then for a short while feeding truckers traveling up Route 9 through the Cherry Valley section of Worcester on the other side of town. The diner's appearance, its long, narrow shape topped off with a railroad-inspired monitor roof, makes it easy to understand why the retired railroad car myth persists to this day. Inside, working-class joes get to eat in a space fit for royalty. Mahogany ceilings, oak trim, ceramic tile floor designed with complex patterns, and inch-thick marble countertops tell of an age where businesses in general and diners in particular seemed to spare no expense in their construction.

Moberly attached the diner to one of a growing number of shuttered factory buildings, turned the building into a club, and opened for business.

It wasn't long before the diner and nightclub became a magnet for scen-esters all over the region to catch an up-and-coming band while also chow-ing down on one of the finest burgers or bowls of chili to be found in all of New England. Eventually the diner adopted the cocky but tongue-in-cheek catchphrase "Eat at Ralph's. Live forever."

Essentially, Moberly had created a near perfect hangout for a town with a gritty but glorious industrial past. The diner served as both an external visual attraction to the uninitiated and a low-key, intimate preshow gather-ing spot where people could enjoy a drink with their burger and chili. From the diner, patrons passed into the lounge, which also served as a museum of sorts to display a sizable portion of Moberly's collection. From the ceilings hung stuffed wild animals, motorcycles, neon signs, and other artifacts. Local artists had painted larger-than-life paintings in the nooks and cran-nies, and the bar itself was built from salvaged diners. It was a perfect place for dating or meeting new people; hardly a space in the room didn't have something to spark a conversation. On the jukebox, you'd find songs you'd never thought you'd see in one of those machines. The Ralph's experience continued upstairs in the club—known as the Blue Moon Cafe—where live acts played, often to audiences drawn from the entire state and beyond.

It took the media far too long to acknowledge this local institution, but in 1994, the *Boston Globe* finally declared Ralph's the best nightclub in the commonwealth, and at the time, Ralph's had already passed its prime. The fact that this club incorporated such an amazing diner surely contributed to its appeal.

The car still retains much evidence of Worcester Lunch Car's capabilities during this period and could benefit immensely from a sustained restora-tion effort. The fact that it still retains such beauty after nearly eighty years of service speaks volumes for the supreme level of artisanship of the French Canadian craftsmen who built it.

As often happens with popular clubs, Ralph's arc of popularity came in for a hard landing in the late 1990s, and the diner's cachet began to fade. A bitter divorce, employee squabbles, and a general decline in the city's live music scene contributed Ralph's ultimate decision to sell the place to his for-mer bartender Vincent Hemmeter. Hemmeter had already supplanted Ralph as the city's toastmaster upon the opening of his own eponymous tavern. When working at Ralph's, Vince's responsibilities had included booking bands as well as serving the best martini in New England. Hemmeter would seem the ideal successor to Ralph's developing legend and likely will do a fine job refurbishing both the diner's physical and fiscal conditions. More gratifying, Hemmeter shares Moberly's appreciation for Americana and pro-clivity to collect, so we can expect the menagerie to continue to grow.

DINER DIRECTORY

CENTRAL MASSACHUSETTS

1921 Diner
53 Shrewsbury St., Rte. 140
Boylston, MA
(508) 869-9921
1927 Worcester 586
Originally placed in Boston as Fahey's
Diner. Taken in trade by Worcester
Lunch Car and sold to Adams, Massachusetts, where it remained until
replaced in 1948 by the new Miss
Adams Diner. Worcester Lunch Car
likely took this diner in trade, refurbished it, and sold it to a Worcester
operator. Eventually, #586 became the
first of two Charlie's Diners on Plantation Street in Worcester. In 1957, Charlie Turner Sr. replaced this with another
used Worcester car removed from service in Wareham, selling #586 for its
move to Boylston.

Though almost entirely covered with vinyl siding,
the 1921 Diner retains a great deal of its
interior charm.

Alice & the Hat Diner
Murray St.
Worcester, MA
1928 Worcester 610
Originally Grove Street Diner. Closed
and used for some undetermined commercial use. According to John Baeder's
book *Diners,* Alice & the Hat was a
favorite of the newspaper crowd in the
city. "The Hat" was the nickname of
Alice's husband, who worked at the
Worcester Telegram.

Art's Diner
541 W. Boylston St.
Worcester, MA
(508) 853-9705
1930s Worcester
Little remains of the original diner. Art's
has become mainly a local watering hole,
with Italian specialties and a full bar.

Blue Belle Diner
Millis, MA
1948 Worcester 814
In storage. The Blue Belle served most of
its life in Worcester, but in 1998, it was
moved from its last location on Prescott
Street to a car dealership in Shrewsbury.
A Milford businessman purchased the
diner in 2001, and hopes to restore the
diner and its operation in that town.

Blue Moon Diner
102 Main St./Rte. 68
Gardner, MA
(978) 632-4333
1949 Worcester 815
Listed on the National Register of Historic Places. Before the Blue Moon
came to Gardner, it served customers

in nearby Winchendon as the Miss Toy Town Diner. In 1988, retired police officer Dennis "Skip" Scipione brought the diner to the Chair City, placing it on the location of the original Blue Moon Diner. In 2000, Skip sold the business to a former waitress, Jamie Brouillet.

Boulevard Diner
155 Shrewsbury St.
Worcester, MA
(508) 791-4535
1937 Worcester 730
Probably this city's most recognizable diner, the Boulevard Diner is one of fourteen diners in the state on the National Historic Register. Lovingly restored by Jim George, a grandson of the diner's original owner. He also restored the diner to a true twenty-four-hour operation, a real rarity in Massachusetts.

Carl's Oxford Diner
291 Main St./Rte. 12
Oxford, MA
(508) 987-8770
c. 1930 Worcester
Carl's serves a fine meal for the money in a smoke-free atmosphere. Known for its huge portions, and anyone who dares to ask for seconds will get them.

Central Diner
90 Elm St.
Millbury, MA
(508) 865-0705
1930 Worcester 673
Second diner on this location, replacing a slightly smaller 1910 Worcester car. (See pages 120–21.)

Charlie's Diner
Worcester, MA
www.charliesdiner.com
1948 Worcester 816

A 1970s-era renovation blankets some of its more sparkling charms, but everyone who knows Carl's Diner knows it for its huge portions.

In storage. Originally Aiken's Diner, located in Wareham, Massachusetts. Closed in April 2003. Awaits permits for installation in new Worcester location.

Chet's Diner
191 Main St./Rte. 20
Northborough, MA
(508) 393-9403
1931 Worcester?
Possibly built on-site by Worcester Lunch Car. Bar with additional back room built on for live entertainment. Also serves breakfast and lunch. Tenuous future.

Corner Lunch
131 Lamartine St.
Worcester, MA
(508) 799-9866
www.cornerlunch.com
1950s DeRaffele/Musi
Listed on National Register of Historic Places. Originally located in Babylon, New York. Largest diner in Worcester, installed in 1967 by Musi Diners, who had converted about a third of the original dining area into a kitchen unit. American food with some Greek specialties. Breakfast and lunch only.

The East Side Diner looks as if a previous owner expanded the diner, knocking out its front wall to allow for booth seating.

East Side Diner
135 Lunenburg St.
Fitchburg, MA
(978) 343-9635
c. 1925 Worcester
Small diner that has undergone some remodeling, which widened the original structure. Usually open for breakfast and lunch only.

Edgemere Diner
55 Hartford Tpk./Rte. 20
Shrewsbury, MA
(508) 752-7054
1948 Fodero
Classic Fodero with winged clock. A rare find for New England. Fodero built some of the industry's most beautiful and stylish diners.

Emerald Isle
49 Millbury St.
Worcester, MA
(508) 754-7676
1946 O'Mahony
Originally Messier's Diner. This diner has a big leprechaun hat on its roof. With a remodeled exterior, the diner has few remaining original features. Blue-collar restaurant in a struggling neighborhood. Full menu.

Fifty-Fifty Diner
440 River St.
Fitchburg, MA
(978) 345-7721
Worcester?
Old barrel roof diner remodeled with the appearance of a 1950s stainless diner, using aluminum panels. Retains few original features. Fun, friendly place featuring good, homemade breakfasts and lunches.

Finely Fran's
Worcester, MA
(508) 756-1122
1936 Sterling 363
In storage. The third diner built by J. B. Judkins in 1936, and the oldest still extant, but with dim prospects for its future. Formerly known as Muggsy's. Closed in 1990 and never reopened. Since then, the diner has suffered extensive decay and vandalism.

George's Green Island Diner
162 Millbury St.
Worcester, MA
(508) 753-4189
c. 1929 Worcester
Classic blue-collar diner with late-night hours. Owner George Army has worked in several of the city's diners.

Home Plate
5 E. Main St.
Westboro, MA
(508) 616-0289
c. 1930 unknown
Though it has few of its original features, the Home Plate still serves up fare true to the tradition. Breakfast and lunch.

Jim's Flyin' Diner
Southbridge Airport
Southbridge, MA
1958 Master

One of Massachusetts' most out-of-the way diners. Located at the Southbridge Airport, it features a deck built to overlook the landing strip for small aircraft. Rare Master diner, and one of only four in the region. Basic grilled diner fare. Breakfast and lunch only.

Joy Asia Restaurant
735 Boston Post Rd./Rte. 20
Marlborough, MA
(508) 481-0100
1952 O'Mahony
Formerly located in Everett. Interior stripped of most original features for use as Marlboro liquor store. Partially restored and reopened as diner in 1995. Converted to Asian cuisine in 2003. Beautiful 1950s classic.

Kenwood Diner
97 Main St./Rte. 9
Spencer, MA
(508) 885-6596
1933 Worcester 713
Worcester diner serving breakfast and lunch in a Main Street setting.

Lou's Diner
100 Chestnut St.
Clinton, MA
(978) 365-9808
1929 Worcester 638
Originally the R&G Diner, located in Portsmouth, New Hampshire. Small car remodeled by Worcester in the 1950s. A real gem in a town on the upswing. Seating capacity less than twenty. Basic breakfast and lunch menu.

Lou-Roc's Diner
1074 West Boylston St./Rte. 12
Worcester, MA
(508) 853-9791
1953 Silk City

Classic Silk City diner, rare to Massachusetts. Completely encased in a box-shaped brick building. Interior still relatively intact. When still in original condition, featured in *New England Roadside Delights*.

Mac's Diner
Shrewsbury St.
Worcester, MA
1931 Worcester
Few discernible vestiges of Worcester Lunch Car construction, but excellent food and still in same location. Italian specialties. Lunch and dinner.

Main Street Diner
311 Main St./Rte. 2A
Athol, MA
(978) 249-8529
1930s Worcester
Probably a small Worcester car that has undergone extensive remodelings. Lengthy counter runs the length of the original diner and the on-site extension, but the narrow width allows no space for table seating.

From the late 1920s into the 1930s, Worcester Lunch Car constructed some elaborate monitor roof diners that still make some believe that diners once rode the rails. George's Green Island Diner clings to precious little of its original features, but it continues to serve the night owls in its blue-collar neighborhood.

Mindy's Diner
Rte. 117
Bolton, MA
(978) 779-2711
1939 Worcester 747
Used as a hot dog stand in Crystal
Springs campground. Not generally
open to the public.

Miss Worcester Diner
300 Southbridge St.
Worcester, MA
(508) 757-7775
1948 Worcester 812
Closed in 2004 in a legal dispute. Listed
on the National Register of Historic
Places. Located across the street from
the factory that built it.

Moran Square Diner
6 Myrtle Ave./Rte. 2A
Fitchburg, MA
(978) 343-9549
1940 Worcester 765
See page 124.

Myriad Ballroom
Lakeview Park/Rte. 16
Mendon, MA
(508) 478-2778
1951 O'Mahony
Incorporated into function hall and
not in general service.

Nap's Diner
W. Main St.
Webster, MA
(508) 943-1525
1931 Worcester 682
Originally Drury Square Diner, located
in Auburn, Massachusetts. Small basic
unit attached to a restaurant as interesting as the diner itself. Breakfast and
lunch only.

Nelly's Diner
Rawlins Ave.
Marlborough, MA
(508) 481-1303
1947 Worcester 802
Recently reopened after a difficult period
that saw several attempts to revive business. Originally located in Shrewsbury,
near the now-defunct White City Amusement Park. Now part of the downtown
historic district and in very original condition. Breakfast and lunch.

Parkway Diner
148 Shrewsbury St.
Worcester, MA
(508) 753-9968
1930 Worcester 670
Exterior completely remodeled and easy
to miss, but interior in original shape.
Almost directly across the street from
the Boulevard Diner. Specializes in Italian dishes, with a meatball sandwich
that has no equal.

Peg's Diner
87 Church St.
Whitinsville, MA
(508) 234-0170
1937 Worcester 723
See page 122.

Ralph's Chadwick Square Diner
95 Prescott St.
Worcester, MA
(508) 753-9543
1930 Worcester 660
Listed on the National Register of Historic Places. In need of restoration, but
still shows the meticulous craftmanship
of Worcester Lunch Car. Once located in
Chadwick Square. In the 1950s, moved
to the Cherry Valley section. It now
serves as a dining area for a larger nightclub complex, with mainly burgers and

chili during the evening hours, Wednesday through Saturday. New owners plan to reopen for lunch as well.

Residence
Dudley/Webster Rd.
Webster, MA
Worcester
Private residence.

Residence (LaPrade's Diner)
Stafford St.
Worcester, MA
1930s Worcester?
Currently used as a residence. Last used as a diner, by the name LaPrade's, in 1968.

Stewart's Diner
148 Main St.
Blackstone, MA
c. 1930 Worcester
Tiny car, drastically remodeled.

Tim's Diner and Chowder House
15 Water St.
Leominster, MA
1949 Silk City 4921
Rare, custom-built Silk City, one of only two in Massachusetts. Small with partial brick facade and attached dining room. Known for chowders and excellent breakfasts. Clean. Early breakfast and lunch on weekdays; breakfast only on weekends.

Tony's Diner
50 Deepdale Rd.
Worcester, MA
1933 Worcester 705
In storage. This diner has traveled quite a bit, from Maine to Lowell and back to

LaPrade's Diner likely closed up for good in the 1960s and subsequently became someone's house. Some historians speculate that LaPrade's could have come from the work of Wilfred Barriere, a diner builder and journeyman who worked for Worcester Lunch Car and for himself in the 1910s and 1920s.

Worcester, where it was restored and set up on the city's common as a visitors information center. In 1998, arsonists nearly destroyed it. The following year, local car collector and restorer Mike O'Connor undertook the task to repair the damage. Currently under restoration.

Yankee Diner
23 Worcester Rd./Rte. 20
Charlton, MA
(508) 248-7370
1939 Worcester 735
Originally installed in Leominster, Massachusetts. Serves many homemade items, including corned-beef hash, in a very friendly atmosphere. Breakfast and lunch on weekdays; breakfast only on weekends.

WESTERN MASSACHUSETTS and VERMONT

The geography of both western Massachusetts and Vermont stands out as among the most bucolic and pastoral to be found anywhere in New England, but sadly, it also represents some of the most economically depressed. New England's longest river, the Connecticut, largely separates this sector from the rest of the region, and as a natural resource, it provided western New England with an early source of power and a later source of waste removal. Thankfully, efforts to clean up the Connecticut in the past thirty years have helped tremendously, as has the closing of most of the mills that once lined its scenic banks.

Springfield, Massachusetts, stands at a major crossroads for western New England. The siting of the armory here by none other than Gen. George Washington ensured the city's eventual industrial prominence and its role as the commercial center of most of the river valley north of Hartford. As it did for most northeastern cities, the coming of the railroad marked the start of a century of industrial growth, and the advent of the automobile generally heralded its decline. Springfield lays claim to a wide variety of historic landmarks. It was the birthplace of Theodor Geisel, better known as Dr. Seuss; the site of the first mass-produced automobile; the place of manufacture of the Springfield rifle; and the birthplace of basketball. It was also the first municipality to ban the lunch wagon from its streets.

Samuel Messer Jones, the first to manufacture lunch wagons, in nearby Worcester in 1884, sold his business there and moved to Springfield to begin again. Jones built forty wagons at his shop on Union Street before the town fathers deemed their presence a nuisance. Perhaps City Hall had just cause for stifling this development, or perhaps established restaurants simply resorted to political methods to seek protection from their upstart competition, but the edict produced a rippling effect throughout the industry. With more cities following Springfield's lead, the lunch wagon industry responded by building larger cars better suited for stationary operation. With the ability to tie in to utilities, diners could accommodate more customers and provide them with

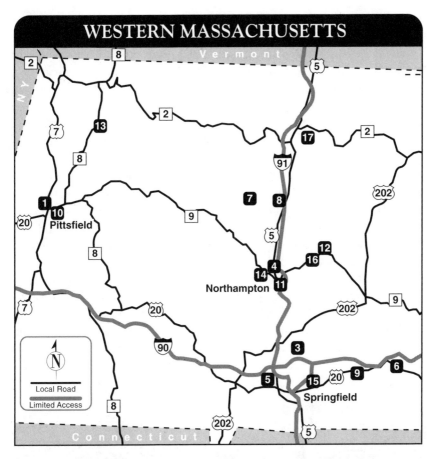

WESTERN MASSACHUSETTS

1 Adrienne's Diner: Pittsfield (BR)
2 Al's Diner: Chicopee (MS)
3 Bernie's Dining Depot: Chicopee (MS)
4 Blue Bonnet Diner: Northampton (BR)
5 Charles Diner: W. Springfield (MS)
6 Day & Night Diner: Palmer (BR)
7 Delligan's Diner: Conway (MS)
8 Fillin' Station: Whately (EM)
9 Gregory's Restaurant: Wilbraham (R)

10 Hudpucker's Grill & Bar: Pittsfield (R)
11 Kathy's Diner: Northampton (BR)
12 McMurphy's: Amherst (R)
13 Miss Adams Diner: Adams (BR)
14 Miss Florence Diner: Florence (BR)
15 Route 66 Diner: Springfield (MS)
16 Route 9 Diner: Hadley (P)
17 Shady Glen: Turners Falls (OS)

a larger menu. Their long, narrow proportions made these later lunch wagons and early diners ideal for slivers of land too small for other traditional uses. Despite this, many operators remained reluctant to remove the wheels still used for shipping in case the location turned sour.

Though a few others built their own lunch wagons to ply the streets in competition with Jones's cars, Wilson Goodrich provided Sam with his only real competition in the building of these cars. Both men bailed out when the city outlawed their products in 1905.

In the 1930s, Springfield played host to one other diner builder, the Wason Manufacturing Company, which had previously built railroad coaches. When the Depression decimated that line of business, the company switched to diners, constructing them under license with the Brill Company of Philadelphia, also more famous for its railroad and trolley cars. With its broad industrial base, the city predictably saw the establishment of many diners over the years, but all except one has passed into history.

The city now has just one diner left—the Route 66 Diner on Bay Street, not far from the Springfield Central High School and across the road from Blunt Park. This classic Mountain View was known as the Bay Diner for much of its existence, until purchased by brothers Don and Norman Roy in 1985. The Roys have transformed the Route 66 into a family-friendly haven for great food in ample portions.

Out in Palmer, the Day and Night Diner stays true only to the "day" half of its name, but it remains an authentic diner in every other sense. The 1944 Worcester car, now owned by Eileen Laurion, makes breakfast and lunch for another struggling mill town. Eileen makes great soups, and I rarely stop in for breakfast without getting a Polish omelet. Her omelets come off the grill as yellow as sunshine, and the grilled onions, peppers, and kielbasa round out a satisfying breakfast.

Owned since 1993 by Eileen Laurion, the Day and Night Diner, a 1944 Worcester car, enjoys a reputation for perfect omelets and a setting just like home—a real treasure.

MISS DINERS

New England has nine diners with names that begin with "Miss," and many more have served the area throughout diner history. The name seems to have a distinctly New England flavor to it, and indeed, until recently, most of these diners remained within its borders. More recently, the resurgence in the diner's popularity and the spreading awareness of its history have led others outside the region to apply the name to their diners as well. Usually "Miss" precedes the name of the town where the diner does business, giving potential customers an important clue for finding it. You will not likely see the Miss Worcester in Fitchburg.

Though no specific documentation exists to prove this, historians generally believe that "Miss" was added to names as an attempt of diner operators in the 1920s and 1930s to soften the image of their male-dominated enclaves. Indeed, my own mother never set foot in a diner until the late 1980s because, as she put it, "Nice girls didn't go to diners."

Savvy operators realized that catering to women represented a potential doubling of their market. Some went so far as to deliberately place their female customers close to the door so that passers-by would see that this diner welcomed the fairer sex. Also, potential customers might further assume that a diner patronized by women must have good food.

Others diners had baked into their exterior enamel "Ladies Invited," "Tables for Ladies," or "Booth Service," all intended to appeal to women. In New England, only Lou's Diner in Clinton maintains its "Ladies Invited" placard. The sign has drawn the scorn of at least one passing woman, who wrote a letter accusing the owners of sexism.

Crossing the Connecticut from Springfield into West Springfield, the ardent diner fan will rejoice at the sight of the Charles Diner, more commonly known as Charlie's. The Alfano family has upheld the tradition in a classic and now very rare 1948 Fodero diner that still retains its prototypical winged clock. The diner's menu features many Italian specialties, as well as the expected diner favorites. The Alfanos have made some changes to the structure, including the addition of a vinyl awning. After the diner's splendid neon sign collapsed in the mid-1990s, it was never returned to its roadside perch.

Back across the river and to the north in Chicopee, the owners of Al's Diner have garnered the "best diner" accolade for almost ten years straight now, and with good reason. Al's Diner represents the "old school" at its finest. A good hot meal, low price, and clean, familial atmosphere will never go out of style, and this diner could write the manual on how that's done.

A recent change of owners brought many changes to Miss Florence, but it remains a true diner in every sense.

Continuing up the Connecticut River Valley, we now bypass Westfield and then Holyoke, the country's first planned city, which lost its last diner in 1991 to a location farther north. Northampton, however, still boasts three diners. One of these, the Miss Florence, enjoys the distinction of a listing on the National Register of Historic Places.

Until 2001, the Alexander family owned and operated both the 1941 Worcester diner and the adjoining dining room, Alexander's. Under their stewardship, the diner became one of the most famous in the country, appearing in the pages of the *New York Times, Boston Globe, Yankee,* and other publications because of its traditional diner experience enlivened by a monumental neon sign, barking waitresses, and chicken croquettes and meatloaf.

The diner fanatic will soon notice the anomaly of the diner's floor-tile pattern, seen to the right upon entering the front door. The seam indicates where the Worcester Company built a later addition to the Miss Flo after its previous owners had moved it to the village of Florence from a location in downtown Northampton, giving the structure an L-shaped dining area that wrapped around the counter.

The Alexanders sold the business and property to Konstantine Sierros, a local restaurateur who says he fully appreciated the celebrated role the diner played in anchoring the local community. Sierros spent the next nine months attending to years of deferred maintenance. When the Alexanders sold the Miss Flo, the diner's original oak booths and marble counters were long lost. Other than that, the diner needed a modicum of restorative work. Sierros bucked a few traditions with his renovations, such as a pink granite counter and counter apron and a revolving pie case, but along with the other improvements, especially the new wooden booths, wood-laminate ceiling panels, and completely renovated kitchen, he did a fine job of preparing the diner for another seventy years of service.

Sierros also made many improvements to the menu, particularly at breakfast. Besides the typical fare, the diner now offers homemade cornedbeef hash. Service is friendly and personable, and you can settle in comfortably for some happy dinering.

A newcomer visiting Northampton today would never believe that only twenty-five years ago, the city suffered the same reputation and prospects of any other northeastern factory town. But with four nationally renowned colleges and a huge state university in the area, it seems inevitable that the economic and cultural power of these institutions would eventually help reverse the city's fortunes. One can mark the beginning of this reversal with the 1977 opening of a restaurant called Fitzwilly's, a "fern" bar on Main Street that generated $3 million in business in its first year. From that point on, the city became a magnet for new shops and restaurants, and every autumn seemed to bring a fresh crop of eateries with the returning students.

In the midst of this cataclysmic gentrification stood the former Red Lion Diner, now known as Kathy's. One might have expected that a little family diner that specialized in $2 hamburgers and homemade soups would have sold out long ago to developers. Showing its age all too plainly, Kathy's Diner, a 1920s vintage Worcester diner with monitor-style roof, represents the Northampton of old, before the onslaught of the boutiques and coffee shops staking their places in the city's hyperactive downtown.

The Bluebonnet Diner, north of downtown on King Street, also fights the tide of progress with its 1950 Worcester car, now augmented by an expansive dining room and function hall. Take note of this diner's rare layout with two entrances with small vestibules on either end of the facade. The Bluebonnet keeps a clean, fresh appearance and retains its original clock. Located now in the heart of Northampton's own particular retail "miracle mile," it makes for a fine respite after a morning of shopping.

Northern New England boasts three diners that typically never close. One of the two in Massachusetts sits in Whately, just off the exit from Route 91. The Fillin' Station sparkles in appearance with its flamboyant, early 1960s space-age design, neon signage, and large plate-glass windows. Truck-

Northampton is currently the only growing community in western Massachusetts, and its red-hot real estate market has meant that most downtown businesses now cater to the upscale markets. Kathy's Diner, the oldest operating diner in western Massachusetts, marks a pointed contrast to that trend.

Kullman Industries, the company that built it, called this model the Princess, a rather precious moniker for such a jet-age design. Today the Fillin' Station stays open around the clock, a rarity for Massachusetts, and remains popular with truckers.

ers and after-hours party hoppers fill the seats in this gorgeous diner built by Kullman at the tail end of the diner's heyday.

The Kullman Company dubbed this style of diner rather incongruously, calling it the Princess model, an appellation that hardly conjures up images of orbiting satellites. This diner represents one of the last examples of the transportation metaphor inherent in diner design since its inception. Until the early 1960s, diners all either moved or looked like something that moved. The Princess style, like many of the Googie-style coffee shops all the rage on the West Coast during this period, looked like a space port from which you might see rocket ships launching somewhere out back.

The Fillin' Station moved up to Whately from its original location in Chicopee Falls, Massachusetts, and is currently owned by F. L. Roberts, a regional oil services company in Springfield that owns a chain of gas stations and car washes throughout the valley.

A quick but vital side trip into the sleepy town of Turners Falls takes us to the Shady Glen. Though the Shady Glen does not have a prefabricated heritage, this book would do you a great disservice by allowing you to pass it by without sampling its wide variety of fresh-baked pies, homemade soups, fresh dinner plates, and the friendliest service in New England. The Glen offers fresh vegetables in season and real mashed potatoes. In all but its architectural pedigree, the Shady Glen looks, feels, smells, and acts exactly like a real diner and often does a better job than many of its prefabricated cousins.

Run for forty years by the affable John Carey, the Shady Glen started out in the 1950s as a drive-in restaurant. In the early 1960s, John joined his sister, who already worked there, and persisted long enough to create one of New England's more popular eateries. At dinnertime, the Glen brings the only real life to Avenue A in this picturesque but quiet mill town, and patrons often must wait long enough to read the entire daily paper before getting a booth here. The Glen draws its business from all over, with people in the know stopping for a meal on their way from Boston to ski vacations in Vermont or up from Connecticut. In 2004, John finally sold the business, ending an era. He looks forward to a long, relaxing retirement.

Heading up the valley, we cross into Vermont, where Brattleboro greets the traveler with its own brand of renaissance and its four rather unusual diners. Brattleboro is often described as a college town without the college, and its countercultural leanings have led to the establishment of all sorts of businesses catering to the neo-hippie. As you head north, the first diner will not make itself obvious from the road. You'll have to walk inside Gillie's Seafood Restaurant to see it, but buried within the building sits one of only two Kullman diners in northern New England. The diner retains many of its original interior features, but its windows were removed when it was enclosed. The

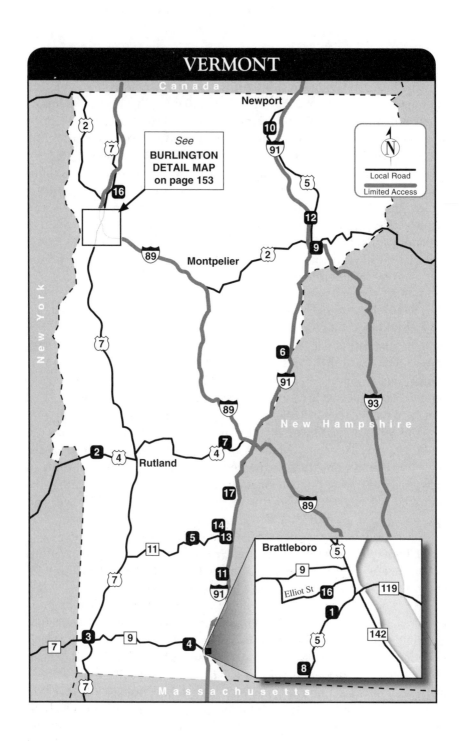

1 Big Mama's Diner: Brattleboro (BR)

2 Birdseye Diner: Castleton (MS)

3 Blue Benn Diner: Bennington (MS)

4 Chelsea Royal Diner: W. Brattleboro (BR)

5 Country Girl Diner: Chester (MS)

6 Fairlee Diner: Fairlee (OS)

7 Farina Family Diner: Quechee (MS)

8 Gillie's Seafood Restaurant: Brattleboro (MS)

9 Locks: St. Johnsbury (BR)

10 Martha's Diner: Coventry (MS)

11 Miss Bellows Falls Diner: Bellows Falls (BR)

12 Miss Lyndonville Diner: Lyndonville (R)

13 Shanghai Garden: Springfield (BR)

14 Springfield Royal Diner: Springfield (MS)

15 T. J. Buckley's Uptown Dining: Brattleboro (BR)

16 Wesson's Diner: In Storage (MS)

17 Windsor Diner: Windsor (MS)

restaurant specializes in seafood, but one can hardly describe it as a neighborhood diner. Farther north on U.S. Route 5, slow down for Big Mama's Green Mountain Diner, a 1920s vintage Worcester car that has undergone several remodelings in the past ten years. Yes, there is a "Big Mama," and the diner serves authentic Mexican cuisine three days a week.

Brattleboro contains another diner anomaly in T. J. Buckley's Uptown Dining. This very small Worcester Lunch Car diner currently serves only upscale prix fixe meals at four tables by reservation only. Though this is hardly classic diner fare, Buckley's has enjoyed a slew of glowing reviews from critics around the region. The diner originally was shipped to Woburn, Massachusetts, as the first diner on the site of today's Main Street Diner. Worcester took the old diner back to the factory and updated it for resale, which eventually put it in Brattleboro.

The builders of the Shady Glen originally designed a drive-in, but since 1962, its current owner John Carey has quietly and diligently turned it into one of the finest diners in New England. Homemade soups, pies, and hot plates rule this popular spot in an otherwise struggling mill town. Not to be missed.

T. J. Buckley's currently serves a prix fixe menu at its four tables, and most reviews give it very high marks. Reservations are required.

Finally, on the town's west side just before Route 9 starts climbing into the hills, the Chelsea Royal Diner occupies a primo location and draws in the crowds. Desserts at the Chelsea reign supreme, but the diner also does justice to classic comfort foods. The diner's counter and other fixtures have been removed relegating it to a mere dining room in a multiroomed restaurant. As you enter, note the vintage photos of the diner in its original location in the center of town, before earlier owners moved it to the outskirts. Also note the handsome neon that hangs by the road. A former owner, Philip Gomez, had the sign sitting in his barn in West Lebanon, New Hampshire. In 1999, Gomez stopped by the diner to drop off a photo of the sign, which eventually led to current owner Todd Darrah's repurchase of the sign for the price of one Spanish omelet. Darrah then contracted with Cheshire Signs of Keene, New Hampshire, to learn that its president, Tony Magaletta, had made the sign in 1958. Magaletta restored the sign to original condition using the same paints and techniques as he had years before.

Bellows Falls, Vermont, is another town that has shown promising signs of rebirth. This former railroad town grew up around the junctions of the Boston & Maine and Central Vermont main lines, and its dam provides electric power to the surrounding area. In the heart of downtown, the Miss Bellows Falls Diner stands ready to serve you. This precious, gray porcelain clad Worcester car is the second diner in the United States individually listed on the National Register of Historic Places.

The menu boards above the counter erroneously date the diner, serial number 771, to 1927, twelve years before it actually left the Worcester Car factory. In fact, the diner started out in Lowell in 1941 as Frankie & Johnnie's Diner, and in 1944, Worcester Lunch Car took it back and resold it to a Bellows Falls operator, who likely operated an older unit already called the Miss Bellows Falls that possibly dated back to 1927.

Typical for a company that tended to waste nothing, Worcester replaced the front exterior panels with new porcelain on which was the new name and put the originals on the diner's rear. While in Lowell, the diner likely stood against a site-built kitchen and didn't need porcelain skin. A small portion of those panels remains visible on the diner's back today.

In 2001, Charlie Jarris sold off his landmark to Ron Bingham, who has been working to revive the diner. Early reports sound good, and if Ron remains true to the simple but honest formula for diner operation, he should do okay.

Springfield, Vermont, lies at the center of an area known as Precision Valley, so dubbed because of the many machine tool companies that once dominated the local economy. Their closures have forced the community to make many adjustments to the new realities, and it generally now markets itself as another part of the greater Vermont industrial tourism complex catering to the perennial parades of leaf peepers that clog up the scenic highways in September.

The few towns in Vermont that grew up because of manufacturing rather than agriculture have suffered the most in the transition, but the fact

The Royal Diner originally came from downtown Brattleboro and lost its counter not long after the move. In 1999, the owner received quite a gift when the diner's original sign suddenly turned up in a barn in New Hampshire. Freshly restored by its original maker, the sign now shines a bright welcome to traffic coming to and from Brattleboro.

that Springfield retains much of its small-town charm and infrastructural utility has helped it attract newcomers seeking a slower pace of life while still enjoying some of the benefits of city living. Springfield now features a trendy coffee shop and a popular bakery on a streetscape benefiting from a renewed emphasis on Main Street retail.

And yes, you can also find Chinese food, and in Springfield, it comes from a diner. The Shanghai Garden occupies a remodeled 1941 Worcester diner, which until 2003 was the city's only extant diner. In that year, local businessman Matt Alldredge and a group of investors brought a real diner rarity to this town and attached it to his Precision Valley Corvette Museum, a local attraction in itself. The newly opened Springfield Royal Diner represents the last of only four diners built by Mahony Diners, a company founded in 1956 by former employees of the once-mighty O'Mahony Diner Company, which had just closed.

Alldredge almost purchased a brand new Starlite Diner from Ormond, Florida, but reconsidered when he found the shuttered and available Royal Diner on Route 28 in Kingston, New York. Worn down but still mostly intact, the sixty-seat stainless steel structure needed little restorative work and would provide the perfect setting for Alldredge's doo-wop dream. Its entry into the Springfield area made quite a splash when it opened in 2003, and business has been brisk. This diner made a brief appearance in a 1992 episode of "Seinfeld."

Slightly weathered but little changed, the Miss Bellows Falls has an atmosphere that reeks of New England cozy.

DINER ARCHITECTURE

Located in the heart of Lynn, a city finally on the mend, the Capitol Diner shines like an oasis in the desert and serves to explain the fascination with this great American institution.

When people think of Worcester, they often think of diners. And when they think of Worcester diners, they probably think of the Boulevard.

When it first opened in 1941, the Salem Diner attracted such large crowds that its employees couldn't go home for days. Though the crowds have definitely dissipated, the diner still attracts plenty of attention thanks to the striking streamlined design.

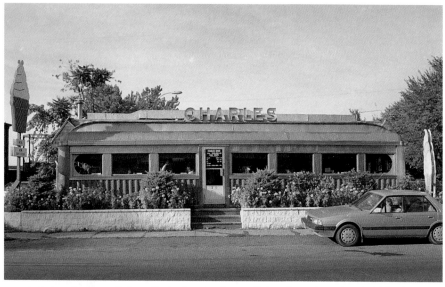

A vinyl awning was added to this classic and quite rare Fodero diner, shown here in 1992. Customers enjoy the Charles Diner's hearty breakfasts and fresh-baked ham.

Who could resist that magnificent neon sign? Al Mac's Diner in Fall River literally outshines every other restaurant in this region.

With its shining stainless steel exterior and simple but direct sign, Zip's Diner attracts both travelers and locals to its "quiet corner" of Connecticut.

DINER INTERIORS

The menu at Haven Brothers has only a few quick items on it, but savor every moment of your visit.

Hot dogs dominate the menu at Tex Barry's Coney Island, a charming 1920s vintage Worcester car.

Lou's Diner in Clinton is a little gem that still "invites ladies."

The diner world owes John Rehlen a huge debt of gratitude not only for restoring this Silk City gem and bringing life to a sleepy Vermont town, but also for proving the culinary potential of the classic diner. The Birdseye Diner was recently expanded into an adjacent storefront, and even more people can now enjoy its wide variety of fresh-made meals and desserts.

Fodero built the Forbes Diner in 1957, installing it the same year the Connecticut Turnpike opened, and it has changed little since.

The postmodern interior of Dave's Diner.

DINER ART

Don Sawyer's rendition of The Blue Benn Diner captures the folksy atmosphere of this Vermont landmark.

Don Sawyer spins a great yarn about his travels and his painting successes.

DINER POSTCARDS

Depot, Fitchburg, Mass.

Disembarking train passengers likely looked forward to a quick bite from the Buffet Lunch. Though the trains still run to Fitchburg, both the depot and the lunch wagon are now long gone.

Above: The palatial Aetna Diner had already been open a good ten years when it issued this post-card. Located near the insurance company of the same name, the Aetna advertised itself as a superior experience. This was no truck stop.

Left: This post card shows Lindy's when still owned by Timolean "Lindy" Chakolous.

The last Mahony diner came up from Kingston, New York, thanks to local businessman Matt Alldredge, who sought to add to the attraction of his Corvette museum. Relatively minor restorations make this diner a real feast for the eyes.

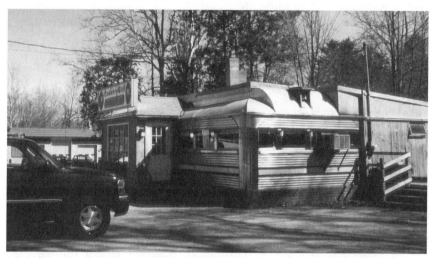

Noted photo-realist painter Ralph Goings immortalized the Country Girl Diner in his work. It has changed little in appearance since then, but owner Matt Stori has made continues improvements to the menu.

To the west of Springfield in Chester, you'll find a well-maintained Silk City and a fine meal at the Country Girl Diner. Owner Matt Stori purchased the diner in 1991 from the Delaney family, who had made the place a popular spot that attracted locals as well as the ski set on their way to and from the slopes. Its interior was twice depicted in paintings by artist Ralph Goings, who often uses diners as subjects and backdrops for his highly detailed realistic renderings.

To the northeast of Springfield in Windsor, another roadside gem awaits—Dan's Windsor Diner, built by Worcester and shipped in 1952 to its first location, Fitchburg, where it operated as Ray's Diner. In 1992, Rich Grano made a run at the business after moving up from Connecticut to the slower life in Vermont. After four years at the grill, he sold the diner to local antiques dealer Si Lupton, who took out a loan to purchase and refurbish the tired diner. Lupton had already made a name for himself in the area and in the diner industry as the man responsible for transporting the Ross Diner up from Holyoke. He did a fine job giving the interior a fresh polish, but he managed to keep the diner open only weeks before closing it and bailing on the business entirely. Dan Kirby then had a one-year stint at running the diner, before handing over the reins to its current owner, Fred Borcuk.

A diner that still enjoys a certain notoriety in the city of Holyoke, Massachusetts, now lies to the north in Quechee Gorge, Vermont. The former Ross Diner came to Quechee thanks to Si Lupton, who planned to open up this rare Worcester streamline model on the busy retail strip on Route 12A across the river in West Lebanon, New Hampshire. Faltering finances forced Lupton to sell the diner to antiques mogul Gary Neil, who set the diner down on his growing Quechee Gorge Village antiques mall and tourist complex near the famous namesake landmark on U.S. Route 4.

DINERS BY DON

Diner artist Don Sawyer has become a regular fixture at art festivals all around New England selling his folksy renditions of diners and other roadside attractions. He's done pretty well for someone with exactly $7 worth of art training that he received in 1994 in a remedial high school art course in Gardiner, Maine. On one of his assignments, the teacher asked him to paint something of architectural interest, so he pointed his canvas at the A-1 Diner. He sold the painting soon afterward for $150 to a local attorney. With that, Don had embarked on a new career, leaving behind a job teaching high school English.

Currently Don maintains an inventory of prints that reverentially depict more than 120 diners and other subjects, among them Curtis's Barbecue in Putney, Vermont; Casey's Diner in Natick, Massachusetts; and the Townsend Dam Diner in Townsend, Vermont. The paintings always capture the mood one might experience sitting on a stool at that counter. Don's customers, of whom he says at least 65 percent are between ages thirty and thirty-five, scoop up his matted $20 prints like hotcakes. To see more of Don's work, visit his website at www.dinerdon.com.

See photos in color section.

It may say Yankee Diner on its exterior, but the Farina family made it their own in 1997. The diner started as the Ross Diner in Holyoke, Massachusetts, and was brought to this area thanks to an entrepreneur's failed attempt to put it in West Lebanon. After a bumpy start, the diner seems to have hit its stride with good, classic home-cooked meals and generous portions.

Freshly restored and beautified, the storied Ross Diner began its new life in the north country in the experienced hands of John Desimone, who owned the Mountain Creamery in nearby Woodstock. While Desimone did a fine job at first offering his mile-high apple pies and some tasty barbecue, he moved on a couple years later to be replaced by Steve Shorey, who owned the Four Aces Diner across the Connecticut River in West Lebanon.

Problems arose when diner fantasy clashed with restaurant reality: Local fire codes prohibited the use of a grill behind the counter. With the kitchen on the opposite end of the dining room from the new diner addition, waitresses had to cover considerable ground to bring a hot meal to the farthest booth. And people preferred sitting in the stylish environment of a real diner.

Shorey removed the diner's original porcelain panels and fitted the facade with fiberglass replacements bearing a new name, the Yankee Diner. Despite his reputation and experience, the precious diner continued to struggle, situated as it was in a complex that was highly dependent on area tourism. Each year the diner's business dropped off considerably after the leaf peepers and skiers went home.

In 1997, the Yankee Diner became Farina Family Restaurant when Jay Farina took over the business from Shorey. Though Jay has since left the restaurant behind, his brother Chris and father, Ron, carry on in capable fashion.

Buried inside this building are the remnants of a Sterling diner, severely damaged by fire. The owners rebuilt around the shell and enjoy a devoted following.

Continuing north up U.S. Route 5 along the Connecticut River, you'll encounter the stick-built Fairlee Diner, which, like the Shady Glen, looks, feels, and serves food as fine as any prefab diner and therefore merits mention. The Gilmans offer amazing fresh-baked pies and other good foods in a cozy space completely devoid of diner pretense. Roadside devotees should also note that Fairlee has New England's last remaining drive-in theater/motel combination still in operation.

U.S. Route 5 in this part of Vermont soon veers away from the river and continues more directly north. Folks from this area seem to flock in great numbers to the Miss Lyndonville Diner in Lyndonville. The exterior of this restaurant gives no indication of what lies within, but once you're through the front door, you'll see the structural outlines and basic shape of the original Sterling diner. In 1979, the diner suffered a fire that nearly destroyed the business. Owner Ashley Gray took the opportunity to clean up the remains and rebuild, doubling the overall dining area. The Miss Lyndonville serves good, old-fashioned Yankee cooking, prepared mostly with fresh ingredients. The busy atmosphere attests to the winning formula of low prices and friendly service.

In the stretch between Lyndonville and Newport, Vermont, the already rural geography only intensifies as you drive farther north. On the trip up the valley, by far most of the diners we've visited have come from the staid but dependable Worcester Lunch Car company with only a few Jersey-built diners sporting the iconic stainless steel look. Thus the sight of Martha's Diner along a lonely stretch of road in this tiny farming community might take you a little by surprise. O'Mahony built this diner in 1953 for the DeCola family, whose Monarch Diner chain spread throughout the Boston area.

The diner came up to Coventry from Saugus, Massachusetts, in 1980. In 2001, Martha LeBlanc sold it to her daughter, Kathy LeBlanc, who runs a friendly place for locals and tourists alike. Except for the usual wear and tear, the diner's interior has changed little in forty years, and it serves few surprises on the menu as well. Single pancakes fill entire plates, and the ready coffee refills come with a big smile.

Until recently, this guide would have described an experience at the splendidly maintained Miss Newport Diner in Newport, formerly located east of town on U.S. Route 5. The diner's fire engine red panels with its name baked into the enamel made for one of Vermont's most precious roadside landmarks. In October 2003, Dave Pritchard shipped the Miss Newport to Salisbury, Massachusetts, adding a third diner to his collection.

This diner trek now heads west across the widest part of the state to Burlington. One interesting stop along this stretch is the Farmers Diner in Barre, established in 2002 by Tod Murphy, who has set the laudable, ambitious goal of using only locally supplied meat, vegetables, and dairy products: Bacon comes from local hog farmers, hamburger comes from beef cattle raised by local ranchers, and milk comes from a local hormone-free dairy. Murphy gets high marks for the thorough execution of this concept. The company philosophy weaves through the entire experience within an inviting space in a Main Street storefront, and the attention to detail indi-

Martha's began its operation as one of the Monarch diners north of Boston. It came to this remote stretch of U.S. Route 5 in the 1970s. The young and energetic Kathy LeBlanc looks forward to a long future in the business, made more likely with the generous portions and excellent pancakes.

cates a high level of passion for his idea. Let's hope the idea catches on. We need places like this more than ever, and in as many locations as possible.

The drive continues west to Burlington, a city that has become a cosmopolitan enclave in a remote area known as New England's west coast. Lake Champlain, whose shores were once lined with railroad tracks and industrial facilities, is being steadily transformed into another year-round residential magnet as well as a major draw for tourists from all over. The economy and growing cultural options of Vermont's largest city have provided an opportunity for restaurateurs of all stripes.

This growth has so far attracted one diner transplant since 1990: Libby's Blue Line Diner just north in Colchester. Owned and operated by Karen Griffin, who named the diner after her mom, the 1953 Worcester car originally served meals as Casu's in Turners Falls, Massachusetts, and a short time after became the Forest Diner in Auburn, Massachusetts, along U.S. Route 20.

Karen bought this unit from diner broker John Keith, who actively sought closed or closing diners in good condition for their eventual resale to others. During a roughly five-year period ending in 1992, Keith was involved in the sale and transport of at least nine diners, with four shipped off to England to become part of a chain of American diners called Fatboy's. One of those diners, the Seagull, formerly located in Kittery, Maine, burned down less than a year after opening in Birmingham, England. Two remain in operation.

Libby's Blue Line sits high above the road on its U.S. Route 7 location near an entrance to I-89. Upon its installation, Karen extended the original seating area out from the diner's right side. The customers who often fill both spaces can delight in Libby's many homemade specials and fantastic baked goods, while enjoying a majestic view east across the Winooski River valley.

All gone now, the Miss Newport left its longtime location on U.S. Route 5 in late 2003 and sits in storage in Salisbury, Massachusetts.

1 Henry's Diner: Burlington (R)

2 Libby's Blue Line Diner: Colchester (MS)

3 Oasis Diner: Burlington (MS)

4 Parkway Diner: South Burlington (MS)

Avid diner hunters should not miss an opportunity to visit the Oasis Diner, a completely original Mountain View car smack in the middle of downtown Burlington. Few vintage diners seem to still thrive in these tight urban locations anymore, but the Oasis has enjoyed a fifty-year run under the same family, and its host community has become Vermont's main economic hot spot.

One block away from the Oasis, also on Bank Street, sits Henry's Diner, an O'Mahony dating from 1925. Most of the diner's original features went up in smoke during a severe fire in the 1980s, and owner Henry Goldstein, who has since retired, restored the building in a southwestern adobe motif.

An oft-photographed diner, another Worcester, awaits the traveler in South Burlington. With a serial number of 839, the Parkway ends a near-unbroken series of Worcester diners that all display the company's struggle to

Libby's Blue Line Diner is hard to miss in this setting on the hill right near I-89.

The mother-daughter team of Libby and Karen Griffin have expertly maintained Libby's Blue Line Diner since they trucked it to Colchester in 1990. Its new location in the land of good food also meant a fresh, contemporary menu of homemade comfort foods and generous desserts.

keep up with its New Jersey competition. The series also included Dan's Windsor Diner (835); Duffy's Diner, once located in Central Falls, Rhode Island (836); the Four Aces in West Lebanon, New Hampshire (837); Libby's Blue Line (838); and the Seagull Diner, which burned down (840).

The Parkway's charms and degree of preservation will delight anyone who sees it today, but at the time, it represented a transitional style for Worcester as the company struggled to keep up with the state of the industry in 1952. The diner's red vertical exterior fluted porcelain panels, intricate ceramic floor tile pattern, and cozy hardwood trim and booths all hark back to design trends more popular ten or twenty years before. As Worcester assembled this beauty, companies such as O'Mahony, Fodero, Paramount, and other premier Jersey builders had successfully transformed their models into gleaming, streamlined, stainless-steel paragons of food-service efficiency and celebrations of America's postwar optimism. The application of stainless steel in this series generally adhered to the patterns and designs of the diner's wood-framed-and-trimmed predecessors. Worcester never built a diner with terrazzo floors and constructed only one multisectioned modular unit.

Fifty years later, diners like the Parkway look quaint and just as attractive as their Jersey-built contemporaries, though in a different way. The diner's owners since 1999, Christine and George Alvanos appear inclined to change little of this splendid structure and have done an excellent job of reviving the business on this busy stretch of U.S. Route 7.

From Burlington going south, you have to drive another 60 miles or so before happening upon another of this state's real gems. In the typically Vermont town of Castleton, also home to a state college, the Birdseye Diner basically anchors the diminutive downtown. The diner was purchased in

In the early 1950s, Worcester Lunch Car began a concerted effort to catch up with the designs of its New Jersey competition. Though the company ultimately failed in that endeavor, it produced diners considered spectacular today. Of that lot, the Parkway tops them all.

1995 by local businessman John Rehlen, who also owns and operates the Castleton General Store, directly across the street. It needed and received extensive restoration work, which mostly removed the plywood box that had enveloped it, decreased its window size, and gave the interior a cavelike atmosphere. The restoration of this 1946 Silk City allowed a diamond to again shine, and thanks to John's business acumen and appreciation for the finer points of diner operation, it has a beauty that goes far deeper than its new skin.

The Birdseye provides lucky locals and wise travelers a wide selection of homemade meals with interesting twists, such as sweet potato fries and fresh seafood chowder in a tomato base. In a place with so much quality on display, you likely will find an old or new favorite on the list and can finish off a fine meal with a slice from a great selection of pies baked on premises.

Vermont offers up one last diner before this tour returns to Massachusetts. The Blue Benn gets many votes as the state's best. The diner has long thrived despite the long-running struggles of its host town, but with excellent meals for great prices, it's hardly a mystery why people flock here. In 1975, Sonny Monroe took over the 1948 Silk City when its previous owner decided to close up, and he's made his forty-seat diner a must stop on any Vermont leaf-peeping tour.

After crossing back into Massachusetts, we make a brief stop in the little town of Adams. Anyone remotely interested in diners who talks to the locals here will get an earful about the too-short run of one of the nation's

Postcard of the Birdseye Diner

Barry and Nancy Garton operated the Miss Adams Diner from 1988 to 1999 and were popular with everyone in the area. Besides their excellent meals, the Gartons also did much to restore the diner's interior, but they sold it without renovating the stone facade.

best diners, the Miss Adams Diner. Though the diner still stands in the heart of downtown Adams, it has closed after a series of operators attempted to fill the very large shoes of Barry and Nancy Garton, who left in 1999.

In 1988, the couple took a run-down, depressed Worcester car and transformed it into a delightful, friendly, and ultimately satisfying diner experience that should serve as a standard for anyone considering a jump into this industry. Their creative menu, aesthetic flair, smoke-free environment, and warm hospitality made this place a magnet for locals and tourists in a town that needed economic activity.

With the business laboring under crushing debt the Gartons had assumed to refurbish the kitchen, they finally sold out to a Boston-area restaurateur with local roots. Things just weren't the same afterward. In one incarnation, the diner became the second store for Jack's Hot Dogs. As of early 2004, Bill England-Horsfall became the latest to try his hand at running the diner.

The Gartons' spark carries on a little to the north in Barry's new café, Brew Ha Ha, where customers find a lot of the same look, feel, and flavors of the Miss Adams. Located on 20 Marshall Street across from the new Massachusetts Museum of Contemporary Art, Brew Ha Ha has contributed greatly to the ongoing North Adams renaissance.

We end this tour in Pittsfield, which clings on to only two more actual diner buildings, though only one operates in that mode. Adrienne's Diner on Wacannah Street near the baseball stadium is a Sterling Diner that came originally from Albany. Pittsfield's only other is enveloped in restaurant space that has changed hands many times in the past decade, taking turns as a retro diner, a pub, a Chinese restaurant, an Italian bistro, and now Hudpucker's Grill and Bar.

ROUTE 66 DINER
1957 MOUNTAIN VIEW #532
950 Bay St., Springfield, MA • (413) 737-4921

Although there is a road in Hampshire County, Massachusetts, designated Route 66, it comes nowhere near the Route 66 Diner in Springfield to the south. The name was bestowed by the Roy brothers, Norman and Don, when they purchased the shuttered hash hangout in 1985. They likely had thought it best to give the tired old diner a fresh identity along with its fresh start. The second to last Mountain View diner built before the company shut its doors in 1957, the former New Bay Diner did a fair business on a location that straddled an industrial park and an aging residential neighborhood anchored by Blunt Park.

Mountain View Diners was one of four builders that stamped serial numbers on their builder tags. At #532, only one more diner followed the former New Bay Diner out of the factory before it shut down.

The brothers figured the business had something for each of them: Norman had worked in restaurants all over the East Coast, and Don's background in investments meant that the diner would enjoy experienced management. The Roys had bought the diner after it lay dormant three years, and in an oft-repeated story, it required a healthy application of elbow grease. They invested in some new equipment, furnishings, and renovations to make the diner good as new.

Norman departed after two years, leaving Don to do all the cooking and manage the operation. The diner struggled during these years. For a while, Don seriously considered selling out, but in 1993, Norman returned and helped get the business back on solid ground. Norman asserted that what was needed was some simple public relations. He knew he had a good product. Changing little on the menu, Norman began to place ads in local publications and generally spread the word that the Route 66 was a true neighborhood diner. He also experimented with longer hours and considered adding on to the structure. Before long, the neighbors started flocking in and business boomed.

Norman died in 1999, but not before helping to generate a thriving business. Route 66 serves meals ideal for those with large appetites and is now well known for its hefty portions, superb home fries, and savory hot plates.

FEATURED DINER

AL'S DINER
1958 MASTER
14 Yelle St., Chicopee, MA • (413) 534-3607

First things first: There is no Al. At least, not anymore. Al Thibeault gave the diner its current name and the once fabulous but now nonfunctioning neon sign still sitting atop the diner. He later sold the business to one of his employees, Anastasios "Toss" Matthews, in 1967.

The diner has occupied its site on Yelle Street its entire operational life, and until the late 1980s, its doors were open twenty-four hours a day, seven days a week, a rarity for a small diner these days. Toss, however, came from a generation that understood that success meant hard work and sacrifice. As a result, the diner business not only made a good living for Toss and his family, but also put two children through college and one of them through medical school. Toss seemed to relish the long conversations he shared with customers when business slowed down. I enjoyed long-running regular Wednesday evenings at the diner, where Toss shared his views on local politics, the restaurant industry, and life in general to these eager ears.

Despite his engineering credentials, Toss's son Gus returned to the family business to assume more and more of the diner's operation. In the early 1990s, Toss entered semiretirement, making his appearance one or two days a week and ending the diner's twenty-four-seven schedule.

The diner's menu has all the usual suspects, along with ample daily dinner specials, homemade soups, and desserts that usually include a bread pudding variety not to be missed. Most first-timers will be pleasantly surprised by the prices. Dinner for two will rarely ring up a check higher than $15.

When Toss died in September 2003, the industry lost one of its last legendary dinermen, guys who thought nothing of working eighteen-hour days at a hard living that required truckloads of patience, resourcefulness, and attention in the face of sometimes surly customers, difficult employees, and temperamental equipment.

Today Gus keeps the diner going. He occasionally adds some interesting new items to the menu, such as a pulled pork sandwich and orange-pineapple bread pudding, but like his father, he remains ever mindful of the importance of upholding the quality of the tried and true. Al's therefore always feels like home—and one to which you can always return.

OASIS DINER
1954 MOUNTAIN VIEW #369
189 Bank St., Burlington, VT • (802) 864-5308

In the past decade and a half, the bustling Burlington streetscape has become home to a plethora of dining options catering to a gentrifying market of young professionals and neo-hippies. With the establishment of an IBM factory and research facility in the area and the increasing economic and cultural influence of the local colleges, the town has become a veritable island of urban sophistication and cosmopolitan living in this remote locale better known for its bitterly cold winters and dairy cattle.

Because of the many changes brought by the new economy, the Oasis Diner on Bank Street more truly lives up to its name than ever. This 1954 Mountain View diner celebrated its fiftieth anniversary of operation by the Lines family in 2004. It was placed in its current location in February 1954 by Harry Lines, who passed it on to his son Stratty later that same year. Since then, the streamlined, with its open-air informal atmosphere, has served as a proxy city hall where customers debate the current issues facing the region and the world.

Indeed, the diner confirmed its role in the community's political arena in July 1995, when President Clinton stopped in for lunch with then-governor Howard Dean. A plaque at their booth commemorates the occasion.

In 1995, Stratty decided to retire, but a two-year search for the "right" new owner proved fruitless. So in January 1997, his sons Jon and David decided to take over. After a period of adjustment, as is typical when a business passes from one generation to another, the brothers have reversed a slow decline in the diner's fortunes by fiscally and philosophically bringing the operation into the twenty-first century. Now the menu recognizes the changing demographic of its local market while still applying the same basic formula for success every good short-order restaurant must use to build business: fresh food, low prices, clean atmosphere, and friendly service.

Jon Lines and his brother David took over the Oasis Diner from their father Stratton in 1996. Since then, they've managed to revive a local institution that had begun to show it age. Here, Jon rests amidst the fruits of his labors.

David views his role in the diner as largely supportive of Jon, who has a restaurant background, and both brothers see their career paths as leading elsewhere. The brothers assumed ownership of the local landmark both to shore up its finances and to stave off potential buyers with little understanding or appreciation of the diner business. Indeed, under their management, the diner feels brand new. The motivated staff and greater use of fresh ingredients provide the hungry traveler with both a fine meal and a sense of Burlington's former days. When the brothers finally do decide to move on, let's hope they find a kindred soul who will embrace and nurture the tradition and always make this Oasis live up to its name.

BLUE BENN DINER
1948 SILK CITY #4815
102 Hunt St./Route 7, Bennington, VT • (802) 442-5140

The southwestern Vermont gateway town of Bennington may finally have pulled out of the economic doldrums, and downtown Bennington's prospects continue to improve. Through it all, one little diner chugged along, seemingly impervious to any cyclical effects of the economy. After a visit or two, you can quickly see how this might be. People will always be hungry, and they will always seek out incredible values. The Blue Benn simply offers some of the finest prepared food for the money to be found anywhere. Who would want to pass that by?

It has been owned and operated since 1974 by Sonny and Marylou Monroe, who tossed out the greasy spoons on day one, opting instead for a creative yet classic menu loaded with organically grown items and locally supplied provisions. The Benn, for instance, has served tabouleh since the 1970s, and vegetarians have long found themselves welcome in a setting that has historically catered exclusively to the meat-and-potatoes crowd. Still, no one does classic comfort foods better than the Blue Benn, to which the ever-present sight of fresh-made donuts in a large glass jar attests.

In recent years, the diner has included more Tex-Mex style meals, including an amazingly wonderful breakfast burrito that will keep you fueled well up until dinnertime. The use of salsa pervades the breakfast menu, exemplified by the strikingly flavorful and ample Mexican omelet, made with free-range eggs and prepared with grilled chicken, peppers, onions, and mushrooms, rounded out with home fries grilled to absolute perfection. The Benn offers you a choice of fresh-squeezed or bottled orange juice, and like most self-respecting diners in this state, it serves real maple syrup exclusively. Just about everything on the menu reflects this level of creativity and attention to detail.

If you visit during the weekend, get here early or you likely will endure an extended wait for a spot in this forty-seat diner. It seems that Sonny could easily double or even triple the size of the restaurant and still fill the place on most days, but the guy already works hard enough. Though he generally goes home well before the lunch crowd settles in, his day actually starts sometime around midnight, when he comes in to prep.

Sonny and Marylou represent the last of a generation who willingly work in this business who fully understand how much effort it takes to squeeze a good living out of a small diner. As such, they must be among the hardest-working people in the business. With many restaurants today serving prepackaged meals, the Blue Benn holds out as a stubborn but welcome anachronism. And with the Monroe's daughter Lisa becoming more of a fixture in the diner, its future looks pretty secure.

DINER DIRECTORY

WESTERN MASSACHUSETTS

Adrienne's Diner
145 Wahconnah St.
Pittsfield, MA
(413) 499-0107
1930s Sterling
Originally located in Albany, and rumored to have served breakfast to Nelson Rockefeller while there. Remodeling stripped many original features. Basic grilled diner fare. Breakfast and lunch.

Al's Diner
14 Yelle St.
Chicopee, MA
(413) 534-3607
1957 Master
Listed on the National Register of Historic Places. One of four New England Master diners, and in excellent condition with few changes. Reasonably priced full menu of American food and homemade desserts. Known for French meat pie.

Bernie's Dining Depot
749 James St.
Chicopee, MA
(413) 539-9268
c. 1950 O'Mahony
Much remodeled and incorporated into larger restaurant. American food. Full menu.

Bluebonnet Diner
324 King St./Rte. 5
Northampton, MA
(413) 584-3333
1950 Worcester 825

Exterior in very good condition. Interior modified with brick-style paneling. Full menu. Closed on Sundays.

Charles Diner
218 Union St.
W. Springfield, MA
(413) 733-8551
1948 Fodero
Beautiful but weathered classic Fodero diner, complete with winged clock. American food with Italian specialties. Known for serving fresh ham off the bone. Breakfast and lunch.

Day and Night Diner
1456 Main St./Rte. 20
Palmer, MA
(413) 283-4536
1944 Worcester 781
Well preserved, with welcoming local personality. Subject of John Baeder painting. Homemade specials and excellent omelets. Breakfast and lunch only.

Purveying classic Yankee cooking has brought much success to the Blue Bonnet Diner. Often overlooked in the shadow of the more famous Miss Florence Diner, this splendid 1947 Worcester continues to gain a following in the growing Northampton community.

Deligan's Diner
Conway, MA
1948 Silk City 4824
In storage. Originally located in Peekskill, New York. Also called the Blue Tone Diner. Brought to Massachusetts in 1995 for private use. Currently under restoration.

Fillin' Station
Rte. 5
Whately, MA
(413) 665-3696
1960 Kullman
Originally located in Chicopee Falls, Massachusetts. Excellently preserved "Princess" model. Popular truck stop, open twenty-four hours, seven days. American food.

Gregory's Restaurant
2391 Boston Post Rd.
Wilbraham, MA
(413) 596-3500
1960 DeRaffele
Rare for this region, but now extensively remodeled. Formerly known as Pizza Pub.

Hudpucker's Grill and Bar
1350 East St.
Pittsfield, MA
(413) 443-3113
1950 Kullman
Encased in larger restaurant that seems to change names and themes about every four years. Retains only its backbar.

Kathy's Diner
6 Strong Ave.
Northampton, MA
(413) 586-2225
1933 Worcester 702
Oldest diner in western Massachusetts, located in the heart of resurging community. Basic grilled diner fare. Breakfast and lunch only.

McMurphy's
Pleasant St.
Amherst, MA
1928 Worcester 614
Barely a shell of a very old barrel roof diner, seen only from inside the tavern. Formerly the Miss Amherst Diner, closed in the 1970s.

Miss Adams Diner
53 Park St./Rte. 8
Adams, MA
(413) 743-5303
missadamsdiner.com
1949 Worcester 821
Delivered to site in 1949. Stripped of its porcelain exterior panels in the 1970s and sided with stone. Booths acquired from another closed Worcester in 1993. Made famous by Barry and Nancy Garton during their eleven-year run, starting in 1989, for their superior food quality and service. Since 1999, under absentee ownership that has installed a series of managers and lessees. Closed in 2003 and reopened in February 2004, attracting many hopeful customers.

Miss Florence Diner
99 Main St./Rte. 9
Florence, MA
(413) 584-3137
www.missflorence.com
1941 Worcester 775
Listed on the National Register of Historic Places. Enlarged by the Worcester company in the 1940s. A famous iconic diner featured in the *New York Times* and *Yankee* magazine, among other media. A real landmark in the area. Large, stylish neon sign. Serves full menu most days. American food with daily specials and Greek specialties.

Route 66 Diner
950 Bay St.
Springfield, MA
(413) 737-4921
1957 Mountain View 532
Listed on the National Register of Historic Places. Originally known as the New Bay Diner. Last diner in Springfield, and the second to last built by Mountain View. Known for large portions, excellent home fries, and low prices. Breakfast and lunch only.

Route 9 Diner
Route 9
Hadley, MA
(413) 256-1222
2000 Kullman
Stunning retro design. Installed as flagship diner of planned chain of Sit Down Diners, and second in the operation after purchase of existing diner in Danbury, Connecticut. Generally popular, but closed in early 2003. Reopened as Route 9 Diner in December of that year. American food with Greek specialties. Full menu.

Shady Glen
7 Avenue A
Turners Falls, MA
(413) 863-9636
on-site
Originally opened in 1950s as a drive-in restaurant. Classic, high-quality diner fare in a quaint setting. Full menu, seven days. Superb homemade desserts and platters. Not to be missed.

VERMONT
Big Mama's Green Mountain Diner
45 Canal St., Rte. 5
Brattleboro, VT
(802) 254-0090
1920s Worcester

Few diners enjoy the fame and recognition of the Miss Florence Diner. Its commanding neon signage, striking chartreuse panels with red lettering, and reputation for good, honest Yankee cooking have all helped get it mentioned on the pages of national publications and painted and photographed by artists of all levels.

Old but retains many original interior features. Breakfast and lunch.

Birdseye Diner
Main St.
Castleton, VT
(802) 468-5817
c. 1946 Silk City
Formerly Jim's Diner. Beautifully restored. Serves a full, varied menu of homemade dishes, with excellent desserts, soups, and sandwiches. Hand-cut french fries.

Blue Benn Diner
102 Hunt St./Rte. 7
Bennington, VT
(802) 442-5140
1948 Silk City 4815
In very good condition, with some recent restorations. Outstanding extensive menu featuring mostly homemade items. One of the original neo diner menus, bucking the usual meat-and-potatoes traditions. American food with Mexican specialties and many natural foods.

Chelsea Royal Diner
Marlboro Rd./Rte. 9
W. Brattleboro, VT
(802) 254-8399
1939 Worcester 736
Originally located in the heart of Brattleboro and moved in the 1970s. Diner in good condition but stripped of counter and used as additional dining area for larger restaurant. Full menu.

Country Girl Diner
Main St./Rte. 103
Chester, VT
(802) 875-2650
1951 Silk City 5174
In very good condition. Subject of painting by Ralph Goings. Full menu with creative, innovative meals. Homemade desserts.

Dan's Windsor Diner
135 Main St./Rte. 5
Windsor, VT
(802) 674-5555
1952 Worcester 835
Well-preserved diner, though now missing its tags and rare clock. Originally installed in Fitchburg, Massachusetts, as Ray's Diner. American food. Full menu.

Fairlee Diner
Rte. 5
Fairlee, VT
(802) 333-3569
1939 on-site
Charming vintage diner atmosphere. Excellent homemade pies.

Farina Family Diner
U.S. Route 4 at Quechee Gorge Village
Quechee, VT
(802) 295-8955
1946 Worcester 787
Operating as the Ross Diner in Holyoke, Massachusetts, until 1991. Purchased and moved in a failed attempt to install in West Lebanon, New Hampshire. Resold to Gary Neil, owner of the Quechee Gorge Antiques Mall, who installed it on the property and has leased it out to a succession of operators. Original panels removed and replaced in 1994. Seven-day operation serving full menu of American food, with daily specials and homemade desserts.

Gillie's Seafood Restaurant
107 Canal St./Rte. 5
Brattleboro, VT
(802) 257-4559
c. 1946 Kullman
Only Kullman in Vermont. "Challenger" model. Encased in larger restaurant, though structure still mostly visible from inside. Seafood menu. Lunch and dinner.

Henry's Diner
155 Bank St.
Burlington, VT
(802) 862-9010
1925 O'Mahony
Extensive fire gutted this diner, which was restored in a southwestern vein. American food. Daily specials.

Libby's Blue Line Diner
1 Roosevelt Hwy./Rte. 7
Colchester, VT
(802) 655-0343
1953 Worcester 838
Originally located in Turners Falls, Massachusetts, then moved to Route 20 in Auburn, Massachusetts, and called the Forest Diner. Purchased and sold by diner broker John Keith in 1989, then moved to Colchester by Karen and Libby Griffin. Dining room was added to one side and a large foyer to the right. Diner is in excellent condition. Full menu of American food with daily specials, homemade soups, and fresh-baked desserts.

Locks
69 Portland St.
St. Johnsbury, VT
(802) 748-3660
1937 Sterling
Few visible vestiges of its diner history.
Used as storefront. Last served food as
Dave's Diner in the early 1990s.

Martha's Diner
Rte. 5 & Main St.
Coventry, VT
(802) 754-6800
1953 Fodero
Former Monarch Diner, located in
Saugus, Massachusetts. Moved to
Coventry in the 1970s. Only Fodero in
Vermont. In good condition, though a
little weathered. Big portions and very
friendly. Breakfast and lunch.

Miss Bellows Falls Diner
90 Rockingham St.
Bellows Falls, VT
(802) 463-9800
1941 Worcester 771
Listed on the National Register of Historic Places. Originally called Frankie &
Johnnie's Diner and located in Lowell,
Massachusetts, until 1944. Taken back
and renovated by Worcester Lunch Car,
which gave it new front panels. Original
front panels moved to back, where they
still can be seen today. Basic grilled
diner fare. Full menu.

Miss Lyndonville Diner
686 Broad St./Rte. 5
Lyndonville, VT
(802) 626-9890
c. 1939 Sterling

Oasis Diner
189 Bank St.
Burlington, VT
(802) 864-5308

This image shows St. Johnsbury's only diner in
better days. Now used by a local locksmith,
only the stained-glass windows remain on this
severely renovated structure.

Only the stained-glass windows betray the
origins of Locks' Sterling diner.

1954 Mountain View 369
A longtime favorite in the Burlington
area. This model is rare in this part of
the country. In original condition and in
excellent shape. Under the same ownership since it opened in 1954. Served
President Clinton in 1996. American
food with daily specials. Breakfast and
lunch only.

The Miss Bellows Falls Diner makes for a welcome sight in this historic small town. Brought up from its original location in Lowell, Massachusetts, the diner got new front panels for its new home.

Parkway Diner
1696 Williston Rd./Rte. 2
South Burlington, VT
(802) 864-9730
1953 Worcester 839
Worcester only made eleven more diners after this one, but made none more beautiful. The detailing, tilework, and woodwork are all of excellent design and craftsmanship. Stained-glass panels have nautical scenes. Full menu of American food. Daily specials.

Shanghai Garden
Rte. 11 East
Springfield, VT
(802) 885-5555
1941 Worcester 768
Chinese restaurant. Originally the Ten Eyck Diner.

Springfield Royal Diner
363 River St./Rte. 106
Springfield, VT
(802) 886-1400
www.springfielddiner.com
1957 Mahony
Only Mahony diner remaining of the four built, and still in excellent condition. Formerly operating as Royal Diner in Kingston, New York. Purchased and shipped to Springfield in 2002, reopening in 2003. Part of a private Corvette museum. American food. Full menu.

T. J. Buckley's Uptown Dining
132 Elliot St.
Brattleboro, VT
(802) 257-4922
c. 1927 Worcester
Originally located in Woburn, Massachusetts. Moved to Brattleboro in 1950s. Currently serves prix fixe menu and very upscale cuisine. Very well regarded, but definitely not diner food. Reservations only. Expensive.

Townshend Dam Diner
Route 30
Townshend, VT
(802) 874-4107
www.virtualvermont/damdiner
on-site

Wesson's Diner
Burlington, VT
1954 Worcester 843
In storage. Closed and awaiting a rebirth. Jersey-style diner formerly located on U.S. Route 7 south of Burlington.

NEW HAMPSHIRE
and MAINE

I n the past fifteen years, New Hampshire has become something of a diner
hot spot. In that period, the state gained six diners while losing two, both
to demolition. With only twenty-eight diners within its boundaries, that
makes for a net gain of 14 percent, a considerable increase in a period well
past the industry's heyday.

Maine's numbers have largely held steady during that period, although
two new Denny's Diners built by Starlite Diners of Ormond, Florida, opened
in Augusta and Bangor in 1999 and continue to do brisk business. Maine
lost three diners, two to demolition and one to export.

For the most part, a diner hunt in these two states takes the lucky traveler through some of the most breathtaking scenery in all of New England.
A few of the finest diners in the country do business in this region, and in
contrasting settings. Your diner hunt here will bring you to the majestic
White Mountains, along the dramatic rocky coastline of Maine, and
through the growing charm of evolving mill cities.

Until the advent of the interstate highway and the construction of the
Maine Turnpike, U.S. Route 1 provided the primary commercial route along
the northern New England coastline. If you have plenty of time and are making your first trip into New Hampshire and Maine, you will do well to stick
to it. Although the initial stretch of the road into New Hampshire has lost all
of its diners over the years, it finally does reward patient diner hunters when
they get to Portsmouth.

Here, tucked into a lot on a side street of downtown, Gilley's Lunch
Cart awaits you. Built by Worcester Lunch Car in 1939, Gilley's certainly
lives up to its name, and it stands alone as the last operating authentic lunch
wagon in the entire country. Ralph "Gilley" Gilbert set up shop every night in
the town square in violation of parking regulations, which eventually earned
Gilley a mention in the *Guinness Book of World Records* for having received the
highest number of parking tickets: 5,000. When Gilley retired in 1974, the
town honored him with a parade and officially forgave his parking fines.

With an era finally closed, the diner fell into the hands of Steve Geno
and John Murray who moved it onto the lot on Fleet Street where it now sits,
complete with the truck still attached. In 1995, Geno and Murray sold the

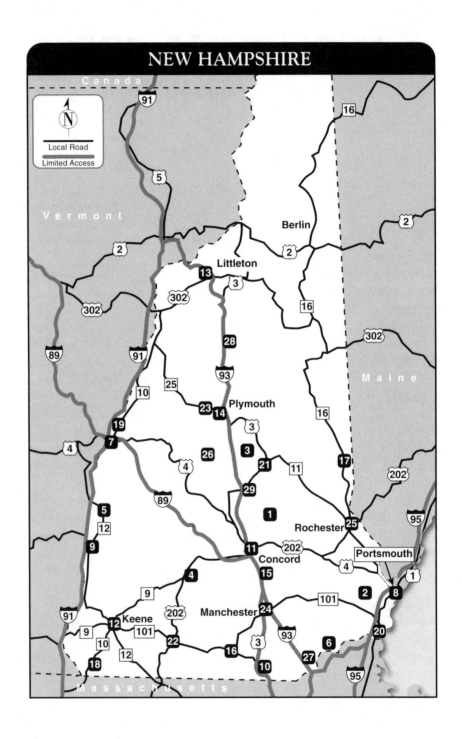

NEW HAMPSHIRE

1 Barr's Diner: Loudon (BR)
2 Betsy & Mike's Diner: Exeter (MS)
3 Bobby's Girl Diner: Merideth (MS)
4 Caron's Restaurant: Hillsboro (MS)
5 Daddypop's Tumble Inn Diner:
   Claremont (BR)
6 Eggie's Diner: Plaistow (MS)
7 Four Aces Diner: West Lebanon (MS)
8 Gilley's Lunch Cart: Portsmouth (BR)
9 Heritage Diner: Charlestown (BR)
10 Jo-Ann's Kitchen: Nashua (BR)
11 L & B Tailoring: Concord (BR)
12 Lindy's Diner: Keene (EM)
13 Littleton Diner: Littleton (BR)
14 Main Street Station: Plymouth (MS)

15 Mayfair Diner: Bow (MS)
16 Milford Diner: Milford (BR)
17 Miss Wakefield Diner: Wakefield (MS)
18 Mt. Pisgah Diner: Winchester (BR)
19 O.K. Diner: Hanover (BR)
20 Ocean Wok: Hampton Beach (BR)
21 Paugus Diner: Laconia (MS)
22 Peterboro Diner: Peterborough (MS)
23 Plain Jane's Diner: Rumney (MS)
24 Red Arrow Diner: Manchester (OS)
25 Remember When Diner: Rochester (P)
26 Riverside Diner: Bristol (BR)
27 Route 28 Diner: Salem (MS)
28 Sunny Day Diner: Lincoln (MS)
29 Tilt'n Diner: Tilton (MS)

business to a young Turk, Robert Kennedy, who stripped the lunch wagon of its last pretensions of mobility by expanding the kitchen to give the structure an L shape.

The experience of eating at Gilley's still provides a more or less primordial diner experience. Pull aside the sliding door and you step back in time to experience the tight spaces, late-night hours of operation, and simple menu of the typical pre-Depression lunch wagon. Hot dogs and burgers rule the menu, and during the warmer months, you can sit on the picnic tables outside. Otherwise, you'll need to scramble for a stool along the counter that lines the windows.

In 1996, the new owner of Gilley's Diner expanded his actual Worcester Lunch Wagon by adding a kitchen. The wagon had already become more or less immobilized on this spot since the retirement of Ralph "Gilley" Gilbert, and the new space allowed owner Robert Kennedy to expand the menu a little.

Since the Henry brothers established the Maine Diner in 1983, they've served more than three and a half million customers.

Across the Piscataqua River, we enter the great state of Maine and soon come across its namesake diner in Wells. Though the Maine Diner does not meet the strict definition of the word, brothers Myles and Dick Henry have nevertheless created a standard the real McCoy would do well to emulate. Since their purchase of the business and property in 1983, the Henrys have built yet another diner institution along the coast that in many ways rivals a similar homemade operation farther up the coast in Waldoboro. Though the Maine Diner does not share Moody's history or reputation for low prices, it does provide a comparable value.

During the summer months, people line up to get inside, and chances are they have one of the diner's lobster dishes on their minds. It is Maine, after all, so you'll find the crustacean in just about every aspect of the menu except dessert. Start the day with a lobster omelet, then come in for lunch and try the hefty lobster roll. At dinner, get a slice of lobster pie or a cup of lobster stew. Or just get the lobster.

Dessert won't disappoint either, especially the blueberry pie. In far too many cases, short-order restaurants rely upon gummy canned filling, making for an unsatisfying end to what might otherwise be a great diner experience. The Maine Diner does it right, with fresh blueberries baked to a perfect consistency inside a flaky crust.

The Maine Diner also has a gift store, where it peddles its own branded merchandise as well as a wide selection of diner- and Maine-related souvenirs.

U.S. Route 1 still retains much of its nostalgic charm, but the advance of progress and the overall growth in the coastline population, both seasonal and year-round, will undoubtedly change things, and not always for the better. Route 1 between the New Hampshire border and Portland becomes almost hopelessly clogged with tourists in the summer. Though Maine can claim more than 5,000 miles of coastline, true sandy beaches occupy only a small stretch of it, and most of them lie between Kittery and Old Orchard Beach.

The Palace Diner in Biddeford stands alone as the last real diner in Maine south of Portland. Nevertheless, this leg of the trip makes for an inter-

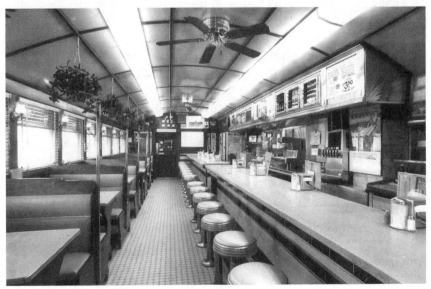

Closed in March 2004, the Miss Portland now belongs to its namesake town, which plans to use it to spur development in its Bayside neighborhood.

Just north of the ever-busy Freeport outlet shops, the Miss Brunswick Diner greets travelers at the gateway to this pretty college community.

esting ride and still has many classic roadside attractions, and the Palace will make the trip there worth your while, especially if you get an early start.

Twenty years ago, Portland provided few reasons to visit. Its seaport had declined precipitously, its older neighborhoods had decayed rapidly, and travelers trekking to the Freeport outlet stores and L. L. Bean now hopped the Maine Turnpike, which channeled them far away from the city's commercial center. But even though the future looked bleak for this old port city, the Miss Portland Diner, a 1949 Worcester car, endured the slide and stuck around long enough to watch the city enter a new renaissance. Unfortunately, because its location is far removed from the rebounding Old Port section of the city, urban revival hasn't exactly sparked a renaissance for the diner. Owned and well maintained since 1981 by Randy Chasse, the diner sits in a rather remote industrial section of town not far from an exit off I-295. During Randy's ownership, he ran a successful operation and served up some fine meals. But as time and age take their toll, he explored the possibility of selling out.

The Miss Portland started its service in the city at a different location, downtown on Forest Street. In 1964, its new owners, Harold Foley and Al Karas, moved it to make way for a new federal building. As of this writing, the diner will have to move once again to make way for new development. With the Portland real estate market heating up, large parcels near interstate exits will go for good prices, and what was once a commercial backwater has now become a prime location.

In 2004, Randy Chasse arranged to give the diner to the city so that he could sell the land beneath it. The city has been accepting proposals for its future use in another section of town.

Leaving Portland behind, U.S. Route 1 passes through Freeport, which until recently reigned supreme as a shopping destination thanks to the outlet stores and Maine retailing kingpin L. L. Bean. Unless you plan a shopping day, continue driving the old route into New Brunswick and pull into the parking lot of the Miss Brunswick Diner. For a period stretching from the 1980s through a change of ownership in 1996, the diner advertised Mexican fare alongside its classic diner meals. New owner Andre Prest reverted the menu back to simple comfort food.

The diner came down from Norway, Maine, where it operated as the Norway Diner. In 1949, it was set up on this Route 1 location as the Norwago Diner. When Ed Buckley took it over in 1972, he changed the name to the Miss Brunswick Diner.

Our route detours from Route 1 up to Gardiner for a true diner delight, in more ways than one. To get there, take the more scenic Route 24, which hugs the Kennebeck River. Once in town, look for the A-1 Diner on 3 Bridge Street, an address that exists only because of some ingenious engineering.

Maine's capital of Augusta regained a diner in 1999 in the form of a Starlite-built Denny's Diner, part of the well-known chain. A fun backroad stretch connects Gardiner to Waldoboro and rejoins with Route 1. Here you'll find Moody's, a long, white, clapboard-sided building with a precious yet brand new neon sign, exemplifying both the classic roadside attraction

Locals tend to prefer Moody's Diner in the winter when all the tourists go home, but no matter the season, this Waldoboro institution makes everyone feel at home. If you go, consider also staying in a Moody's cabin. Though spartan, their rustic charm and low price make them high in demand. Reserve early.

and restaurant institution. Moody's has enjoyed ample word of mouth and positive publicity in just about every form of media invented. Its longevity alone would make for good copy these days, but the Moody family has earned every accolade it has ever received. Classic Yankee cooking gets no better than it does at Moody's, and it probably doesn't get any less expensive.

Moody's began as tourist cabins along a lonely stretch of Route 1 back in 1927. Percy Moody charged $1 a night, and by the end of the summer, he had raked in a whopping $630—good money for those days—and reinvested in the business by constructing more cabins and a tearoom to serve the

YOUR OWN PRIVATE DINER

The restaurant industry's increasingly onerous burdens has largely made more and more of the remaining prewar diners obsolete. With less than fifty seats, their small capacity severely hampers their viability, and most of the remaining structures no longer meet modern fire or health codes. When the door locks up for good, the odds do not favor a reopening any time soon, no matter what the diner's degree of preservation. Usually too small, too dilapidated, or too remotely located, these business opportunities find fewer and fewer takers with any serious experience in the field. And if conditions force these diners from their sites, they face an especially doubtful future.

Several museums have adopted and restored these diners for use as working exhibits in their facilities, but in New England, at least six people have purchased diners strictly for their own personal use. Apparently, New England is the hotbed for this particular trend. While some may have diners rotting away in a field with hopes of eventual sale, these private diner owners generally have no interest in putting their diners back into service, even if they could.

In 1993, Dave Waller of Boston, Massachusetts, undertook an extreme form of home renovation when he installed the fabled Apple Tree Diner inside his converted firehouse. With barely an inch to spare, the 1929 Worcester diner slipped into one of the two bays originally designed for emergency vehicles.

Waller's own personal history largely explains the dramatic preservationist gesture. For one thing, his grandfather Jack Hines owned and operated the Yankee Flyer Diner in Lynn, Massachusetts. Famous and hugely successful, the diner had a long twenty-five-year run in the community under Hines and his partner, Jack Welsh, finally closing in 1958. New owners demolished it soon after.

Waller claims that a full-size diner such as his makes a poor replacement for a residential kitchen. In a sense, the diner now serves as a rather dramatic conversation piece. Largely restored after fifty-two years in service in its former Dedham, Massachusetts, location, the diner is now in retirement safe from the elements, the wrecking ball, and the demands of customers—at least during Waller's lifetime.

lodgers. When the state diverted Route 1 down the hill on the other end of his property, Percy constructed a small roadside stand on the new road and sold simple homemade meals with reminders about the cabins up the hill.

Three quarters of a century later, the business has grown quite a bit, but not excessively. In 1994, the Moody family nearly doubled the size of the diner, which worried many locals, already upset over the encroachment of so many tourists in the area. But the Moodys first polled their customers on the impending expansion, and patrons overwhelmingly requested that the family retain the original well-worn counter. Indeed, the counter area remains

David Clem originally purchased half of a double Worcester car (#666) that operated in Shrewsbury, Massachusetts, with the intention of putting it back into service in Cambridge's Kendall Square. Failing to make that happen, Clem trucked the diner to his own property, first in Norwich, Vermont, in 1993, and then over the river to his backyard in Hanover, New Hampshire, in 1998. With Clem's barbecue grill on the deck extending off its front, the diner looks like a fine place to relax on a warm summer evening.

The owner of this Worcester #663 keeps this little gem in his backyard for purposes of private entertainment.

The other half of that diner has met a similar fate. It is now located in Andover, where Doug Johnson is slowly working to restore it to useful condition.

When Mike O'Connor got his diner, some may have questioned his judgment. This Worcester #705 had spent most of its service as Tony's Diner in Rye, New Hampshire, but it returned to Worcester in the form of a gift thanks to Henry Ciborowski, who offered it to the city to use as a civic mascot. But the birthplace of the diner industry couldn't find a suitable use for the old car, so it bounced around in various uses, such as a visitors' information kiosk, a "First Night" celebration concession, and finally a snack bar for the now-defunct Forum Theater, a nonprofit group that staged productions in city parks.

When youths set fire to the diner in 1999, some wanted to write it off as a total loss. One contractor who claimed to specialize in diner restoration estimated $100,000 for its refurbishment. The diner's legal owner, Preservation Worcester, instead handed it over to Mike O'Connor, a local businessman known for his classic car restorations and his love of these roadside gems. Since taking

(continued on page 180)

one of the diner's best features. The rest of the diner stayed pretty much the same, except that now there was more of it.

Homemade remains the rule of the day, for the soups, the specials, and especially the pies. Perhaps best of all, the Moodys still accept reservations for their cabins, which are almost more of a bargain than the meals. A room in a cabin, which all have screened porches and a TV with rabbit ears but no phone, still costs less than $40 a night.

In Ellsworth, a truly hidden gem among Maine's diner collection sits inside a larger restaurant, Maidee's International Cafe, which offers both

(continued from page 179)
over, O'Connor has slowly but lovingly restored the diner to its original condition with the expert help of historian and carpenter Gary Thomas. O'Connor says that he may put his diner back into service. Many diner enthusiasts are grateful to O'Connor for keeping this diner a part of Worcester's heritage.

Another private diner came to New England from New Jersey by way of Cleveland. The former Pole Tavern Diner represents a remarkable achievement for restorer Steve Harwin, who took the crumbling Silk City, stripped it to its bare steel frame, and promptly rebuilt it to remarkably original condition. Since the buyer of the diner didn't have to worry about health codes or restaurant industry formulas, he could alter the diner's layout somewhat for the purposes

of entertaining guests. Nevertheless, the retiled floors, walls, and trim and the new, replica design cherry wood booths are completely convincing to all but the most discerning eye. Redubbed by its new owners as Betsy & Mike's Diner, it now sits on a large estate in Exeter, New Hampshire.

In 1993, Brian Bram, a friend of Dave Waller's, perhaps succumbed to a form of peer pressure when he purchased the former Deligan's Diner for a mere dollar. At the time, some thought he paid a dollar too much, but nine years later, Bram seems pleased with his prize. Bram's background as an illustrator and designer likely honed his aesthetic sensibilities and entrenched his appreciation for all things retro.

The Pole Tavern Diner (top) was restored and renamed Betsy and Mike's Diner (bottom).

Chinese and French cuisine. Maidee's lounge is actually the former Pineland Diner, a 1938 O'Mahony that operated in various places under various names in Maine until 1989. Indeed, Will Anderson, in his book *Good Old Maine*, refers to the Pineland as "Maine's most moved diner." Though it spent most of its existence in Augusta, in 1970 it moved to Waldoboro and then in 1982 to Ellsworth, where it became an upscale diner. When it closed in 1988, Maidee Chang took a shine to it and incorporated it into her new restaurant. Even the most experienced diner hunter searching for any exterior architectural vestiges of the original diner will

---

The 1948 Silk City entered service as the Blue Tone Diner, a name that played off its cool aqua color scheme, in downtown Peekskill, New York. In 1952, it moved out to the Bear Mountain Parkway, and in 1962, it became Deligan's after its owners Gus and Connie Deligan. After Gus died in 1976, the diner entered into a period of slow but steady decline. By the late 1980s, with the land already in state hands, the diner looked increasingly like bulldozer fodder. Then along came Bram seeking information. Told by the state to call the family attorney, the lawyer promptly told him, "You are a gift from Jesus!"

For his money, Bram got a leaky, vandalized, twenty-ton antique full of old broken equipment, trash, and a copy of *Diner* magazine. He then hired O. B. Hill to move it to a temporary lot in Ashland, Massachusetts. In 1995, Bram hired Hill to move the diner again to the site of his future house in Conway. With his new house completed, Bram began the project of restoring Deligan's to "working condition" and estimates he's already spent $35,000 over ten years toward that effort. When I visited it in 2003, Bram had set the diner on a foundation and given it a new roof, but the future holds many, many weekends working to complete the restoration.

Private Diners
None of these diners are available to the general public, and you are urged to respect the privacy of the owners.

Apple Tree Diner	**Tony's Diner**
North Boston Metro, Massachusetts	Worcester, MA
1929 Worcester #641	*1933 Worcester #705*
Deligan's Diner	**Betsy & Mike's Diner**
Conway, MA	Exeter, NH
1948 Silk City #4824	*1946 Silk City*
Midway Diner	**O.K. Diner**
Andover, MA	Hanover, NH
1935 Worcester #666	*1932 Worcester #636*

In the 1980s, the Minute Man Diner, as it was originally called, came all the way up to Springfield, Maine, by way of Lynn and then Ware, Massachusetts, as well as a series of other towns lost to history. Its remote location makes it a must-see only for true diner fanatics.

miss this place. Not until you step inside will the original structure become obvious.

Maidee's energy and passion make a positive first impression upon any-one who meets her, and her menu reflects much of her personal history, which took her from China, through France, and finally into the United States. Though she's made significant cosmetic changes to the diner, she's saved all the parts and panels she's removed and has covered up the rest. The diner lounge features a fine selection of local ales, and the built-in charm of O'Mahony craftsmanship help establish a convivial atmosphere.

North of this point, there are few diners. In Bangor, a new Denny's Diner built by Starlite awaits. Beyond that, the hamlet of Springfield, 80 miles north, has a tantalizing find for the most ardent fan—the remains of a car originally called the Minute Man Diner. According to diner historian Gary Thomas, the Worcester Diner first saw customers in Lynn, Massachusetts, in 1929. Owners then traded down to a used, older diner, sending the Minute Man back to the Worcester factory for refurbishment and resale to new owners in Ware, Massachusetts. Its history becomes clouded at this point, but it probably ended up in this remote stretch of woods in Springfield in the 1980s. Its future doesn't look so bright. Though its owner appeared to begin work on reopening it at some point, at last look, this prospect seemed unlikely.

Doubling back across the interior of Maine, you'll encounter ruggedly beautiful scenery, charming small towns on the downslope from prosperity, and three diners of note: the Farmington, the Wirebridge, and the Deluxe Diners. The Farmington Diner sits at a crossroads in the town of that name. Rare, run-down, and rustic apply to this late 1940s Mountain View Diner that had previously mystified diner historians who debated its manufacture. For budding roadside historians, a brief study of this structure provides a quick lesson in diner archeology.

The Farmington Diner sports mostly rounded corners that square off at the bottom, a feature commonly referred to as cowcatcher corners. These are unique to 1946–49 Mountain View diners and mimicked the bovine removal devices railroads once employed on the fronts of their locomotives. Despite this, the diner's ragged appearance and the replacement aluminum exterior skin possibly indicated on-site construction. The diner sits on a

The Farmington Diner is Maine's only Mountain View. It has undergone some significant renovations.

squared foundation, however, which follows the outlines of the cowcatchers, an architectural feature a cost-conscious builder would not likely bother to include. Most likely, the previous owner stripped the original skin when the stainless suffered damage, either from the weather or from an accident of some kind, such as an automobile collision.

The remote village of New Portland hosts one of those welcoming respites in the middle of nowhere. The Wirebridge Diner, a 1932 Worcester car featuring a monitor roof, remains popular with the ski set on their way up to the Sugarloaf ski area and with locals who still remember the diner's days in its original location in Waterville. The diner moved to its current location in 1971 after six sorry years in storage, and though it barely retains its basic shape and few obvious original architectural features, it continues to provide a welcoming atmosphere for those looking for a classic experience.

The town of Rumford, Maine, grew up around its paper mill, which still operates, and it also was the birthplace of Edmund Muskie, governor, U.S. senator, and statesman. The town's tidy, scenic downtown still shows plenty of life, but its single jewel of a diner sits in a blue-collar neighborhood close to the industrial section. The Deluxe Diner, another jazz-era model, came up from Worcester Lunch Car in 1928. Over the years, the diner's exterior acquired new coverings, and though a pitched roof and a vinyl-sided facade encase the structure, the interior retains a great deal of its original features, including ceramic tiled floors and walls, marble countertop, and Monel metal hood.

This trip now reenters New Hampshire. Most of New Hamsphire's diners are located along the north-south corridors west of Lake Winnipesaukee, but one of the two exceptions (other than Gilley's) is one of several recent transplants. In 1991, Dick Benner, a former navy cook, purchased a closed and beaten-up 1949 O'Mahony formerly called Pat & Bob's Diner from a site on Route 20 in East Greenbush, New York. Benner proceeded to clean and restore his new Miss Wakefield Diner, reopening it to a grateful public in 1992. Benner ran a tight ship for the next six years or so, but difficulties with finding good help and probably other business-related issues prompted him to find a new buyer. In 1999, Scott and Grace Bramer stepped into the kitchen and have kept the customers on their way up Spaulding Highway to the Conways and the White Mountains happy with their efforts.

The Lake Winnipesaukee region has traditionally been one of New England's premier vacation and recreation areas. In the heart of it all, Laconia serves as a gateway to the lakes and the White Mountains to the north. In a strip plaza on the east end of town stands the Paugus Diner, a 1951 Worcester car in magnificently original condition despite its envelopment within the plaza architecture. First installed in Concord, it was moved to its current

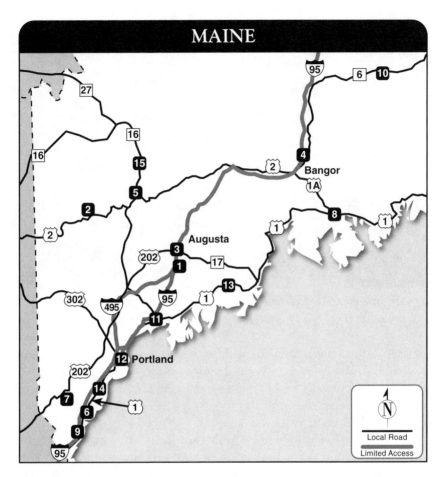

MAINE

Bangor

Augusta

Portland

N

Local Road

Limited Access

1 A-1 Diner: Gardiner: (MS)

2 Deluxe Diner: Rumford (BR)

3 Denny's Classic Diner: Augusta (P)

4 Denny's Classic Diner: Bangor (P)

5 Farmington Diner: Farmington (MS)

6 Flo's Hot Dogs: Cape Neddick (R)

7 Lois' Diner: Sanford (MS)

8 Maidee's: Ellsworth (MS)

9 Maine Diner: Wells (OS)

10 Minute Man Diner: Springfield (BR)

11 Miss Brunswick Diner: Brunswick (BR)

12 Miss Portland Diner: Portland (MS)

13 Moody's Diner: Waldoboro (OS)

14 Palace Diner: Biddeford (BR)

15 Wirebridge Diner: New Portland (BR)

location in the early 1960s. The diner's somewhat anachronistic design, exemplified by a brown marble counter in a room brightened with pale yellow and light blue ceramic tile walls, looks classic and cozy today.

This diner shares these features with others in northern New England: the Windsor Diner in the town of that name and the Parkway Diner in South Burlington, Vermont. Like the others, the Paugus showed the com-

Yet another northern New England diner under another roof, the Paugus Diner, sits near the junction of Routes 3, 107, and 11 in the popular Winnipesaukee lake region.

pany's inability to keep up with the times, which demanded a more stream-lined design. The Paugus has some exterior stainless trim, but it primarily advertises itself with its forest green porcelain panels. In 1994, owner Allan Fullerton expanded the business into an adjacent space. That, the good food, and the excellent crossroads location keep the Paugus hopping.

In 1991, the Tilt'n Diner just outside Laconia in Tilton marked a kind of a rebirth for the idea of a diner chain in New England, not seen since the demise of the Monarch Diners in the Boston area during the 1930s to 1960s. The Tilt'n belongs to Alex Ray's Common Man restaurant chain, which has twelve family-style restaurants spread out between Manchester and Lincoln. The Tilt'n, ironically enough, began as a Monarch Diner located in Waltham, Massachusetts. It replaced the first Monarch on that site, a 1940 Worcester now in Lowell operating as the Four Sisters. Built in 1951 by O'Mahony, the diner then was moved to Salisbury, becoming the Lafayette Diner. In 1989, it was moved to temporary storage in Concord before Ray secured its new loca-tion at the Tilton exit of I-93.

The Tilt'n Diner inspires some debate among diner purists. In a sense, Ray uses the diner purely as front to the larger restaurant operation. Renova-tions removed the diner's backbar, which now affords those sitting at the counter a broad view of the main dining room behind the diner. And therein lies the rub: The diner itself isn't the heart of the operation. It does not serve as the primary dining area, but as a prop to bring an air of authenticity to a theme restaurant. And although Alex Ray enjoys a measure of fame in the New Hampshire restaurant world, customers will not likely find him behind the counter at the Tilt'n.

Nevertheless, the Tilt'n Diner packs 'em in, and Ray likely will find similar success with his next diner project, slated for launch in 2005. In 2001, Ray purchased a 1940s-vintage Kullman diner formerly located near Binghamton, New York. Ray plans to restore the unit and install it in Ashland, New Hampshire.

The Red Arrow Diner represents another attempt to turn a diner business into a chain operation. At one time, at least three Red Arrows operated in southern New Hampshire from Manchester to Keene, starting in 1922. Today the lone Red Arrow in Manchester never closes, a rarity in northern New England. Though lacking a prefab pedigree, the Red Arrow looks and feels like the real thing, and its menu, staff, and smoke-free atmosphere make it a don't-miss for anyone traveling—or living—in this area.

The diner is run by the friendly and creative Carol Lawrence, who banned cigarettes from its cozy environs in 1998. Carol had many doubters, but like other smart and enlightened operators who took their own initiative on this matter, she saw the damage smoking did, not only to the health of her patrons and help, but to her business as well. When she banned the butt, she did it with great fanfare, garnering some major publicity points in the local paper and celebrating the event with a street party, repeated annu-

This Monarch Diner now serves customers in Tilton, New Hampshire.

ally. Carol estimates that her business has increased as much as 20 percent since going smoke-free.

Nashua, New Hampshire, paid homage to one of its long-gone diners in 1997, when it mounted a mural of the Yankee Flyer Diner on the side of a building near City Hall. This Sterling Streamliner served the city from 1939 to 1965, when it made way for "progress." In the mid-1990s, a former mayor launched an effort to raise funds for the mural, and to the best of anyone's knowledge, it remains the only piece of public art that so prominently features an actual diner. Unfortunately, folks connected with this effort seemed to forget that Nashua still had an actual diner right in the heart of downtown. Jo-Ann's Kitchen sits perpendicular to the street, wedged between two larger buildings, with its street end mostly covered by a facade. Inside, the diner retains many of its original features, except that an expansion removed an outer wall to accommodate booth seating.

The state recently completed a bypass that now takes U.S. Route 202 traffic around the town of Hillsborough, but travelers who elect to take that road will miss Caron's Diner near the heart of town. Mary Caron heads this smoke-free operation and serves up all the traditional diner favorites in a rare 1940s Kullman diner, the only one in New Hamsphire.

Thornton Wilder wrote his Pulitzer-winning play *Our Town* in Peterborough, New Hampshire, and it's tempting to imagine him taking breaks at

Though built on-site, the Red Arrow Diner would fool all but the sharpest eye. After one bite of the diner's wonderful homemade pies or a serving of one of its big omelets, the distinction becomes trivial.

A rare Kullman in northern New England, Caron's Diner serves up some excellent Yankee cooking in a small-town setting.

the Peterboro Diner. The current diner didn't emerge from the Worcester factory until 1950, but Wilder may have sipped his coffee at its predecessor, Worcester #549, which today survives as the Ever Ready Diner. A later renovation that likely enlarged the diner's kitchen also removed the restrooms from the original structure, giving the diner space for more seating. The floor tile indicates the original layout.

Lindy's Diner, in the heart of Keene, serves as a major stop along the presidential campaign trail during the primaries, and just about every president and hopeful has walked its terrazzo floors since its installation in 1960. Even George W. Bush flipped a burger or two at the grill in the 2000 campaign. George and Arietta Rigopolous kept this rare Paramount diner thriving since the 1970s, when they purchased the diner from Timolean "Lindy" Chakolous.

In December 2003, they sold the diner, business, and property to Keene residents Chuck Criss and Nancy Petreillo. Chuck has extensive experience in the restaurant industry, managing the former Peter Christian's restaurant in town (which eventually became 179 Main Street) and later the Springfield Royal Diner in Springfield, Vermont (see page 146). The owners of that project had drafted Chuck into the effort, but he harbored ambitions to run his own place. When Lindy's hit the market in 2003, he found his opportunity and looks forward to proving his mettle in the trade. Criss and Petreillo have continued in the Greek diner tradition, gradually putting their own stamp on the operation.

RECOMMENDED WEBSITES

Given the ephemeral nature of the Internet, I recommend the following web-sites with crossed fingers. The main criteria for inclusion here are current longevity, utility, accuracy, and user experience. You can find all of these sites linked from my own site at www.roadsideonline.com.

John Baeder　　www.johnbaeder.com
One of the founding fathers of diner appreciation finally has his own website displaying his groundbreaking, awe-inspiring paintings.

Diner City　　www.dinercity.com
Ron Saari maintains extensive listings and photographs of diners coast to coast and beyond. This website also includes reader reviews of diners.

Dream Diner　　www.dreamdiner.com
Fun, energetic site for a fun, energetic diner experience.

Maine Diner　　www.mainediner.com
A most comprehensive site describing the diner's operation. Also includes an online version of the diner's gift shop.

Red Arrow Diner　　www.redarrowdiner.com
The Red Arrow's website got a little quiet in 2003, but Carol Lawrence has a great idea going nonetheless. Lively and full of information, the site promises much future interactivity.

Rosie's Diner　　www.rosiesdiner.com
Jerry Berta's creation launched when he still ran the actual diner. Since 2002, he sold the business to Tammy Fitzgerald but retains the website. The site remains primarily yet another self-promotional vehicle for Jerry himself and his artwork.

Lindy's offers the basics and does them well. While the Greek diner pre-vails in southern New England through New York and New Jersey, Lindy's is one of few in this region. Greek diners typically distinguish themselves with large and varied menus, longer hours, consistent food quality, and feta cheese in the salads and omelets. Since 2002, Lindy's also offers a smoke-free atmosphere.

The Heritage Diner claims to be the oldest operating Worcester diner in the country, but this distinction more likely belongs to Casey's Diner in Natick, Massachusetts (see page 63). In 1997, the efforts of the LaPierre family allowed this beautiful diner to reemerge after years of being hidden behind a clapboard facade and pitched roof. When known as Alice's Trolley Stop, the diner's exterior revealed little of its true origins, with the possible exception of the window proportions, although its interior still had many of its original features.

The diner came to Charlestown in 1946 and opened as the L&Y Diner, but in the early 1970s, its owners wrapped it in artificial siding. In 1997, Carol LaPierre and her husband came to the rescue. They purchased the property with the diner and attached house and negotiated a land swap with a local bank across the street. The bank owned an 1820s vintage federal-style house and wanted the diner property to construct a new branch. The LaPierres wanted the house to convert it into a tavern and restaurant, which would incorporate the diner. As the LaPierres uncovered the diner, they also revealed one of the original wheels used to move it.

Since then, they've successfully revived the diner and created a fine place to eat. The LaPierres proved their abilities early on, with fresh sandwiches and wonderful homemade pies. The diner is clean and well maintained and retains much of its 1920s vintage atmosphere.

The Daddypop's Tumble Inn Diner, in the town of Claremont, has appeared in just about every book of diner photographs and paintings published over the last twenty years, and for good reason. Save for the automobiles parked just outside, the sight of it seems perpetually lifted from a vintage postcard. The diner sits atop a high foundation, and from the street, photographers get an angle that includes the handsome nineteenth-century hotel that looms in the background. Since 1997, the mostly unspoiled 1941

One of the oldest operating Worcester diners, the Heritage Diner in Charlestown, New Hampshire, got a new life in 1996 thanks to its new owners, the St. Pierre family. The diner still had its original wheels when later remodeling was removed.

The Heritage came to Charlestown in the 1940s and operated as the L&Y Diner in service to locals and transients plying busy Route 12.

Worcester car has belonged to a Pennsylvania resident and New Hampshire expatriate who already owns another famous diner with a catchy name, Daddypop's in Hatboro. After purchasing the Tumble Inn, Ken Smith put it in the able hands of his daughter Debbie Carter, who not only has kept this diner from leaving Claremont, but also has made it an anchor in the town's spreading renaissance.

The unique heritage of the Riverside Diner in Bristol, New Hampshire, seemed long forgotten until its new owner, Christos Stamnos, embarked on a restoration project in the mid-1990s. His work revealed the diner's origins in the Pollard factory in the 1920s, meaning that the Palace Diner in Biddeford could no longer claim to be the last surviving example of a Pollard diner. The work on the Riverside hasn't finished, but the diner, which occupies a location overlooking the raging Newfound River, is open most days for breakfast and lunch.

In the nearby town of Plymouth stands another rare Worcester streamliner model that has seen the partial undoing of some previous renovations. Former owners had draped Fracher's (pronounced FRAY-zer's) Diner in a coat of red brick, covering its cozy yellow porcelain panels with red lettering and trim. Though the mansard-style roof remains, the original wooden shake shingling was replaced with green-coated aluminum roofing panels. The diner, in the heart of this busy little college community, first came to town in 1946 and now fronts a much larger restaurant called the Main Street Station, which features an eclectic combination of Mexican, Asian, and pub cuisine.

While New Hampshire's White Mountains region offers the visitor a cornucopia of attractions, including the excitement of the primordial flume, the majesty of Mount Washington, the drama of the Kancamangus Highway, and the classic fun of Clark's Trading Post and the Hobo Scenic Rail-

The Riverside was identified by historians in the mid-1990s as a Pollard diner. Its owners have since begun the diner's restoration.

road, it also provides one of the most satisfying rewards of any diner hunt. Tucked away at the base of this mountain range in Lincoln is a diminutive, forty-two-seat Master diner, where Chris and Bruce Balch and Kelly Ann Kass have created a special oasis of quality. The Sunny Day Diner raises the culinary bar for every diner, large or small, that does business on the American roadside.

The grand tour of this grand region ends at a seat in the Littleton Diner, a Sterling built by J. D. Judkins. Getting there from the south brings you past the former site of New Hampshire's trademark Old Man in the Mountain, a once-natural rock formation with the appearance of a rugged masculine profile that was discovered by European explorers in colonial times. The state began to artificially prop up the facade in the 1930s in an attempt stave off its inevitable demise, which finally came in 2003.

The diner's history is described on its website in some detail. It came to Littleton in 1940 thanks to Eugene and Stella Stone, who wanted to replace an older, and presumably smaller, diner they had purchased and installed ten years before. Not long after installation, the Stones modified the diner's interior, removing the equipment behind the glass-topped counter to a new kitchen, and then closing in the space by moving the counter and stools forward. The alteration allowed for the addition of twenty more seats.

The Stones kept the diner in operation until 1960, when they sold it to their daughter Eileen and her husband, Louis Burpee. Eileen and Louis kept

In 1995, Fracher's Diner reemerged from its brick facade to reveal intact porcelain panels.

The Littleton Diner brings further charm to an already thriving downtown in northern New Hampshire.

the grills hot until 1975, when the diner entered a period in which it saw several ownership changes. In the meantime, the town underwent similar ups and downs, although today visitors will find a bustling tourist-oriented boutique community, complete with charming bookstores, fancy restaurants, and a brewpub.

Everett Chambers stabilized things a bit at the diner in 1992, but he finally sold it in 2003 to Chris and Patti Williford. The Willifords appear to have a firm handle on things, offering up all the classic diner staples and making them fresh and homemade for another generation of grateful customers.

FEATURED DINER

PALACE DINER
1926 POLLARD
18 Franklin St., Biddeford, ME

No one outside of Biddeford can seem to find the Palace Diner, which is tucked almost out of sight behind one of the commercial blocks at Main Street and Franklin Street. You can easily find the diner by asking any cop how to get to the police station, which shares the same parking lot.

Rick Bernier and his wife took over the rare and well-maintained Pollard diner in 1998 from longtime owner Reynald Beaudoin, and by all accounts, they have made a very successful transition. The diner keeps very early and rather short hours, opening at 5:00 A.M. and closing at 1:00 P.M.

Since 1926, this fifteen-stool diner has had only four owners. Its first, Louis Lachance, helped build it as well. A friend of the Pollard family in Lowell, Massachusetts, Louis found himself laid off from his job as a fire-man with the Boston & Maine Railroad. The Pollards had recently entered the diner-building business and hired Louis to help in their construction. Eventually they suggested that Louis might give diner operation a try. Bidde-ford has a major French Canadian community, and early morning conversa-tions heard in the Palace are spoken in the Canadian French dialect.

Louis learned the trade quickly and well and had a good run. He finally retired in 1962, after thirty-six years of twenty-four-hour operation. Louis sold the diner to Roland Beaudoin, who also owned Roland's Diner, which returned to Worcester in 1988 to become a visitors information kiosk, among other things, and more recently was the restoration project of Mike O'Connor. Rolands's son Pete took over the Palace only four years later.

Maine roadside history maven Will Anderson describes the Palace as Maine's oldest operating diner and speaks of the place with his highest regard.

SUNNY DAY DINER
1958 MASTER
Route 3, Lincoln, NH • (603) 745-4833

The Sunny Day Diner in Lincoln, New Hampshire, proves that good things often do come in small packages. And it proves yet again that it is often the smaller diners that set the standard for the entire industry.

The reputation of this authentic gem beams down warmly upon the entire region, and it stands as a testament to the small diner's potential. Just take three good-natured people, well trained in the culinary arts, plant them in the kitchen of a small diner, and watch the wonders unfold. Though the ardent diner fan should enjoy the inconsistencies of visiting various diners, reveling in each one's distinct personality, a visit here will make you wonder why some diners three and four times the size of the Sunny Day often seek only to satisfy the lowest common denominator.

Customers find themselves welcomed by a friendly staff, fronting an operation for Bruce and Chris Balch and Kelly Ann Kass, who ensconce themselves behind the scenes in the kitchen and bakery. Besides busy waitresses, a spotless environment, and an unspoiled rare diner, you will also notice upon entry all the baked goods placed almost everywhere. While some diners fill the place with nostalgia items, the Sunny Day decorates with dessert. In cake dishes on the counter and the pie case at the backbar is a full frontal assault of fresh-baked fruit and cream pies, cookies, muffins, whoopie pies, cakes, and puddings. Memo to small diners everywhere: Desserts—don't serve customers without them. In fact, the diner's reputation for desserts has allowed for its entry into the retail market. Bruce and Chris have accepted jobs catering various local affairs and recently baked a wedding cake. One item that has brought added glow to the Sunny Day is its delicious banana bread french toast.

Not too many diners offer gazpacho, and although cool soups aren't for everyone, first-time visitors should go with the flow and trust the menu. Besides a nice sprinkling of the unexpected, the Sunny Day rounds out the lunch menu with pasta dishes with homemade sauces, hearty sandwiches, and fresh-cut fries. Most of the Sunny Day's standard menu is basic comfort

The Sunny Day Diner pleases in just about every respect, from its near pristine Master-built interior to the fact that almost everything on its menu is homemade. The diner particularly shines with its desserts, all of which come from the bakery in the basement.

food, although culinary experts have applied their talents to it. The diner makes most items from scratch in the kitchen and the basement bakery.

Despite its white tableclothed foundations, the Sunny Day welcomes all. On any given day, one might find bikers, SUV-transported families, and longtime locals commingling in this showcase diner. Although a few regulars initially voiced their objections to the nonsmoking policy, they still continue to enjoy the Sunny Day experience as much as anyone.

The Sunny Day arrived in Lincoln in 1988 thanks to Jay Bartlett, who found the former Stoney's Diner in Rochester, New Hampshire, closed and for sale. Jay ran a popular business, serving a basic meat-and-potatoes menu, but he ultimately sold out in 1995.

Through all the ownership changes, this diner underwent few aesthetic changes. A tie-rod with turnbuckle extends across the width of the diner, holding the front and back walls in place. Whoever moved the diner for Bartlett cut into the diner's main steel floor cross beams to lower it on the flatbed. This weakened the diner's floor, causing the outer walls to bow out under the weight of the roof. Despite this damage, the Sunny Day looks much as it did when it left the Master factory.

Seeing the possibilities and potential that Kelly, Chris, and Bruce have fully realized here, other diners could learn a lesson from the Sunny Day. In the diner world, size definitely does not matter.

FEATURED DINER

A-1 DINER

1946 WORCESTER #790

3 Bridge St., Gardiner, ME • (207) 582-4804

Finding diners like the A-1 makes road trips and lengthy diner hunts completely worthwhile. This rare Worcester semistreamliner breaks the cliché about little diners in depressed mill towns. The uninitiated could be forgiven for expecting to find standard meat-and-potatoes fare in a smoke-filled setting as worn as its hardworking but tired owner.

Instead, the lucky customer finds one pleasant surprise after another. Meat loaf and mashed potatoes join standard breakfast items on the regular menu, but a scan of the specials menu always makes a visit to the A-1 notable. On any given day, customers might have the choice of gorgonzola risotto cakes, crispy Asian game hen, or spiced pork with orange mango salsa. Such a menu might seem more fitting in a Manhattan bistro, but Michael Giberson and Neil Anderson pull off this culinary feat without a hint of irony.

The natural-foods movement that took hold in the 1970s took its time entering the conservative bastion of the neighborhood diner, but today any diner operator hoping to succeed in the business serves heart-healthy meals. In 1988, Giberson and Anderson boldly brought innovation in a place few people would have dared.

It all works because Michael and Neil haven't forgotten the basic rules of any successful restaurant: Give people a good value, and they will reward you back. The pair have the added advantage of a unique setting. Their

Worcester diner style is one of only seven left in operation, and it sits on 18-foot stilts that raise it to the same level as the bridge it faces. A stairway to the left of the diner descends to the street below and provides a rare opportunity to inspect the underside and get a unique view of a vintage diner. The diner's interior is as lush as the exterior is interesting.

The A-1 began service in 1946 as Heald's Diner, as indicated on the front porcelain panels. The cream and maroon diner represents the Worcester Company at its peak of design, when it applied a broad palette of interior finishes. Customers walk through the front door and step on an intricate pattern of ceramic tile. They then sit either on solidly constructed oak booths or super-heavy-duty chromed stools at a marble-topped counter wrapped with the same ceramic tile that adorns the walls below the large windows. The streamlined hood holds inset menu boards displaying the day's specials and sits atop a stainless steel backbar with panels expertly bent into a scalloped pattern. The woodwork trim and blue laminate ceiling panels in comfortably ornate fashion are fit for royalty but designed for the regular Joe. The experience provides an encompassing visual feast to foreshadow the one that soon will arrive on the plate.

Michael and Neil have done an excellent job of trashing the diner stereotype, but they also endured its difficulties. After fifteen years, they've built up a successful business and have been mentioned on public radio's "Splendid

The A-1 Diner in Gardiner, Maine, distinguishes itself in many ways, including the use of steel "stilts" to raise it to bridge level.

Table" as well as in a slew of positive notices in regional publications. They will be the first to admit, however, that bringing this level of creativity to their customers requires imagination and a lot of hard work—probably too much for just one person.

As if they weren't already working hard enough, in early 2003 the guys planted even deeper roots in the town of Gardiner's revival with the opening of the A-1 Market, a retail shop that extends their retail philosophies into a new venue. The smartly designed space provides a wide variety of specialty foods, deli items, and easily the finest wine selection likely ever seen in Gardiner. Located on a prominent corner of town, the store backs up against the diner, and a footbridge connects the two businesses.

Since both places provide meals, one wonders whether the local market has enough people in the right demographic to make it all worthwhile, but Michael believes the concepts complement each other. The store's deli accommodates folks in a hurry and those planning to cook at home. The big risk comes from carrying so much inventory. Michael voiced his concerns about the new burden of diversifying but decided the time for an expansion had arrived. Gardiner had recently joined the National Trust's Main Street Program and had begun to offer low-interest loans to businesses willing to invest in downtown. In 2002, the diner won a facade improvement grant of $5,000 that will aid in further restoration of the diner.

The jury remains undecided about the ultimate success of the program or of the A-1 Market, but the town and the guys get an "A" for effort. Of all the diners in Maine, this one deserves the highest priority when you are in the area.

DADDYPOP'S TUMBLE INN DINER

1941 WORCESTER #778
1 Main St., Claremont, NH • (603) 542-0074

Many books and guides seem eager to direct readers to the Tumble Inn Diner in Claremont, and for good reason. Diner buffs certainly appreciate the rarity of the diner's style of construction and its history. When Worcester built this unique diner, for a reason lost in time, they fashioned it after its streamliner models, but without the slanted sides. Inside, the Tumble Inn reveals Worcester Lunch Car interior design at its absolute finest. Resplendent with its tilework of cobalt blue and fire engine red, the Tumble Inn's visual feast prepares you for its culinary one.

Since 1997, the Tumble Inn has belonged to Ken Smith of Hatboro, Pennsylvania. In that town, people know all about his Daddypop's Diner on York Road and its reputation for large meals, superfriendly service, and Ken's penchant for collecting small machinery. When Ken purchased the Tumble Inn, it ended some agonizing speculation in the diner world over the diner's future. Claremont's best days seemed to lie behind it, and its downtown featured few retail businesses that one might describe as thriving. Though New Hampshire is generally regarded as a prosperous state, this region, which once served as a center for machine tool manufacturing, continues to suffer from the closure of most of those factories. Indeed, in the early 1990s, Claremont had fallen on such hard times that its school system faced discreditation.

In that decade, the diner passed through at least four owners. Brenda Rubera sold the diner to local restaurateur Larry Beswick, who had some success with it for about three years. He in turn sold it to Sue Durfey. She ran it reluctantly for another two years, during which time she kept the diner on the market, but the depressed local economy didn't attract too many qualified buyers. It began to look more and more likely that the diner would leave town, as had so many others in the area. In 1989, the Streamliner Diner in Newport, another Worcester streamliner, headed south to Atlanta, where it was sold at auction and moved to Savannah, where it remains as a neighborhood diner operated by the Savannah College of Art and Design.

But in stepped Ken Smith, a New Hampshire native who often vacationed in the area and who purchased the diner in 1997. Ken took on the new challenge by handing over responsibility for the diner's operation to his daughter Debbie Carter and her then-husband, Paul. With the diner closed for a few months for repairs and cleaning, Ken and family gave the rare diner a new shine while tending to some of the deferred maintenance. It reopened as Daddypop's Tumble Inn in 1998, with almost exactly the same menu as its sister diner in Hatboro, including the hard-to-beat home fries, large fluffy pancakes, and fresh-roasted turkey club sandwiches. The two diners also keep the same breakfast and lunch hours of operation, and if you take a pen from one diner to the other, you'll get a free cup of coffee.

In 2002, Debbie took the initiative to make the Tumble Inn smoke-free, which she claims increased sales by more than 15 percent. A straight talker, Debbie seems to share her father's Yankee sensibilities and values, which can only help her in this tough business.

In the meantime, the town of Claremont also looks as though it has turned the corner. Though the downtown theater was demolished, its other storefronts have shown signs of life, with the antique shops leading the way and a new café and other retail ventures in their wake.

PLAIN JANE'S DINER
A 1954 O'MAHONY
Route 25, Rumney, NH • (603) 786-2525

BOBBY'S GIRL DINER
1957 WORCESTER #850
Route 104, Meredith, NH • (603) 744-8112

In 1990, Bob and Gloria Merrill began to make their mark on the North Country diner scene with the installation and restoration of what would become Glory Jean's in Rumney, New Hampshire. This relatively small 1954 O'Mahony, formerly known as the Bell's Pond Diner, had last operated near Hudson, New York. At the time that Bob finished his restorations, Rumney looked more like the middle of nowhere than it does today. Though it may have seemed like a foolish endeavor to spend so much time and money on a restaurant in an area with so few people, the Merrills proved skeptics wrong and drew crowds of grateful customers eager to give the spiffed-up classic a try.

Bob's experience in the construction trades certainly qualified him to build a restaurant, but he had no previous experience with diner restoration

Bob and Gloria Merrill brought this O'Mahony to Rumney in 1990, restored it, and called it Glory Jean's. They sold out in 1994, and the diner closed in 1998. In 1999, it reopened with new owners Steve and Jane Greene, and a new name: Plain Jane's Diner.

The Merrills, who returned Bobby's Girl to New England, deserve high praise for their efforts for restoring not one, but two diners. In 2003, they exited the diner scene yet again, leaving the last Worcester built in the capable hands of Ron and Mary Elliard.

specifically. Nevertheless, he did a tasteful job, giving the diner a cool and calming seafoam green hue and adding an unobtrusive dining room off the back. Unlike other projects that have grafted old diners onto new buildings, here the diner took center stage. For the diner's menu, Bob and Gloria stuck with the tried-and-true staples of a good short-order restaurant, which made customers feel comfortable and at home.

After three years of success in the business, the Merrills sold their diner to Charlotte and Ed Kimball and moved into another, slightly more formal restaurant. The Kimballs struggled with their new venture for the next five years, finally closing in 1999. After a couple years in mothballs, the diner was purchased by Jane and Steve Greene, who gave the place a new lease on life and yet another refurbishing. Jane originally hails from the area but had moved out to the West Coast, where she met her husband. Her experience in the restaurant industry brought them both back east, and a stint in the diner world seemed like a good idea.

Though the Merrills did well with their second restaurant, Gloria later admitted that they missed the diner terribly. Both of them remained fascinated with doo-wop culture, having been born into that generation, and in 1995, they began a search for yet another diner. At about the same time, Alexis Stewart had just about given up on her dream to install her recently acquired vintage diner in the upscale community of Bridgehampton, Long Island. Although she was the daughter of Martha Stewart, the town fathers deemed her diner tacky and denied her the required permits, ultimately forcing her to sell.

Before Bobby's Girl Diner wound up in Meredith, New Hampshire, it spent several lonely months in this Bridgehampton, New York, field awaiting permit approvals that never came.

Bobby's Girl started out as Lloyd's Diner in Johnstown, Rhode Island, in 1957, and aside from some renovation work, it was the last effort of the Worcester Lunch Car Company. Though today we marvel at the beauty of this interior work, it still shows many vestiges of the company's 1930s vintage diners, hence the company's fall from favor in the marketplace.

Bob and Gloria initially balked at the $40,000 price tag, but in the end, they decided they had to have not only another real 1950s diner, but the last one built by the Worcester Lunch Car Company (#850). Bob cut the check and never looked back, installing the diner on newly acquired land on Route 104 in Meredith and calling it Bobby's Girl Diner. The couple set up an operation nearly identical in tone to their first diner operation, but this time the layout of the overall restaurant didn't quite give the same prominence to the diner, which barely needed any restorative work.

After forty years in four locations, the last Worcester had held up rather well. It had begun as Lloyd's Diner in Johnstown, Rhode Island. Then it was closed, sold, and moved to Kingston, Massachusetts, where it became something of a theme restaurant called Sh'Boom's. Diner broker John Keith purchased the diner in 1991 with the intent of shipping it to England, but when that deal collapsed, it attracted the interest of Stewart. She planned to add the diner to her kitschy retro motel business, but instead had to watch her dream return to New England.

This time, the Merrills really seemed to turn up the doo-wop in their new business. The main dining room built off the back of the diner housed an even larger collection of fifties memorabilia, while the diner, accessed from behind, remained the preserve of smoking customers.

In 2002, Bob suffered a 14-foot fall from a rooftop and never quite recovered. The drain on his energy proved too much, forcing the Merrills to sell yet another diner operation, this time to Ron and Mary Elliard, who promptly banned smoking from the entire establishment.

The Merrills had left quite a mark on the area, inspiring others to follow in their wake, and one might easily suspect that Bob and Gloria will once again start looking for another diner gem to polish.

DINER DIRECTORY

MAINE

A-1 Diner
3 Bridge St.
Gardiner, ME
(207) 582-4804
1946 Worcester 790
Famous for many things, including its well-done, innovative, neo diner menu, its rare streamliner style, and the fact that it sits on 20-foot stilts to level it with the bridge. Originally Heald's Diner. Full menu. Daily specials.

Deluxe Diner
29 Oxford St.
Rumford, ME
(207) 369-9561
1928 Worcester
Well-preserved interior encased inside remodeled exterior. Small, stools-only diner features basic grilled diner menu. Breakfast and lunch only.

In 1998, Denny's restaurants underwent a major change in image by ordering a slew of actual diners from Starlite Diners of Ormond Beach, Florida. Two of these landed in Maine. The Denny's Diners typically have streamlined menus compared with the standard Denny's restaurants.

Denny's Classic Diner
27 Civic Center Dr.
Augusta, ME
1998 Starlite
Part of Denny's chain. American food.

Denny's Classic Diner
120 Haskell Rd.
Bangor, ME
1998 Starlite
Part of Denny's chain. American food.

Farmington Diner
Intervale Rd.
Farmington, ME
(207) 778-4151
c. 1949 Mountain View
Substantially renovated. Standard diner fare.

Flo's Hot Dogs
Rte. 1
Cape Neddick, ME
unknown build
Mostly hot dogs and grilled lunch fare.

Lois' Diner
Salisbury, ME
1951 O'Mahony
Former Monarch Diner. Closed and in private storage.

Maidee's
156 Main St.
Ellsworth, ME
(207) 667-6554
1938 O'Mahony
Very narrow diner encased in larger building, mostly intact. Formerly operating as Pineland Diner in Pineland, Maine. Serves as bar and lounge area for larger restaurant. Asian cuisine with French accent. Lunch and dinner.

Maine Diner
2265 Post Rd./Rte. 1
Wells, ME
(207) 646-4441
www.mainediner.com
on-site
Budding Maine institution. Full menu
of American food with seafood specialties. Known for award-winning chowders and outstanding desserts.

Minute Man Diner
Rte. 6
Springfield, ME
1929 Worcester 649
Originally called the Minute Man Diner
when installed in Lynn, Massachusetts.
Moved later to Ware, Massachusetts, and
then to various locations on its way up
to Springfield, where it arrived in the
1980s. Remarkably intact and partially
restored, but apparently abandoned.

Miss Brunswick Diner
101 Pleasant St./Rte. 1
Brunswick, ME
(207) 721-1134
1942 Worcester
Very modified diner with clapboard
exterior, but retains its barrel roof. Backbar was pushed back to accommodate
booths in this formerly all-stool diner.
Features Mexican cuisine. Full menu.

Miss Portland Diner
49 Marginal Way
Portland, ME
(207) 773-3246
1949 Worcester 818
In excellent condition, but closed
since 2004.

Moody's Diner
Rte. 1
Waldoboro, ME
(207) 832-7468
1930s on-site

Moody's at night.

Landmark Maine institution, well known
for low prices, homemade Yankee cooking, and fresh desserts. Full menu weekdays, twenty-four hours weekends.

Palace Diner
18 Franklin St.
Biddeford, ME
(207) 284-8200
1926 Pollard
The Palace is one of two remaining
Pollard diners, manufactured in Lowell,
Massachusetts. Barrel roof diner with
no booths. In excellent condition.
Serves wonderful home-cooked meals.
Breakfast and lunch only.

Wirebridge Diner
Rte. 27
New Portland, ME
(207) 628-6229
1932 Worcester 698
Originally located in Waterville and
moved to its current location in 1971.
Extensively renovated but retains basic
structural outlines. Basic grilled diner
fare. Breakfast and lunch only.

NEW HAMPSHIRE

Barr's Diner
Rte. 106
Loudon, NH
1938 O'Mahony
"Monarch" model. Closed and used for storage.

Betsy & Mike's Diner
Exeter, NH
1946 Silk City
In private collection. Former Pole Tavern Diner in Upper Pittsgrove, New Jersey. A total wreck when purchased by Steve Harwin but now fully restored.

Bobby's Girl Diner
Rte. 104
Meredith, NH
(603) 744-8112
1957 Worcester 850
Last diner built by the Worcester Lunch Car company. Originally installed in Johnstown, Rhode Island, and known as Lloyd's. Moved to Kingston, Massachusetts, as part of Sh'Boom's nightclub, and moved again in 1991 to Bridgehampton, New York, by Alexis Stewart, daughter of Martha, in a failed bid to reopen. Sold in 1994 to Bob and Gloria Merrill, who brought it to Meredith and reopened. Still in excellent condition. Full menu of American food.

Caron's Diner
83 Henniker St.
Hillsboro, NH
(603) 464-3575
1940s Kullman
One of two Kullman diners in all of northern New England. Diner was moved up from New Jersey in the 1960s and attached to a dining room. In very good condition. American food with daily specials. Breakfast and lunch only.

Daddypop's Tumble Inn Diner
1 Main St.
Claremont, NH
(603) 542-0074
1941 Worcester 778
One-of-a-kind car. In excellent, very original condition. Subject of two paintings by John Baeder. Serves simple American food. Breakfast and lunch only. Smoke-free.

Eggie's Diner
127 Plaistow Rd.
Plaistow, NH
(603) 382-5063
c. 1953 Mountain View 317
Originally operating as Pent's Diner in North Reading, Massachusetts. Exterior renovations stripped diner of most stainless work. Serves basic diner fare. Breakfast and lunch menu.

Four Aces Diner
23 Bridge St./Rte. 4
West Lebanon, NH
(603) 298-6827
1952 Worcester 837
Moved from the center of town and built into a larger building that encloses all but the diner's facade. Still in excellent condition. American food, standard diner fare. Full menu most days.

Gilley's Lunch Cart
175 Fleet St.
Portsmouth, NH
(603) 431-6343
1939 Worcester
One of two real Worcester lunch wagons still in existence, though the only one still in operation. Gilley's no longers roves the streets of Portsmouth, but all else is exactly as it was when it was built. Now permanently parked in location. Serves basic sandwich menu and some grilled items. Open late-night hours.

Heritage Diner
Main St./Rte. 12
Charlestown, NH
(603) 826-3110
1925 Worcester
Formerly L&V Diner and Alice's Trolley
Stop, located across the street from present location. Partially restored and
incorporated into larger restaurant.
Excellent homemade desserts. Diner
is breakfast and lunch only.

Jo-Ann's Kitchen
219 Main St.
Nashua, NH
(603) 883-3032
1930 Worcester
Little diner shoehorned into downtown
location. Early renovation expanded
interior, but diner retains much vintage
charm. Breakfast and early lunch only.

L&B Tailoring
18 S. Main St.
Concord, NH
(603) 227-9299
1920s
Renovated but free-standing car. A tailor
shop. No food.

Lindy's Diner
19 Gilbo St.
Keene, NH
(603) 352-4273
1960 Paramount
The only Paramount diner in northern
New England. Space-age style with
colonial elements. Sold in late 2003
after nearly thirty years owned by the
Rigopolous family. American food with
Greek specialties. Full menu.

Littleton Diner
170 Main St.
Littleton, NH
www.littletondiner.com

(603) 444-3994
1940 Sterling
A lot of character despite considerable
renovation of interior. Back bar
removed, but glass counters retained.
Great Main Street location. Full menu
of American food. Daily specials and
homemade desserts.

Main Street Station
105 Main St.
Plymouth, NH
(603) 536-7577
1946 Worcester 793
Rare streamliner, originally Fracher's
Diner. Partially restored in mid-1990s.
Now part of a larger restaurant with
Tex-Mex cuisine. In this context, diner is
something of an afterthought. Full menu.

Milford Diner
2 Union Square
Milford, NH
(603) 673-1815
1931 Ward & Dickinson?
Remodeled, but retains vintage charm.
Basic grilled diner fare. Breakfast and
lunch only.

Interior of the Four Aces Diner.

Miss Wakefield Diner
Rte. 16
Wakefield, NH
(603) 522-6800
1949 O'Mahony
Formerly operating as Pat & Bob's Diner on U.S. Route 20 in East Greenbush, New York. Moved to current location in 1992 and restored. Popular breakfast and lunch spot.

Mt. Pisgah Diner
18 Main St.
Winchester, NH
(603) 239-4101
1941 Worcester 769
Facade of this quaint diner was covered over and the interior has been painted, but it retains a warm atmosphere. Basic diner fare. Homemade soups. Short breakfast and lunch hours, even shorter on weekends.

Ocean Wok
Rte. 1A, 7 Ocean Blvd.
Hampton Beach, NH
(603) 926-6633
c. 1949 Worcester?
Severely remodeled. Serves Asian cuisine.

O.K. Diner
Hanover, NH
1930 Worcester 663
Originally Arlington Diner, part of a double diner operation in Shrewsbury, Massachusetts. Current owner had planned to reopen diner in Kendall Square in Cambridge, Massachusetts. Moved to Norwich, Vermont, in mid-1990s, and then to Hanover by late 1990s. Currently on private residence.

Paugus Diner
1331 Union Ave.
Laconia, NH
(603) 528-8418

1951 Worcester 831
Originally Manus's Diner, located in Concord, New Hampshire. A later model with a black marble counter. Suffered a minor fire in 1991 but was repaired to excellent condition. Enclosed within a shopping plaza, but facade is plainly visible. Full menu of American food.

Peterboro Diner
10 Depot St.
Peterborough, NH
(603) 924-6202
1950 Worcester 827
Lengthy car in very good condition. Past alterations removed original kitchen to expand dining area. Full menu of American food with Greek specialties.

Plain Jane's Diner
Rte. 25
Rumney, NH
(603) 786-2525
1954 O'Mahony
An excellent example of a restoration. Originally operating as the Bell's Pond Diner at the intersection of U.S. Route 9 and Route 9H in New York State. Bought and moved to its current site in 1990 by Gloria and Bob Merrill, who restored the diner and reopened it as Bobby's Girl Diner. Became Plain Jane's in 2001 with new ownership. Subject of a John Baeder painting as the Bells Pond. Full menu of American food.

Red Arrow Diner
61 Lowell St.
Manchester, NH
www.redarrowdiner.com
(603) 626-1118
1940s on-site
Small, lively diner. Once part of small Red Arrow Diner chain in southern New Hampshire. Homemade soups, desserts,

and hot plates. Open twenty-four hours, seven days. Smoke-free.

Remember When Diner
Rte. 11
Rochester, NH
2001 Starlite
American food.

Riverside Diner
9 S. Main St.
Bristol, NH
(603) 744-7877
1926 Pollard
One of two Pollard diners known to exist. Near fully restored. Breakfast and lunch menu.

Route 28 Diner
282 N. Broadway/Rte. 28
Salem, NH
1940 Sterling 406
Formerly operating as Hesperus Diner in Gloucester, Massachusetts. Moved to Salem in the 1970s. Closed in 2003. Threatened with demolition.

Sunny Day Diner
Rte. 3
Lincoln, NH
(603) 745-4833
1958 Master
The only Master diner in northern New England. Brought up in 1988 from Dover, New Hampshire, where it was known as Stoney's Diner. Under the stewardship of Bruce and Chris Balch and Kelly Ann Kass, it became one of the best diners in the country. Well known during this time for amazing desserts and a quality menu of home-made items. Currently on the market. Breakfast and lunch only.

Tilt'n Diner
Rte. 3
Tilton, NH
(603) 286-2204d

The Red Arrow Diner is one of the only diners in northern New England that never closes.

1951 O'Mahony
Formerly operating as the Lafayette Diner and at one time part of the Monarch chain of diners in the Boston area. Originally installed in Waltham, Massachusetts, where it replaced the Worcester now known as the Four Sisters located in Lowell, Massachusetts. Restored in 1992 with a large restaurant-nightclub addition. Full menu of American food.

Village Chef Diner
Rte. 3
Bow, NH
1940 Kullman
In storage. Originally the Mayfair Diner, installed in Elmira, New York, in 1940. Moved to Binghamton, New York becoming the Village Chef Diner. Moved in 2002 to Bow when purchased by the Common Man restaurant chain.

CONNECTICUT

onnecticut's close proximity to the Big Apple often calls its very New England-ness into question. The character of the state varies wildly from the "quiet" northeastern corner of Windham County to its brash bedroom communities for New York City. At its center, its state capital, Hartford, wrestles with its long decline from the time Mark Twain described it as the most beautiful city in America. The city also marks a kind of gateway into this Jersey-like urbanization. Though it's technically part of New England, Fairfield County draws much of its prosperity, and therefore its character and culture, from New York City. Here you will likely find more Yankee than Red Sox fans, and in one sense, you can use that simple demographic to help you draw the true borders of New England.

Diners here largely follow along the same pattern. Of the six New England states, only Connecticut has so many examples of the diner's departure from its lunch wagon roots. The big Greek diner makes a presence in Connecticut like it does in no other New England state, but even the dominance of this ethnicity has begun to subside. Throughout the Northeast, large, later-model diners now see the entry of a new wave of immigrants as managers and owners, many with Middle Eastern origins, such as Turks, Syrians, and Egyptians.

Several of the smaller, older diners in Connecticut, particularly those located in transforming ethnic neighborhoods, have assumed corresponding ethnic flavors. This evolution is completely consistent with the history of the industry. Early lunch wagons in the Blackstone Valley region of Massachusetts and Rhode Island saw French Canadians and Irish at the reins. Italians in New Jersey and Germans in Pennsylvania chased the American dream behind the counter through middle of the last century. Greeks entered the diner industry for all the same reasons. Immigrants began in entry-level positions such as dishwasher, waitress, or busboy. Those men and women who

1 Collin's Diner: Canaan (MS)
2 Folly Cafe: Burrville (R)
3 Laurel Diner: Southbury (MS)
4 Lumani's Diner: Southington (R)
5 Main Street Diner: Plainville (MS)
6 Skee's Diner: Torrington (BR)

7 Tony's Diner: Seymour (MS)
8 Twin Colony: Torrington (E)
9 Valley Diner: Derby (E)
10 Windmill Diner: New Milford (E)
11 Winsted Diner: Winsted (BR)

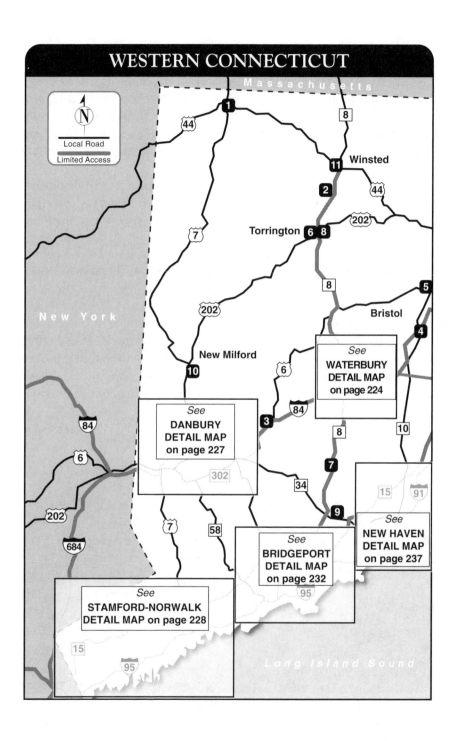

worked hard and proved their aptitude for the complexities of food service advanced quickly and made good livings. Stories abound of diner owners who started out working eighteen-hour days, advanced through successively responsible positions in the operation, and then went on to buy their own run-down diners, fixing them up, building reputable businesses, and eventually becoming prominent citizens in their communities with the ability to send their children to college. This story is repeated throughout the history of the industry.

In the 1950s, a wave of Greek immigration happened to coincide with the peaking popularity of diners in the Northeast. Diners already owned by Greeks hired recently immigrated relatives, who rose up through the ranks to open their own diners, establishing a pattern that would come to dominate the industry in the Mid-Atlantic states and Connecticut. From a culture that already prized good food, community, and hard work, these individuals showed ample aptitude for the demands of the business.

Throughout the 1960s and well into the 1990s, many owners of gleaming streamlined stainless steel beauties either replaced them or transformed them into Early American fantasies or opulent Greco-Roman palaces. Often an owner's sense of style resulted in an unclassifiable design that looked like nothing before seen on the roadside. In response to the spread of fast-food chains, these diner owners drafted voluminous menus featuring a

COLLECTION OF ARTHUR GOODY

The Country Diner seen here in the early 1960s has changed little on the outside, though the new owners have updated the interior some. The diner is now called the Parkway because of its close proximity to the Merritt Parkway in Stamford, Connecticut.

multitude of dishes. The days of diner builders offering a standard style of diner influenced by the broader trends of culture and technology had given way to custom construction dictated by the desires of this newly Americanized ownership and market. Of the six New England states, this development has been most evident in Connecticut, and there mostly in the corridor connecting Hartford, New Haven, and New York City.

On the other hand, the state also has a few of the best-preserved diners still in operation in the country. If you drive a diner-hunting path across the state in the shape of a giant W, you begin and end at two of them.

Along Connecticut's western border with New York, U.S. Route 7 treks south from some of the state's most pastoral scenery to its most congested. The drive from the Massachusetts border south runs mostly parallel with the Housatonic River, and riding this road affords travelers one of the more exhilarating rides in New England—at least until they reach New Milford.

In this corner of the state, the classic Collin's Diner still stands tall and pretty on a gentle slope that faces the historic Canaan train station. O'Mahony built this once-popular style of diner in 1942, of which only about ten others of similar design and vintage still stand. Only the former Riverview Diner displays a similar degree of preservation, but you'll have to fly to England to see it. In 1991, the Fatboy's restaurant chain in that country purchased it and several other vintage diners for use in their ultimately doomed venture.

Collin's Diner and its owner, Mike Hamzy, have both had their share of press. A prominent article published in the *New York Times* featured the diner, and just about every guide to the region gives at least some mention to this sky and cobalt blue monument to the streamline moderne design movement at its peak. Hamzy purchased the diner in 1970, but according to his wife, Aida, he retired from the day-to-day operations in the early 1990s, leaving the business in her hands, with help from their son and daughter.

The diner concentrates on the typical sandwich and comfort food fare. A section of the menu also lists Lebanese specialties such as hummus, tabouleh, and loobi, a mixture of green beans, tomatoes, and garlic, but Aida will only prepare these items in summer. The best thing on the menu here is the diner itself, and the family deserves emphatic kudos for their efforts to preserve this gem. It appears that almost everything affixed by O'Mahony workers remains in place—the black marble countertop, the hardwood booths, the streamlined sconces—and the sweeping lines of the diner inspire awe.

The diner sits in a national historic district that includes Canaan's long-shuttered train station. The New Haven Railroad once served these northwestern Connecticut hill towns and their prosperous industries. Another of those towns, Winsted, to the east along U.S. Route 44, thrived well into the 1960s. The town had at least two diners until that time, when one moved a little farther south to North Torrington on old Route 8 for use as a tavern. Winsted's sole holdout provides another excellent opportunity to enjoy a diner at its best and most basic.

ROUTE 12 DINER DRIVE

New England gave birth to the American diner, and the region remains the home of some of its finest examples. Instead of spending weeks searching out the 300 authentic diners that dot the landscape, you can take a brief diner drive along Route 12. This old north-south commercial route through the heart of New England incorporates plenty of rural and urban scenery, serves up some excellent meals, and introduces the uninitiated to a variety of diner styles, designs, and cuisine.

Keep in mind these important rules for the road:

- Most of the diners mentioned here serve only breakfast and lunch most days, so call ahead for hours.
- Pace your appetite—a good diner tour can end too quickly without proper pacing. You don't have to sample everything on the menu; aim for one course per diner.
- The coffee quality is usually a good indicator of the whole menu.
- You only live once, so go ahead and have two desserts if the experience warrants.
- Pack plenty of film, but don't take pictures inside without the permission of the owners.
- Don't steal the menu—or anything else. Ask for a menu and they might just give you one.

Start your tour in Groton, Connecticut, by taking Exit 85 off I-95. Follow the ramp to Bridge Street. The ramp winds right and almost to the front door of Norm's Diner, one of two diners that continue to serve the town as they have for the past fifty years. You'll find very basic home-cooked meals here in a clean setting—a good value. Up the road, Rosie's Diner sports a classic neon sign and offers hearty home cooking. Both Groton diners allow smoking in their relatively small spaces, and both run a twenty-four-seven operation.

Beyond Norwich, in the small town of Jewett City, you'll find the 1920s vintage Charlene's Diner. Owner Charlene Schultz still runs this much-loved local institution, as she has for the past thirty years. I visited on a Friday, allowing me to try the light and tasty fish sandwich and Charlene's own clam chowder.

The route does not present another diner until Dayville, but what a diner awaits you. The big neon "EAT" sign serves as a welcome beacon for Zip's Diner,

The Winsted Diner sits obliquely on its sliver of property on Main Street, and though some remodeling obscures its original architecture, diner enthusiasts should not miss this place. Run since 1972 by Bob Radocchio, the Winsted Diner takes its customers on a loving trip into the past in a lively but professional setting. The diner's interior, which retains much of its

a classic 1954 O'Mahony stainless diner with a full-service menu served seven days a week in a smoke-free atmosphere. The Yankee-style cooking is simple, honest, and consistent.

The rest of Route 12 in Connecticut offers no diners but plenty of appealing scenery. Leaving the state and entering Massachusetts, in the border town of Webster you'll find Nap's Diner, a precious 1931 Worcester diner. It abuts the sidewalk and serves much the same fare as its sibling restaurant next door. Don't stop here without visiting the restaurant as well. It has a cozy atmosphere and shares the diner's menu, heritage, and degree of preservation.

Talk to anyone who lives within 50 miles of Carl's Oxford Diner, in Oxford, and they'll all mention the portions—they're huge. When asked how they get away with shoveling out such heaps of food and still stay in business, owner Paul Bremmer replies, "We are a nonprofit organization!"

Worcester not only gave birth to the smiley face and the diner-building industry, but it also boasts the fourth-highest number of actual diners in the country. Within Worcester city limits, Route 12 bypasses the city's sampling, but several are worthy of side trips.

When people think of Worcester's Diners, they immediately conjure up the image of the recently restored Boulevard Diner (now a national landmark) and its glorious neon. Though it's not as pristine as its across-the-street competition, sitting at the window of the Parkway Diner affords a lovely view of the Boulevard while eating a piece of lasagna as big as your head. Plunked down in the 1960s, when the nearby Wyman-Gordon plant still hummed away, the steel-clad Corner Lunch (also recently listed as a national landmark) boasts having the most seating capacity of any diner in the city. I've always loved the burgers at the Corner Lunch. The 1940s vintage Miss Worcester Diner, offers typical Worcester diner fare—big, cheap, and satisfying. The Miss Worcester sits across from the factory that built it, which closed in 1961.

Continuing north along Route 12, you'll enjoy more scenic vistas of the Wachusett Reservoir, pastoral New England farmland, and a brush with Mount Wachusett, a popular winter playground for central Massachusetts. In Leominster, Tim's Diner, now operated by Tim Kamataris Jr., continues the tradition begun by Tim Sr. of the quintessential home-cooked meal with a twist: the

(continued on page 220)

original character, invokes smiles and chuckles thanks to all the little signs and placards, and it often seems that a visit to the Winsted allows strangers to learn more about the local community than they ever wanted. The chatter comes as fast and furious as the service in the Winsted, but thanks to Bob's gracious demeanor, it stays civilized and friendly. And long before

(continued from page 219)
trademark clam chowder. Though some brickwork covers this unique Silk City diner, the interior remains as fresh, clean, and original as the day it left the factory in 1949.

Leominster's sister city to the north, Fitchburg, features a good art museum, grand older mill buildings, and the Moran Square Diner. In one of the best-preserved, prettiest diners anywhere in the country, the food served by Chris and Mary Gianetti is fresh and varied. Over to the other side of town, the 50/50 Diner on the west end reopened in 2000 to rave reviews from the local paper and residents and looks to have a bright future.

Route 12 then winds northwest on its way to Keene, New Hampshire, where the geography becomes more rugged. In Winchendon, you can't miss the large wooden rocking horse preserved to commemorate the town's toymaking past. Known as Toy Town, the town once featured a diner called the Miss Toy Town Diner, now in nearby Gardner and called the Blue Moon Diner. The diner's food, preservation, and atmosphere warrant a side trip, which easily accommodates another diner. Take Route 68 north to Route 32 north to Route 119 west to Winchester, New Hampshire, a detour of 10 miles. Here you'll find the Mt. Pisgah Diner, run by the most amicable Joni Otto.

If you stay on Route 12, you'll pass through East Swanzey, New Hampshire, and see a rustic on-site restaurant called the Swanzey Diner. Open and busy since 1988, the Swanzey bakes all its own pies from well-crafted recipes. Also try the tasty onion rings.

Keene's is an easy town to love. Boasting a Main Street 132 feet wide, an operating single-screen theater (the Colonial), a great coffee shop (Brewbaker's), and a solid sense of its small-town identity, it also is home to Lindy's Diner. During election season, all presidential prospects seem to warm a seat here, shaking hands and getting earfuls with their mouthfuls. If smoking bothers you, at least stop in briefly to appreciate the early 1960s Paramount design work and the hearty chicken rice soup.

With three diners, as well as two brewpubs and a thriving downtown shopping district, Brattleboro, Vermont, warrants a detour. Stop at both Big Mama's and the Chelsea Royal Diner, each of which alone will make a detour worth the trouble. Otherwise, from Keene, Route 12 continues northwest to Bellows Falls,

the issue ever became a national trend, Bob made his little twenty-stooler smoke-free.

The little diner has a widespread reputation for its food quality. Though everything on the menu, including the big hearty lunches and the homemade desserts, deserves a try, the Winsted's signature meal is the Ra-Doc-A-Doodle

---

where you'll find the Miss Bellows Falls, built in 1941 and added to the National Register of Historic Places in 1983.

Continuing back up Route 12 on the New Hampshire side of the river, you might miss the Heritage Diner in Charlestown without a little guidance. Installed into the north side of an early eighteenth-century home, it now serves as a separate breakfast-and-lunch room for a larger restaurant.

Next stop is Claremont, yet another mill town in transition. This town plays host to the uniquely styled Daddypop's Tumble Inn Diner, a stunning Worcester with richly colored blue and red ceramic tilework. In the able hands of Debbie Carter since 1997, when she and her father, Ken Smith, restored not only the diner's original beauty, but its reputation as well. Get the pancakes and don't miss the home fries—among the best out there.

After Claremont, leave Route 12 for 12A. Staying close to the river affords visits to more diners as well as better views. Hug the eastern bank of the Connecticut River until you reach the country's longest covered bridge at Cornish. It crosses the river into Windsor, Vermont, where you'll find the namesake Windsor Diner, which reportedly has been developing a devoted following.

The tour ends in West Lebanon, New Hampshire. Just before the bridge across the Connecticut River, you'll find the Four Aces Diner, enveloped by a larger building, which ultimately protects the vintage Worcester workmanship. Here you'll find ample portions and good prices in an exquisitely preserved structure.

Route 12A ends at Route 4 in West Lebanon. The actual Route 12 long ago veered northwest up to Quechee, Vermont, a perennial favorite of leaf-peeping tourists. At this point, I recommend an extended tour up Route 4 to the Farina Family Diner in Quechee, Vermont, now a part of Quechee Gorge Village. The diner offers fluffy pancakes, luscious desserts, and professional service.

If you began your trip in Connecticut, you've probably reached White River Junction late in the day and are looking for a place to rest and digest. I recommend the Coolidge Hotel, at 39 South Main Street in downtown White River Junction. Also on the National Register, this hotel once served the throngs of railroad passengers that coursed through one of the three rail routes that converged here. The Coolidge is still in excellent condition, clean, and reasonably priced, and its location provides easy access to most of northern New England. Call ahead for reservations, and rest easy once you get there: (802) 295-3118 or (800) 622-1124.

sandwich, a deceptively simple egg sandwich with fresh Tennessee sausage and American cheese on an English muffin. The Radocchios came across this particular sausage on a trip through the South some years ago and established a permanent supply line with the farm that produces it. As a result, the humble little meal is imbued with a tradition of obvious care and pride that serves to embellish the flavor and the experience.

Sadly, in 2000, Bob's wife and partner in the business died, leaving him to run it with the help of his daughter Trudy. In 2001, advancing in years, he put the diner on the market, but its small size combined with the slow pace of Winsted's revival have made finding just the right buyer a serious challenge. In this high-tech era, finding anyone to fill Bob's shoes won't come easy. Bob's personality and charm have always made his diner hard to leave. With the prospect of such a transition looming, any diner trek into this region should probably begin here. Keep in mind that few of the Connecticut diners visited afterward will leave a similar impression.

The next major town heading south holds perhaps the world's oldest viable diner: Skee's Diner in Torrington. The sight of Skee's immediately sparks a wistful ache. This diner has appeared in almost every guide and photojour-

Arguably the oldest O'Mahony in existence and still in remarkable condition, the landlord of Skee's, Saint Maron's parish, mulls its future.

nalistic publication featuring diners, and it has been painted by John Baeder and photographed by countless amateur historians and photographers.

In 1996, *Roadside* magazine featured a profile of its then-current owner, but since 2001, the circa 1920 vintage O'Mahony has idled on a busy north-end intersection across from a new Walgreen's, the construction of which destroyed the old North End Diner, another 1920s vintage O'Mahony. The Saint Maron Church, which looms behind it, currently owns the diner and property, leasing it to a succession of hopeful individuals since the 1980s. As of 2002, the diner has joined the ranks of historic places listed on the National Register.

The diner got its name from Ed and Tony Cisowski, brothers who purchased the diner in 1946, only two years after Rudy Cielke, Tom Ryan, and John Miran moved the diner from its original location in Old Saybrook, Connecticut. Under the Cisowski brothers, the business prospered in the midst of the North End's bustling factories. During that time, according to Tony, lines almost always snaked out the front pocket door, and "the seats never got cold." The Cisowskis sold the diner and retired in 1975.

The wondrous interior of Skee's exemplifies the diner industry's craftsmanship of that period, and despite some modifications, it will still amaze even those with the most jaded eye. Etched-glass windows, intricately styled ceramic tile, marble countertop, and attention to every detail will cause anyone to wonder why we give up such places. Companies such as O'Mahony essentially built little palaces for the common man, affording them the opportunity to sit and eat in the architectural equivalent of a Rolls-Royce and, for at least half an hour every day, call it their own.

As this is written, the uncertain fate of the diner has caused some nail biting in the community. The church hasn't decided what it plans to do with the structure, and the city's historical society frets over its future. Skee's is not much larger than Casey's Diner in Natick, Massachusetts, its closest rival in the "world's oldest" department, and anyone considering reviving the operation would do well to keep the meals as simple as possible. Any menu that requires too much preparation will overburden the diner's ability to make money. Diners such as these have increasingly landed in private hands or museum exhibits, thanks to the onerous requirements of contemporary restaurant operation, but Skee's Diner has stood so long at the nexus of this neighborhood that its removal would be a painful loss for the community.

To the south, Waterbury typifies the conversion of a wealth-producing industrial economy to a wealth-consuming retail economy. The early 1990s saw the demolition of the vast brass mill, the export of its equipment to China, and the eventual construction of a large shopping center in its place. Waterbury's location along the I-84 corridor marks a frontier of sorts for the

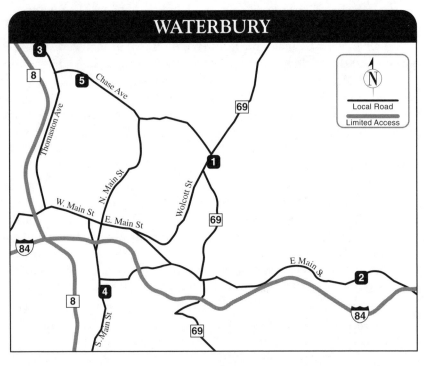

1 Athenian IV Diner: Waterbury (E)
2 Silver Diner: Waterbury (MS)
3 Ted's Diner: Waterbury (BR)
4 Valley Diner: Waterbury (MS)
5 Waterbury Diner: Waterbury (E)

state's large number of big Mediterranean and colonial style diners. Two of the town's five diners fall into this category. Of the remaining three, two still operate. One of those, Ted's Diner, keeps very short, breakfast-only hours. Assumed by Ted Viegas in 2003, the very old 1920s vintage structure, possibly built by Tierney or O'Mahony, has undergone several renovations but retains its basic structural outline. Viegas began with a breakfast-and-lunch operation but cut back the hours when too few showed up for lunch.

The Silver Diner came late to this city's diner collection. In 1994, diner broker Steve Harwin brokered the sale of the former Lafayette Diner, which previously operated in Easton, Pennsylvania, to Nick Agolli, who set it up on East Main Street near the Waterbury city line. Built by Mountain View in 1951, the diner sports a Manno tag, probably because the company had once received it as a trade-in for a newer model.

These days, about the only purpose served by the former Valley Diner is to help diner enthusiasts expand their photo collections. This 1950 Mountain

View sits on a lot with a commanding view in a distressed neighborhood on South Main Street (old Route 8), overlooking mostly idle factories along the banks of the Naugatuck River. A Portland, Maine, based mortgage company holds title to the property and would like to sell the diner, which has been boarded up and vandalized, but substantial unpaid real estate taxes currently hamstring those efforts. The Valley Diner poured its last coffee in 1994.

Just south of Waterbury in Seymour, a rare mid-1950s Kullman dinette stands in the shadow of the Route 8 expressway. Though covered with vinyl siding on the outside and faux-wood paneling on the inside, Tony's Diner still makes for a memorable respite in this mill town. Its owners, Tony and Carmella Librandi, serve a surprisingly varied menu for such a small diner, with a full complement of breakfast items, including blueberry pancakes and a dozen or so omelet varieties, one garnished with asparagus, as well as a lunchtime sandwich selection. The atmosphere allows for the locals to share their concerns over and cures for all the world's problems.

To the west along the I-84 corridor, the bucolic village of Sandy Hook includes another of the state's oldest operating diners. Originally called Corrigan's Diner, much of its remaining history has faded into obscurity, this 1920s vintage barrel roof diner likely originated from Tierney or O'Mahony. Its exterior shows little of the original design, but the cozy interior still has the original vaulted ceiling, marble counter, and twenty vintage stools.

In stark contrast to this most basic of diner forms, the Blue Colony Diner, just up the hill along U.S. Route 6, exemplifies the latest and greatest

A relatively recent addition to the Connecticut list, the Silver Diner was brought from Easton, Pennsylvania, to serve the patrons of the growing number of hotels and big-box stores cropping up on Waterbury's east side.

Just after World War II, the diner companies responded to the return of GIs by turning out a new wave of small diners like Tony's Diner in Seymour. This Kullman dinette model specializes in breakfast with an Italian bent.

of the DeRaffele Company. Completed in 2003, an extensive renovation updated a colonial Manno design and brought the diner's image into the twenty-first century, albeit with a 1950s retro flair. A quick glance around this new construction shows how the industry has come light-years from its lunch wagon roots. Nevertheless, the Blue Colony still has its counter, at which you can sample its lavish desserts and soak in the richly appointed interior furnishings.

Though time has stripped this gem of its jazz-age charms, the Sandy Hook Diner typifies the down-home, local hangout and serves up good homemade desserts.

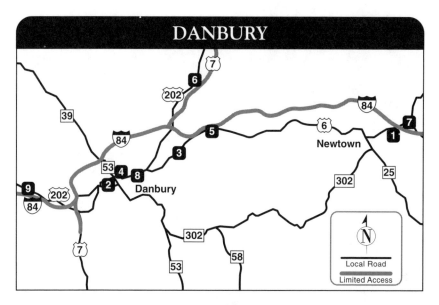

1 Blue Colony Diner: Newtown (P)
2 El Sabor Ecuatoriano: Danbury (MS)
3 Harold's Diner: Danbury (E)
4 Holiday Diner: Danbury (R)
5 New Colony V Diner: Bethel (E)

6 Red Colony Diner: Brookfield (E)
7 Sandy Hook Diner: Sandy Hook (BR)
8 Three Brothers: Danbury (E)
9 Windmill Diner: Danbury (E)

Danbury has five diners, all but one of which fall into the Greek-style category. In the heart of town, a 1952 DeRaffele diner followed a developing trend with vintage diners and changed ethnicities from Greek to Hispanic, becoming El Sabor Ecuatoriano, or the Ecuadorian Flavor. This development in the diner's history reflects the growing Hispanic population in this former hat-making center. The well-preserved diner was originally called the New Englander, and then for a short time the Little Athens.

Also in Danbury, Harold's Diner merits a particular footnote in diner history because of its role in an ambitious but failed plan to establish a regional diner chain called the Sit Down Diners. The energetic Jim Tourtelloite, a University of Massachusetts graduate, initially purchased this 1985 Mediterranean-style Kullman in 1999 to test recipes and theories before the construction and installation of a brand new retro-style flagship diner in Hadley, Massachusetts. The enterprise lasted only three years and shut down before he could establish a third outlet. The Danbury diner reopened in 2003 under new ownership as Harold's.

North of Danbury stands the state's only known Musi diner. The Carteret, New Jersey, company began in the mid-1960s, when Ralph Musi quit his job

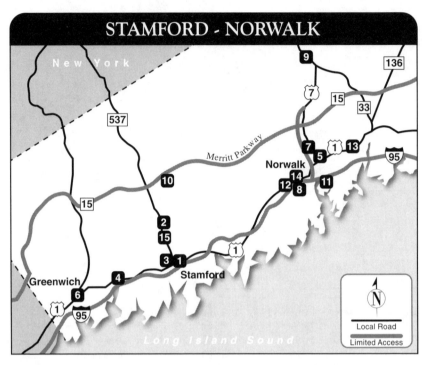

STAMFORD - NORWALK

1 Brasitas: Stamford (BR)
2 Bull's Head Diner: Stamford (P)
3 Curley's Diner: Stamford (R)
4 Emmanuel Upholstery: Cos Cob (BR)
5 Family Diner: Norwalk (MS)
6 Glory Days Diner: Greenwich (P)
7 Jimmy's Diner: Norwalk (R)
8 John's Diner: S. Norwalk (BR)

9 Orem's Diner: Wilton (P)
10 Parkway Diner: Stamford (MS)
11 Penny's Diner: Norwalk (E)
12 Post Road Diner: Norwalk (MS)
13 Sherwood Diner: Westport (E)
14 Silver Star Diner: Norwalk (P)
15 Stamford Diner: Stamford (E)

at Kullman Industries to set out on his own. Musi's early jobs look almost like carbon copies of the diners built by his former employer, and the Red Colony in Brookfield takes most of its design cues from a typical Kullman colonial diner. The Red Colony displays a remarkable degree of preservation for a diner of its vintage.

South of Danbury, the drive down U.S. Route 7 winds through the wealthiest corner of the state. It takes a while to reach the first diner on this particular leg. In 2003, the owners of Orem's Diner in Wilton decided to upgrade and expand in a new location with a brand new DeRaffele-built diner. The diner's rather subdued gray and white exterior, in contrast to DeRaffele's usual broad application of mirror-finished stainless steel, resulted from a town-imposed design restriction. In the diner's interior, however, DeRaffele pulled out all the stops. Marble tiled floors, granite countertops, and expertly fashioned stainless trim all come together for a pleasing and very dinerlike setting. Orem's is a large Greek-style operation that serves a wide selection of sandwiches, hot plates, breakfast items, and Mediterranean specialties, all prepared with above-average quality.

Norwalk presents surprisingly diverse examples of diners from various periods in the industry's history. It is in Norwalk that Kullman Industries inaugurated the 1980s by building the world's first million-dollar-diner for the Savvidis family. The expansive, corporate-friendly, ultramodern structure would look completely natural as an airport terminal. Indeed, by that time, Kullman Industries had already diversified its operation to construct exactly those types of buildings, as well as other institutional structures such as banks, schools, and even prisons.

The Silver Star's interior has hardly changed since then. Gleaming and new in 1980, the broad interior application of mirrors, decorative glass panels, and polished marble in this multisectioned diner-restaurant looks like a set for *Saturday Night Fever.*

The two diners in the immediate vicinity of the Silver Star have a more classic design. Though closed since 1995, John's Diner contrasts sharply with megaplex diners such as the Silver Star. This small 1927 vintage Tierney had a long life as a classic roadside eatery along the old post road, though its fate remains undecided as of this writing.

A little farther west on U.S. Route 1, a happy diner restoration story unfolds at the Post Road Diner. Its purchase in 1996 by the Giapoutzis family also marked the beginning of a slow but steady restoration of the 1947 Paramount. The Post Road is now a successful, fun, family-friendly diner and restaurant.

Another significant vintage find in this city is the Family Diner on 71 Main Street, as you head north out of town. Few mid-1950s Mountain Views exist in this part of the state, particularly one in such original condition. Indeed, Connecticut currently has only nine examples of this particular diner make.

New England's only Bixler found in Stamford still serves food, but only the trained eye would recognize it as a diner structure. Until the mid-1990s, it was called Post Road Luncheonette and then the Pin Stripes Diner. In 2002, it became Brasitas, serving upscale Spanish Latino fare—and doing it extremely well—with recipes that originate from all parts of South America. Remodeling over the years has left the diner with none of its original interior features, and from the outside, only the outlines of the diner's barrel roof and overall proportions remain intact. For more information and a peek at the menu, visit the café's website at www.brasitas.com.

In the heart of Stamford's transformed downtown beats the diner heart of Curley's, a stubborn little holdout against urbanization. In the mid-1990s, Curley's Diner faced a date with the bulldozer as the city attempted to condemn the property for the benefit of a private developer who planned to build a luxury residential high-rise. The city had offered Curley's owner, Maria Aposporos, whose business had occupied the location since the early 1980s, $233,000 for the property; they then planned to sell the site to the developer for $4.6 million. Aposporos fought back, and after a protracted legal battle, the diner emerged unscathed, a community landmark and now rather famous thanks to the national coverage of this controversy.

Curley's Diner was extensively renovated not long after its purchase by Aposporos. The Mountain View had been kept in its original condition up until that point by its initial owner, Herluf "Curley" Svenningsen. Today little but the basic dimensions remain of the original diner.

Stamford's best-preserved classic diner draws customers and its name from its location at the north end of town near the Merritt Parkway. The majestic Parkway Diner on High Ridge Road exemplifies the optimistic DeRaffele flair of the late 1950s, and an interior renovation did little to change the general feel. Its owner, Lusche Gjuraj, manages an operation responsible for some excellent meals, such as a fine chicken marsala. If you're in a hurry, grab a homemade doughnut and a cup of strong coffee to go.

Toward Greenwich, another very old diner withers away on U.S. Route 1. In Cos Cob, a 1920s vintage Tierney teeters on the verge of oblivion. It entered the 1990s as Than's before becoming Ginny's for a short while in

This former diner reportedly came from the Tierney plant, but it last served meals in the early 1990s. Its structural viability somewhat in doubt, this diner won't likely survive to feed another customer.

PHOTO BY PEDAR NESS

Larry's Diner in its heyday.

Mulino's Italian Restaurant is the latest blow to the demise of the once-precious Larry's Diner in Fairfield. Moved from its Main Street location in 1990 by a restaurateur with plans to go upscale with the 1920s O'Mahony, Larry's has instead devolved into a shell of its glorious self.

1996, finally closing around 1998. It is currently used as storage space for Emmanuel Upholstery.

The ultimately affluent community of Greenwich also has a diner in its midst, but you'd be hard-pressed to identify it without a guide. The Glory Days Diner shows the results of a very stringent design code the town enforces

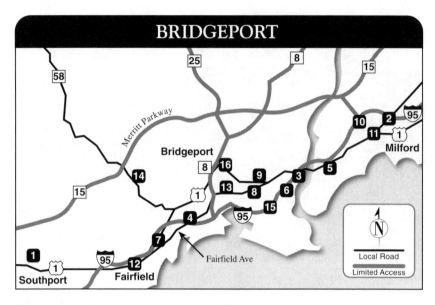

BRIDGEPORT

1 Athena Diner: Southport (E)
2 Athenian Diner III: Milford (P)
3 Blue Sky Diner: Stratford (E)
4 Bridgeport Flyer: Bridgeport (E)
5 Bridgeport Flyer: Milford (E)
6 Duchess Diner: Stratford (P)
7 Fairfield Diner: Fairfield (E)
8 Frankie's Diner: Bridgeport (E)

9 Hi Way Diner: Bridgeport (E)
10 Kimberly Diner: Milford (EM)
11 Milford Diner: Milford (MS)
12 Mulino's Italian Restaurant: Fairfield (BR)
13 New Colony Diner: Bridgeport (E)
14 Penny's II Diner: Fairfield (E)
15 Two Guys Diner: Stratford (E)
16 White's Diner: Bridgeport (MS)

upon its businesses. This inconspicuous DeRaffele betrays its heritage only through the subtle use of stainless steel as trim around the windows and the tag in its entryway. The diner serves a standard menu of comfort food, large breakfasts, and Greek specialties. The larger diners in this region of Connecticut also offer matzo ball soup, and the Glory Days serves one of the better versions.

East of Norwalk, time has removed most of the older diners from along the old post road between there and Fairfield. Two DeRaffele diners, the Sherwood (1970s) and the Athena (1980s), await visits on this segment of highway. Both serve competent Greek-influenced fare.

In Fairfield, locals still remember the fabled Larry's Diner, a 1928 O'Mahony that had appeared in the pages of *Diners of the Northeast* and a John Baeder painting. *Diners of the Northeast* recounts that the diner's original owner, Larry Doyle, lost it in a poker game to Charlie Kadar, who kept the diner's name and its neon sign shaped like a coffee cup.

In 1986, restaurateur Ross Proctor purchased the worn-out diner and moved it to its current location on Miller Street. He then renovated its interior as a high-gloss interpretation of a 1930s restaurant, with black-and-white-checkered tiles along with its original woodwork, ceiling, and nickel grill hoods. Proctor put the neon sign in the attached dining room. Subsequent ownership installed French doors in place of the windows and removed the counter, backbar, and most other vestiges of this classic. Today the building houses Mulino's Italian Restaurant.

As you enter Bridgeport from the west along Fairfield Avenue, the diner parade begins at the Bridgeport Flyer. The city's namesake diner is a 1968 Swingle replacement for a 1941 Sterling Streamliner that once sat on the site, hence the illustrative moniker now incongruously applied to this colonial design.

Of Bridgeport's remaining examples, only White's Diner on U.S. Route 1 in the north end of town predates the Kennedy administration. The late 1950s DeRaffele exhibits the same postwar styling as the Parkway Diner in Stamford, although the interior has been renovated. The above-average food and service this diner offers do justice to the tradition.

At the Bridgeport-Stratford line, you'll encounter the faded beauty, the Hi Way Diner. The colonial style, adopted early on by Kullman and copied here by Musi, has begun to acquire a significant degree of kitsch value in the past few years. The fact that so few remain intact from their mid- to late-1960s heyday will ultimately frustrate the research of future diner historians in the years to come. The Hi Way, which has seen at least one major interior renovation, continues to leave a bright, cheerful impression upon regulars and new customers alike. Its service and food quality are good, and the diner serves a tasty breakfast in a neighborly atmosphere.

This colonial-style Swingle replaced a Sterling Streamliner in 1968, hence the incongruity of the name. Find the Bridgeport Flyer just off Exit 25 of I-95.

This flamboyant design comes from DeRaffele in the late 1950s. White's Diner on U.S. Route 1 in Bridgeport serves excellent Italian specialties.

The Blue Sky Diner hasn't changed much since Fodero installed it on this location in Milford. The diner industry struggled through the 1960s, offering larger colonial and Mediterranean designs such as this one.

Stratford's three diners all date from the 1970s or later. The Blue Sky Diner's quasi-colonial design shows one of Fodero's last styles before it folded in 1981 and remains barely altered. The others are both DeRaffele products, the Duchess Diner from 1986 and the Two Guys Diner (now closed) from the late 1970s.

DeRaffele did and still does rather well in this region. One of its newest and more striking projects came to Milford in 2001, when George Daoutis added another location to his growing Athenian Diner chain near the I-95 entrance. The venerable diner builder had generally resisted the retro diner trend of the past fifteen years, choosing instead to roll out its own contemporary supermodern designs that have typically featured broad exterior applications of mirrors, colored glass, and highly polished stainless steel fashioned into completely new styles. In recent years, the company has allowed many retro aspects to slip into its designs, but diners such as the Athenian III show a distinctive DeRaffele style that still looks very much like a diner.

By the time this book hits the shelves, the venerable Milford Diner should have reopened at its new location. The only Silk City between New Haven and the New York line closed in 2003 when its lease expired and the owners refused to pay an increase in rent. The diner remains idle at this writing, with a "for lease" sign in the window.

Still another 1950s DeRaffele continues to operate in West Haven, tucked away on Elm Street, well off the Route 1 diner trail but well suited for local traffic destined for and returning from New Haven to the east. The Elm Diner has happily retained the originality of its exuberant exterior, though inside, half of its counter was removed to accommodate more seating. The diner serves a comfort food menu complete with the requisite sandwich selections, breakfast items, and Greek specialties.

New Haven faces serious challenges in the postindustrial economy, with many impoverished neighborhoods despite the wealthy presence of Yale University. As a result, the university has begun to take a much more proac-

DeRaffele goes boldly into the future with this striking design of the Athenian IV Diner in Milford.

tive role in the community by investing in its redevelopment, but more progress awaits. The city still has three diner classics. The latest to arrive, the New Star Diner, came to New Haven in 1995, soon after a fire consumed the Hi Way Diner, a Mountain View on Water Street not too far away.

Helmi Ali purchased the shuttered New State Diner in Ansonia, Connecticut, and moved it to New Haven, renaming it the New Star. This well-maintained early 1960s Fodero was futuristically designed for the space age, with a glance back at the colonial period. Large plate-glass windows and flared roof overhangs contrast with wood-grain interior paneling and brown naugahyde upholstered booths for an interior only a diner company could build. Ali keeps the New Star bright all night on weekends and closes after dinner on weekdays.

In the heart of the city near the Yale campus, Tandoor currently serves fine Indian cuisine. Before the transition in 1993, Ross Proctor had fashioned the 1955 Mountain View after the diner-as-bistro precedent established by Manhattan's Empire Diner in 1976. In that case, Jack Doenias took a run-down midtown diner in a depressed neighborhood and introduced haute cuisine. The irony struck chords in both the New York art and restaurant scenes, with repercussions throughout the country. Proctor attempted something similar with the Elm City, introducing subdued mood lighting, a dress code, a baby grand piano, and gourmet menu items. Customers sipped fine wines while listening to live jazz. But unlike the Empire

Removed from this longtime location, the Milford Diner is a Silk City, fairly rare for the Nutmeg State.

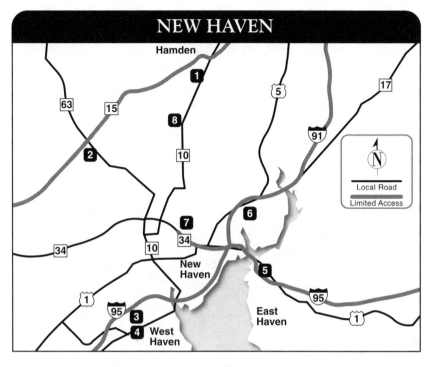

NEW HAVEN

1 Acropolis Diner: Hamden (E)
2 Athenian Diner I: New Haven (E)
3 Duchess Diner: West Haven (E)
4 Elm Diner: West Haven (MS)

5 Forbes Diner: New Haven (MS)
6 New Star Diner: New Haven (EM)
7 Tandoor: New Haven (MS)
8 Three Brothers Diner: Hamden (E)

Diner, here the concept didn't take. Today the diner remains remarkably intact, and the new owners have been successful with the South Asian cuisine they introduced in 1994. For diner fans who enjoy Indian food, Tandoor comes well recommended.

Since Richard Ezold closed Forbes Diner in 1995, the stunning, showroom-quality, three-sectioned 1957 Fodero spent the remainder of the decade collecting dust. Set down the year before I-95 opened to traffic, it replaced an older, smaller diner that likely served both the local workforce and the Route 1 transient trade. The path of the brand new I-95 practically passes through the diner's backyard, and an on-ramp to the westbound side is located within a few hundred yards of the diner, but traffic in this direction will not see a corresponding off-ramp. To access the diner from I-95 westbound today, drivers must exit nearly 2 miles before the diner ever comes into view and drive along a congested frontage road through several traffic lights. The diner reopened in 1999, and thus far its new owner, Adam

Ismaill, has made no major renovations. He serves basic diner fare with Greek specialties.

On the north side of New Haven, Routes 63 and 5 both will bring you past newer Greek-style diners with similar menus. On Route 63 near the entrance to the Wilbur Cross Parkway, the Athenian I Diner, an early 1990s DeRaffele, sits in the middle of several shopping plazas and operates round the clock. On U.S. Route 5 between New Haven and Meriden is another large Greek-style diner, the Athena Diner II, built in the 1970s and recently renovated.

Tandoor serves excellent Indian cuisine, but the operators have made few changes to this very original Mountain View in New Haven.

Few Fodero diners remain that display the same degree of originality as the spectacular Forbes Diner in New Haven.

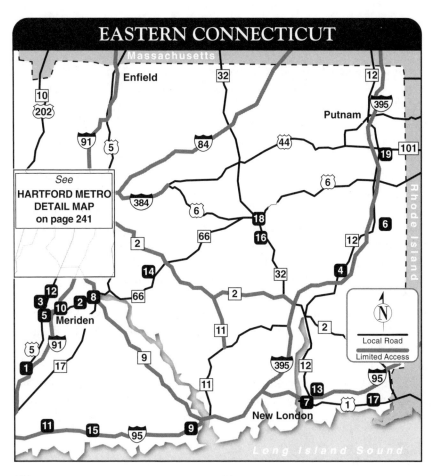

EASTERN CONNECTICUT

1 Athena Diner II: North Haven (E)
2 Athenian Diner II: Middletown (E)
3 Cassidy's Diner: Meriden (BR)
4 Charlene's Diner: Jewett City (MS)
5 Dragon Phoenix: Meriden (MS)
6 Hangout: Moosup (BR)
7 Norm's Diner: Groton (MS)
8 O'Rourke's Diner: Middletown (MS)
9 Old Saybrook Diner: Old Saybrook (P)
10 Olympos Diner: Meriden (R)

11 Parthenon Diner: Branford (P)
12 Quality Time Food & Spirits: Meriden (BR)
13 Rosie's Diner: Groton (MS)
14 Route 66 Diner: East Hampton (MS)
15 Shoreline Diner: Guilford (E)
16 South Windham Diner: South Windham (MS)
17 Stonington Diner: Stonington (BR)
18 Trolley Stop Restaurant: Willimantic (BR)
19 Zip's Diner: Dayville (MS)

Meriden, a city once known for its silversmithing industries but more recently for its struggles with urban renewal, has four diners still in operation. The Dragon Phoenix, a 1960 Silk City on the south end of Broadway, serves Chinese food. On the other end of Broadway, a prewar diner of indeterminate make operates as a tavern called Quality Time. On the far end of

East Main Street is another circa late 1950s Silk City called the Olympos Diner. A renovation has encased the original building and expanded the diner area.

Downtown, a 1949 Silk City has become Cassidy's, named for the son of owner Jay Eagle Delaney. Eagle bought the business in 2002 after a relatively long run as the Justin Time Diner. During that period, owner Steven Prescott created a series of stirs in the local community with antics that included piping country music outside the diner. Prescott purchased the diner after a short stint as a Jamaican restaurant, which followed a similarly truncated period as the Court House II Diner. In 1988, John Baeder painted the diner as the Palace and selected it for his revised edition of *Diners*.

To the east in Middletown, the steamed cheeseburger seems to have put O'Rourke's Diner on the map, but it's only one of several places that serve this curious sandwich in this part of the state. Ground beef is placed in a special steam box until cooked and then topped with a healthy dollop of melted New York cheddar cheese. Brian O'Rourke prefers his with mustard, but many eat it with lettuce and tomato. Though O'Rourke's still serves one of the better examples of this burger around, the past decade has seen the diner aspire to a more vaunted level of cuisine, thanks to Brian's desire to experiment with the full potential of his diminutive Mountain View Restaurant on the north end of Middletown's Main Street.

Connecticut has precious few classic diners, but one hopeful prospect has surfaced in Kensington, just south of New Britain. Now largely bypassed along the east-west corridor by the Route 9 expressway, the town's center

Cassidy's Diner hopes to ride a downtown revival in Meriden.

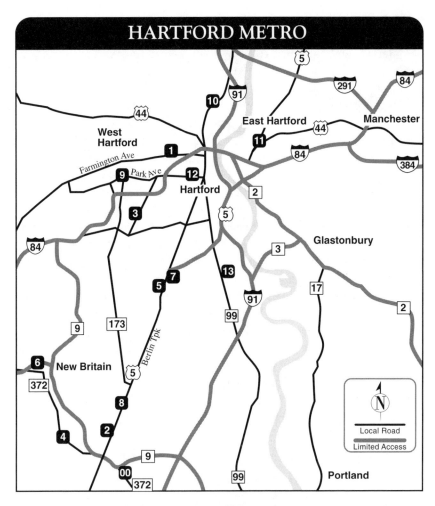

HARTFORD METRO

1 Aetna Diner: Hartford (MS)
2 Berlin Pizza: Berlin (R)
3 East West Grill: West Hartford (EM)
4 Even Stephen's Restaurant: Kensington (BR)
5 Makris Diner: Wethersfield (MS)
6 Miss Washington Diner: New Britain (EM)
7 New England Country Collectibles:
  Wethersfield (EM)
8 Olympia Diner: Newington (E)
9 Quaker Diner: West Hartford (BR)
10 Rajun Cajun: Hartford (MS)
11 Triple A Diner: East Hartford (E)
12 Washington Diner: Hartford (E)
13 Wethersfield Diner: Wethersfield (MS)

has clung onto a rare 1939 O'Mahony Diner that recently has come back to life thanks to another trained chef turned diner cook.

When Stephen Jagiello returned to his native Kensington, he had already spent almost two decades in the food service industry, and like many others with his degree of experience, he wanted his own place. Joe's Diner had closed in 1997 after the death of its owner. Jagiello decided to revive the restaurant only after much consideration, but ultimately he took the leap and purchased the diner. He and a devoted corps of volunteers spent months cleaning and repairing the diner and attached kitchen worn down from years of deferred maintenance. In 2001, the diner reopened as Even Stephens.

Several past renovations have changed or removed all but the general outlines of the vintage structure, leaving only the original door and ceiling. The diner's menu is heavy on sandwiches and breakfast items, and its neighborly atmosphere embodies everything a diner represents in this area. Even Stephens also provides catering, and every three weeks it takes reservations for a full-course dinner where Jagiello can showcase his talents. He sees the diner eventually branching out into a more upscale menu.

In all of Connecticut, few diners inspire as much reverence as the Olympia Diner on the Berlin Turnpike in Newington, built around 1955 and likely the largest O'Mahony diner in existence. Its roadside majesty is crowned with one of the most fabulous neon signs on a diner anywhere. The Olympia made quite a bit of news a few years ago when it announced that it would start closing at 11:00 at night, ending a long-standing tradition of round-the-clock service. The diner's menu lists a broad selection.

A few miles north is another large O'Mahony, the Makris Diner, which came to the turnpike a few years earlier than the Olympia and also has considerable roadside frontage. Closed and vandalized in the late 1980s, it came back to life in 1991 thanks to Rejean Viel, who maintained a good, basic, well-

Probably the largest diner that O'Mahony ever built, the Olympia created quite a local stir when it decided to close down its graveyard shift. Still, the awesome sight of that neon sign continues to draw them in, making it a perennial favorite for the late-night crowd.

In its last years of operation, O'Mahony built some big diners. The Makris would eventually be surpassed by the Olympia down the road, but the eighty-plus seater still serves a good breakfast and lunch to a rebounding Berlin Turnpike.

run diner until he sold it in 1998. Although Viel has left the scene, his wife works for the new owner as a waitress. She now works forty-hour weeks but describes this as part-time in comparison to when she and her husband owned it. "I no longer work weekends, and now at the end of the day, I can go home."

In New Britain, the Miss Washington Diner on Washington Street remains unscathed in the wake of major urban renewal. This pristine Kullman Princess model lies shoe-horned into a side street location and serves standard diner fare with competence. Though it's hard to find, it won't disappoint the fan of the classic diner, with its expansive

The Main Street Diner replaced the 1920s vintage Cunningham's in the 1960s.

Harry Bassilakis, grandson of the original owner, restored his family's diner to its original 1930s charm in 1988 and subsequently sparked a neighborhood renaissance.

plate-glass windows and flamboyant space-age design where George Jetson would feel right at home.

In Plainville, fans of both diners and neon should not miss the Main Street Diner. The late 1950s Master diner, one of only four in New England, sits proudly on West Main Street in the heart of town, adorned with one of the more amazing neon signs on any diner. The outsize words "Main" and "Street" straddle a center vertical neon "Diner," atop which sits a coffee cup. According to the town's historian the diner actually got its name from its former location—Main Street in Hempstead, Long Island. Currently operated by Nicole Ouellete, the Main Street serves an excellent seafood chowder.

The Quaker Diner in West Hartford is a free-standing 1931 luncheonette. The clean, happy, bustling neighborhood grill shows its pedigree with its vaulted ceiling, glass counters, and high-backed wooden booths. Freed from the restraints of over-the-road transport, the builders allowed for a wider interior and seemed to spare no expense on classic diner ornament. Harry Bassilakis's grandfather had the diner built but later sold the business outside the family. The new owners then made some modernizing renovations. Harry bought the diner back in 1987, restoring this gem to its original condition and helping to spark a still-growing revival in the Park Street neighborhood. The diner's easy access off I-85 (Exit 43) make it a must-stop for anyone traveling to or from points south. The Quaker serves home-cooked meals, including an award-winning meat loaf.

A Paramount in West Hartford, the East West Grille, now serves Asian cuisine. According to published accounts, it seems to have built up a healthy following.

Hartford's former status as the most beautiful city in America continues to make itself evident in its Victorian-era neighborhoods, despite the city's recent economic troubles, which unfortunately led to the closure of the city's three remaining diners, all built by Paramount. The city currently remains the home of one of the most spectacular examples of Paramount construction, the former Aetna Diner, so named because of its proximity to

A recent development among vintage diners sees them becoming ethnic restaurants. Here, the East West Grille, a 1962 Paramount, features Thai cuisine.

Aetna Diner, now closed, awaits new owners in this struggling Hartford neighborhood.

the insurance company headquarters. This flamboyant, double-wide expression of the streamline moderne styling has not served a single cup of coffee since at least 2000, when its last short-lived incarnation as the Hog River Grille came to a close. The Aetna is one of only three remaining Paramounts with a burnished circle pattern on the exterior skin. Preservation groups and the *Hartford Courant* have urged the city to save this landmark as part of an eventual urban revival. Its current owners, who live in New Jersey and Florida, made an attempt in 2002 to auction the building off the site but failed to attract any bidders.

The Washington Diner, a 1960s colonial model on Washington Street, closed in 2000. Hal's Aquarius Diner, another postwar beauty in Hartford's Terry Square, closed in 2003. These diners also lie in struggling districts, but a recent report in the *Hartford Courant* has the Terry Square Diner reopening in 2004 as the Rajun Cajun Restaurant.

The economy of Connecticut's southeast corner once hinged upon the success of the General Dynamics submarine plant in Groton and the navy base up the river. Groton and New London, across the mouth of the Thames River, prospered for years as thousands of workers earned good wages building nuclear-powered submarines and other vessels for the navy. In recent years, however, casinos have come to dominate the economic affairs of this region, with the establishment of the Foxwoods and the Mohegan Sun resorts. Their construction dovetailed with the end of the Cold War and the decline of the submarine market. The piles of money now pouring into the region enter through slot machines instead of defense contracts, and the effects of the economic impact have yet to completely unfold. The two diners

Terry Square Diner

About the only thing that changed on the typical Silk City diner between 1936 and 1954 was the color scheme and the encroaching use of stainless steel trim. The cool aqua atmosphere of Norm's perhaps is fitting for a community known for building submarines.

in Groton, which originally served the skilled tradesmen who built boats, now cater mostly to retirees on their way gamble away their pensions.

Depending on your orientation, Groton serves as either the end or the beginning of one of the best diner drives in New England. Route 12, which terminates here, extends through some of the region's most scenic and historic cities, towns, and villages. Along the way, the route affords the traveler the opportunity to visit a fascinating cross section of diner history dating from the Roaring Twenties to the late 1950s.

Both diners in Groton sport Silk City tags, and both operate twenty-four hours most days. Reportedly, they both also do a brisk business, but Norm's Diner has the added benefit of an attached restaurant and lounge area, so it also serves as a kind of after-hours club for its bar patrons. Norman and Ann Brochu have owned this 1954 diner since 1961. Norm's serves the standard diner menu in a setting so aqua in hue, the customer almost feels submerged in tropical waters. Prices for the home-cooked meals are reasonable, and the diner offers a good view of the massive Gold Star Memorial Bridge, which carries I-95 and U.S. Route 1 over the Thames.

Rosie's Diner has no connection to the diner or character in the paper towel ads; it got its name from a real person named Rose Scott, who bought the business in 1986. Today her son Steve handles most of the day-to-day operations for this bustling little diner. Rosie's serves big plates of standard diner fare and packs in the business at all hours of the night.

In the little town of Jewett City, another of New England's oldest diners still keeps customers satisfied. Charlene's Diner, named for its owner, Charlene Schultz, has seen a renovation or two over the years, but the 1920–1930s vintage barrel roof diner retains plenty of historic charm and serves an excellent Rhode Island style clam chowder. Places like Charlene's are still a perfect place to go to take the pulse of society. Debates about the growing influence of casinos continue to surface in little diners such as this one while customers

This Silk City diner became Rosie's after Nancy Walker played the role on television, but there is a real Rosie behind the name. Open twenty-four hours, Rosie's is usually bustling at any given hour.

Customers come to Charlene's Diner for the friendly talk and homemade chowders.

chow down excellent sandwiches (Friday's fried fish is particularly good) and hearty breakfasts. On the diner's walls are vintage photographs of the diner in its more pristine state.

This tour comes to a close at one of Connecticut's most famous, best-preserved, and highly regarded diners, Zip's Diner in Dayville. Enthusiasts will not find a more welcome sight than that of the neon "EAT" sign towering above the entrance of this 1954 O'Mahony. Casually mention "classic American diner" to anyone around the world and the term evokes images that look much like Zip's.

POST ROAD DINER

1947 PARAMOUNT

312 Connecticut Ave., U.S. Route 1, Norwalk, CT • (203) 866-9777

A happy diner restoration story unfolds at the Post Road Diner. Sometime in the 1970s, former owner John Papadatos encased the 1947 Paramount in brick and stripped its interior of the lavish design work common in the company's diners of the time. In 1996, it was purchased by the Giapoutzis family, and since then, the Post Road Diner has earned a reputation as a solid, honest, family-style restaurant that serves a surprising array of good, home-cooked meals any hour of the day. Today the diner benefits from its proximity to expanding retail development along its stretch of the road, and its late-night hours attract many from the South Norwalk's popular and trendy entertainment district.

Family members—Kathy, Maria, Olga, or Teddy—greet customers at the door and guide them to their seats, which since 2002 are either brand new booths or shiny new stools in a completely renovated interior that was designed by the DeRaffele Company and installed by the family. The sparkling, comfortable seating area pays loving homage to the diner's golden age.

The Giapoutzis family's attention to detail didn't stop at the kitchen door, however. In fact, it began there in 1999 when the family shut down the diner for seven weeks to completely renovate the kitchen. Stylish new menus offer a range of meals, including both classic diner fare and Greek specialties, all prepared with care. Desserts come from the diner's own bakery and get particularly high marks here. In 2001, the diner became smoke-free.

ZIP'S DINER
1954 O'MAHONY
Routes 101 & 12, Dayville, CT • (860) 774-6335

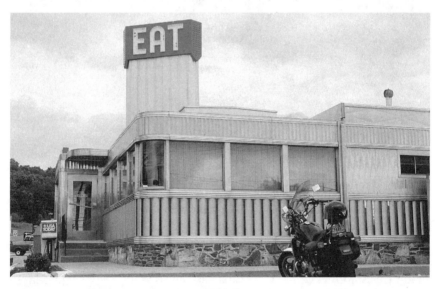

Picture a perfect stainless steel diner with a cool, uncluttered, streamlined interior and a uniformed staff of smiling waitresses serving good home-cooked meals. That's what you'll find at Zip's Diner.

Route 6, Danielson, Conn.

ZIP'S

"New England's Most Modern Dining Car"

The first Zip's Diner came to Danielson, Connecticut, just after World War II. Henry Zipzerra eventually replaced this striking diner with a newer O'Mahony at a new location in Dayville in 1954, but operated both simultaneously for a short time.

Zip's has been part of the Jodoin family since 1965, when they purchased the business from the retiring Henry Zipzerra. It expertly represents the particular style of diner that places most of its emphasis on consistency. Certainly a few of the items on the menu shine, but customers return repeatedly to this diner because of the friendly service, the impeccably clean environs, and the rigidly maintained level of food quality.

Tom Jodoin, current patriarch of the family and the man responsible for the diner's sparkling reputation, manages a well-oiled machine that benefits from its crossroads location. It also now benefits from the year-round north-south casino traffic and wintertime vacationing skiers, as well as the east-west local and interstate trucking trade, as there still is no interstate highway connecting Hartford and Providence.

Polished and businesslike, Jodoin is a restaurant manager who keeps a close eye on all aspects of a rather complex business. Diner owners confined to the kitchen don't often have the opportunity to properly market their businesses, and some of that marketing simply means lots of handshakes with longtime and first-time customers, as well as playing a proactive role in the local community.

In recent years, Dayville and the surrounding towns have seen a rapidly developing residential population growth as well. Increasingly, the diner attracts locals who have settled into Connecticut's "quiet corner," made so by the disappearance of the area's mills and other industries around the Great Depression.

The bustling operation maintains a relatively simple and consistent menu, and the kitchen excels with its homemade soups and the bread pudding. Every visit to Zip's also comes with a friendly smile and a genuine concern for your comfort, and the diner has been smoke-free since 1995.

Zip's Diner still stuns all who see it for the first time, and save for the worn patch of terrazzo in front of the cash register, its pristine condition exemplifies the durability of these special buildings, particularly when, as the Jodoins do, their owners fully appreciate the value of what they have.

O'ROURKE'S DINER
1946 MOUNTAIN VIEW #223
728 Main St., Middletown, CT • (860) 346-6101

Meriden and Middletown form a curious culinary axis for the steamed cheeseburger, found nowhere else in the country, and O'Rourke's Diner serves one of the best examples. Yet despite this particular distinction, Brian O'Rourke has managed to make his diner known today for much, much more than this simple but sublime little sandwich. His love of cooking and creative nature has made O'Rourke's Diner one of the finest in the country. Not only does John Baeder describe it as the best, but it has also received accolades from *Gourmet* magazine, the *New York Times,* and just about every local newspaper and relevant periodical.

O'Rourke practically grew up in the diner, starting at age ten as a "gofer" for his uncle John O'Rourke, well loved and remembered as the man who brought this 1946 Mountain View to town. The brand new diner replaced an older model, continuing the location's diner history, which had begun in the 1920s if not before. O'Rourke's may likely be the oldest Mountain View still in use, a pedigree easily identified thanks to the rounded, glass-block corners that rest upon the company's trademark "cowcatcher" corners.

Brian eventually grew to fill his uncle's shoes and built upon the diner's solid reputation with some amazing culinary feats of his own.

Brian O'Rourke leads the way proving that diners aren't just meat loaf and mashed potatoes. His diner offers up one of the most creative brunch (yes, brunch) menus available anywhere, while retaining the diner's signature item, the steamed cheeseburger.

Though the diminutive diner was long known for its good sandwiches and hearty breakfasts, as well as that cheeseburger, Brian's curiosity and drive would take it into areas rarely explored by diners anywhere up until that time.

The building remained mostly intact until the 1980s, when Brian built a sympathetically designed addition that allowed for a slightly larger dining area and kitchen. Today the relatively small restaurant features an L-shaped dining area that wraps around a new galley kitchen where customers can watch the master work his magic. The expanded capabilities also have allowed Brian to introduce many welcome changes to his menu.

As late as 1980, O'Rourke served a fairly spartan diner menu with no soups or platters, only sandwiches and omelets. Today customers can eat such fare as blackened yellowfin tuna steak with rice, pesto, and cole slaw or a crock of sweet potato soup with greens. Under Brian's management, O'Rourke's has

O'Rourke's Diner caps off the north end of Middletown's Main Street.

established itself as a trendsetter in diner cuisine and has won a "best of" award in just about every relevant category.

Thanks to recent trips to New Orleans, Brian has transformed the diner into a spice lover's haven. His gumbo would satisfy even the most ardent aficionado of Cajun cooking. This high degree of experimentation, mixing traditional fare with the latest and greatest in food trends, often results in some amazing meals. Every visit means a surprise of some sort, but at the same time, there's no guarantee you'll find it on the menu upon future visits. On the other hand, it is perfectly consistent with Brian's nature to make it for you anyway.

O'Rourke's is no longer a twenty-four-hour operation, but it opens at 4:30 in the morning, earlier than most breakfast-and-lunch diners. By that time, Brian has already spent two hours finishing most of the day's baking and likely has begun to prepare a pot of soup for the lunch special. In the early 1990s, Brian added an array of fresh baked goods to the menu, including muffins of many varieties and several breads, with the lemon poppyseed a real favorite.

Though the diner may have originally made its mark with the steamed cheeseburger, O'Rourke's today truly shines on the weekends, when Brian, in deference to the changing dining habits of his local market, serves an absolutely outstanding brunch. The menu includes three typed pages of specials, featuring everything from the classic eggs and homemade hash to a creatively garnished omelet of some type.

Despite all these vaunted culinary aspirations and achievements, O'Rourke's remains a true diner, through and through. This is because, at the end of the day, when the tables are bused, the waitresses count their tips, and the floor is washed, O'Rourke's Diner has spent another day cultivating that precious connection to the community. No one knows the importance of this better than Brian O'Rourke, and thanks to his gregarious nature, this diner has inspired chapters of truly colorful diner lore. Friends and casual customers can usually count on Brian for a good story, much like one might expect from any true Irishman, and eventually hear a heartfelt yarn not likely to be heard in a fast-food joint. What truly separates the diner from the chain is the narrative inspired from the thousands of conversations and handshakes that take place over the marble counters of places such as these.

People like Brian O'Rourke don't come along too often anymore. Those with similar abilities typically seek their fortunes in larger, higher-profile restaurants—that is, if they even enter the food-service business at all. O'Rourke's Diner, with Brian's inspiring presence behind the counter, exemplifies the important role played by the small, locally run diner, and what we stand to lose if it should close and get trucked away.

Today Brian O'Rourke could be considered the grand old man of the neo diner movement. Of all the diners in New England, only the Blue Benn Diner in Bennington, Vermont, another college town, shares a similar heritage and style of operation. Most other diners that fall into this category came along well after O'Rourke and Sonny Monroe first took up their spatulas, but happily, they still inspire others to further redefine the classic diner.

DINER DIRECTORY

CONNECTICUT

Acropolis Diner
1864 Dixwell Ave./Rte. 10
Hamden, CT
(203) 288-0400
1970s Unknown
Mediterranean-style diner with Greek-influenced menu.

Aetna Diner
267 Farmington Ave.
Hartford, CT
1949 Paramount
Formerly the Oasis Diner. One of a handful of Paramounts with burnished, circle-embossed stainless steel skin. Large, double-wide layout, lavishly appointed. Closed since 2000 and located in a distressed neighborhood, though not far from the Mark Twain house.

Athena Diner
3350 Post Rd.
Southport, CT
(203) 259-0603

For a long time, DeRaffele resisted the retro diner trend, but lately the company has put its own spin on the trend, as seen here in the expansive Blue Colony Diner in Newtown.

c. 1989 DeRaffele
Mediterranean-style, multisectioned diner. American food with Greek specialties. Twenty-four-hour operation.

Athena Diner II
320 Washington Ave.
North Haven, CT
(203) 239-0663
Kullman
Mediterranean style. American food with Greek specialties. Open twenty-four hours, seven days.

Athenian Diner I
1426 Whalley Ave./Rte. 63
New Haven, CT
(203) 397-1556
c. 1990 DeRaffele
Mediterranean style. American food with Greek specialties. Open twenty-four hours, seven days.

Athenian Diner II
864 Washington St.
Middletown, CT
(860) 346-2272
1996 DeRaffele
Mediterranean style. American food with Greek specialties. Open twenty-four hours, seven days.

Athenian Diner III
1064 Boston Post Rd.
Milford, CT
(203) 878-5680
1997 DeRaffele
Expansive, multisectioned diner in distinctive quasi-retro style. American food with Greek specialties. Open twenty-four hours, seven days.

Athenian IV Diner
998 Wolcott St./Rte. 69
Waterbury, CT
(203) 419-0242
c. 1985 DeRaffele
Broad menu featuring American food
with Greek specialties. Twenty-four-
hour operation.

Berlin Pizza
196 Berlin Tpk.
Berlin, CT
(860) 828-1321
1953 Mountain View
Pizza joint, heavily remodeled. Lunch
and dinner.

Blue Colony Diner
Church Hill Rd.
Newtown, CT
(203) 426-0745
c. 1980/2003 Manno/DeRaffele
Manno diner renovated by DeRaffele
in 2003. Easy access from I-84. Broad
menu featuring American food with
Greek specialties. Good bread pudding.
Twenty-four-hour operation.

Blue Sky Diner
273 Ferry Blvd.
Stratford, CT
(203) 377-5644
1960's Fodero
Large, eighty-plus-seat diner built in
the transitional post–space-age colonial
style. American food with Greek specialties. Open twenty-four hours, seven days.

Brasitas
954 E. Main St.
Stamford, CT
(203) 323-3176
www.brasitas.com
c. 1930 Bixler
Only Bixler in New England. Thoroughly
remodeled. Formerly the Post Road Lun-

The only Bixler in New England shows little
of its original design, but Brasitas serves up
an expertly prepared Hispanic-inspired menu.

cheonette and the Pinstripes Diner. Full
menu of upscale Hispanic fare.

Bridgeport Flyer
1726 Fairfield Ave.
Bridgeport, CT
(203) 334-6669
1968 Swingle
Colonial style. Replaced Sterling Streamliner in 1968, hence the somewhat
incongruous name. American food with
Greek specialties. Open twenty-four
hours, seven days.

Bridgeport Flyer
249 Bridgeport Ave.
Milford, CT
(203) 878-5121
1973 Swingle
Colonial style. American food with
Greek specialties. Open twenty-four
hours, seven days.

Bull's Head Diner
High Ridge Rd.
Stamford, CT
1993 on-site
Grand retro diner styling. American
food with Greek specialties.

Charlene's Diner, though not perfectly preserved, is loaded with charm.

Cassidy's Diner
82 W. Main St.
Meriden, CT
(203) 238-3301
1949 Silk City # 49212
Stainless steel. In economically distressed downtown location. Basic grilled
diner menu. Homemade cheesecake.
Breakfast and lunch only.

Charlene's Diner
53 Main St.
Jewett City, CT
(860) 376-9465
1920s O'Mahony?
Cozy, weathered jazz-age diner, largely
intact. Serves no-frills Yankee menu and
known for its broth-based chowders.
Breakfast and lunch only; breakfast only
on weekends.

Collin's Diner
Rte. 7 & Rte. 44
Canaan, CT
(860) 824-7040
1942 O'Mahony
Stunning, iconic, golden-age diner in
a historic district. Probably the finest

example of this style still in operation
in this country. American food, with
grilled diner fare. Lebanese specialties
served in the summer only. Breakfast
and lunch only.

Curley's Diner
62 Park Place
Stamford, CT
(203) 348-2020
1949 Mountain View
Heavily renovated with few original
features remaining. Local landmark.
American food with Greek specialties.
Open twenty-four hours, seven days.

Dragon Phoenix
191 Broad St.
Meriden, CT
(203) 634-8884
1960 Silk City #6066
Late model car. Fast Asian fare. Lunch
and dinner.

Duchess Diner
1000 Stratford Ave.
Stratford, CT
(203) 375-7366
1996 DeRaffele
Modern style.

Duchess Diner
706 Campbell Ave.
West Haven, CT
(203) 933-9128
1993 DeRaffele
American food with Greek specialties.
Open twenty-four hours, seven days.

East West Grill
526 New Park Ave.
West Hartford, CT
(860) 236-3287
1962 Paramount
In very good condition. Thai-Asian
cuisine. Lunch and dinner.

Elm Diner
427 Elm St.
West Haven, CT
(203) 933-9966
1957 DeRaffele
Well-kept and striking space-age design. Broad menu featuring American food with Greek specialties. Open twenty-four hours, seven days.

El Sabor Ecuatoriano
101 Railroad Place
Danbury, CT
(203) 748-1020
1952 DeRaffele
Well-kept classic. Formerly the New Englander Diner. Hispanic menu since 2001.

Emmanuel Upholstery
118 River Rd. Ext.
Cos Cob, CT
(203) 869-6081
c. 1925 Tierney
Closed and used for storage. Dilapidated and threatened.

Even Stephens Restaurant
797 Farmington Ave.
Kensington, CT
(860) 829-1130
www.evenstephensusa.com
1930s O'Mahony
Ceiling and front door only remaining original features. Serves very good diner and pub-style fare, with daily specials and homemade soups. Breakfast and lunch.

Fairfield Diner
90 King's Highway Cut-Off/Rte. 1
Fairfield, CT
(203) 335-4090
c. 1990 Kullman
Mediterranean style. Vegetarian food plus American food with Greek specialties. Full menu. Open twenty-four hours, seven days.

Family Diner
71 Main St.
Norwalk, CT
(203) 831-0990
1955 Mountain View 480
In mostly original condition. L-shaped dining area and distinctive terrazzo floors. Basic grilled diner fare with Greek specialties. Full menu. Sundays, breakfast and lunch only.

Folly Cafe
Old Rte. 8 at Greenwoods Ave.
Burrville, CT
(203) 482-8388
c. 1959 Fodero?
Covered over, mansard roof. Stainless still underneath, but interior gutted. Tavern.

Forbes Diner
189 Forbes Ave.
New Haven, CT
(203) 469-9225
1957 Fodero
Stunning classic diner with factory kitchen. Located on old east-west gateway route into New Haven and marked with a fabulous neon sign. Full menu of American food with Greek specialties. Closed on Sunday.

The growth of Danbury's Hispanic community has led to this diner's conversion into a café featuring Spanish cuisine. Formerly the New Englander and the Little Athens, it typifies the ebbing of Greek influence in the diner industry.

Frankie's Diner
1660 Barnum Ave.
Bridgeport, CT
(203) 334-8971
1981 DeRaffele
Mediterranean style. Replaced 1940s
Silk City. American food with Greek
specialties.

Glory Days Diner
69 E. Putnam Ave., Rte. 1
Greenwich, CT
(203) 661-9067
2002 DeRaffele
Town ordinance imposed traditional-
style exterior, with classic diner homage
interior. Replaced the Greenwich Colonial Diner. Broad menu featuring American food with Greek specialties.
Twenty-four-hour operation.

Good & Plenty Diner
869 Mill St.
East Berlin, CT
860-828-5020
1949 O'Mahony
Large car, formerly the Route 72 Diner,
encased in brick facade and incorpo-

The Glory Days Diner shows the adaptability of
the diner concept. Host community Greenwich
would never allow something as gauche as a
stainless steel diner, so the DeRaffele company
designed this conservative structure.

rated into strip mall. Breakfast and
lunch only.

Hangout
Rte. 12
Moosup, CT
1920s Worcester
Converted to tavern. Heavily remodeled.

Harold's Diner
69 Newtown Rd./Rte. 6
Danbury, CT
(203) 778-0887
1985 Kullman
Mediterranean style with arched windows and stone facade. Full menu featuring American food with Greek
specialties.

Hi Way Diner
2025 Boston Ave./Rte. 1
Bridgeport, CT
(203) 333-5269
c. 1967 Musi
Colonial style. Full menu of American
food, basic grilled diner fare.

Holiday Diner
123 White St.
Danbury, CT
(203) 748-9798
unknown build
Major renovations to a likely early-
1960s diner design. Broad menu
featuring American food with Greek
specialties. Twenty-four-hour
operation.

Jimmy's Diner
197 Main St.
Norwalk, CT
(203) 847-5422
1930s O'Mahony
Severely remodeled and bricked over.
American food with Greek specialties.
Breakfast and lunch.

John's Diner
136 Connecticut Ave.
South Norwalk, CT
1927 Tierney
Old, largely intact barrel roof diner.
Closed and threatened.

Kimberly Diner
459 Boston Post Rd.
Milford, CT
(203) 874-9541
c. 1961 DeRaffele
Exuberantly styled, space-age DeRaffele
with folded-plate roof. Some renovations. Full menu of good comfort food
and friendly service.

Laurel Diner
544 Main St. S.
Southbury, CT
(203) 264-8218
on-site
Streamline-style car built on-site, with
broad use of interior porcelain enamel.
Standard diner fare with daily specials.
Breakfast and lunch only.

Lumani's Diner
383 Queen St./Rte. 10
Southington, CT
(860) 628-0282
c. 1952 DeRaffele
Heavily remodeled, stuccoed, and
mansarded. Except for basic structural
outlines, retains no original features.

Main Street Diner
40 W. Main St.
Plainville, CT
(860) 793-1618
1950s Master
Weathered but rare Master diner with
true classic neon sign. Third diner on
the site. Originally located on Main
Street in Hempstead, Long Island.

John's Diner, on U.S. Route 1 in Norwalk,
closed in 1994 and has sat idle since. The hot
real estate market likely will force it from this
location, if it hasn't already.

Good chowders and comfort food.
Full menu.

Makris Diner
1795 Berlin Tpk.
Wethersfield, CT
(203) 257-7006
1951 O'Mahony
Large, well-kept eighty-seater, featured
in *Diners of the Northeast.* Closed for a
short time in the late 1980s to 1991.
Basic grilled diner fare. Breakfast and
lunch only.

Milford Diner
13 New Haven Ave.
Milford, CT
(203) 877-2093
1953 Silk City
Well preserved, with newer vestibule.
Moved from original downtown Milford
location in 2004 after purchase by local
businessman for its longtime operator,
Iljas Memaj.

Miss Washington Diner

Miss Washington Diner
10 Washington St.
New Britain, CT
(860) 224-3772
c. 1962 Kullman
Beautiful, lavishly designed "Princess"
model diner in heart of what's left of
downtown district. American food with
Greek specialties. Open twenty-four
hours, seven days.

Mulino's Italian Restaurant
55 Miller St.
Fairfield, CT
(203) 254-2869
1927 O'Mahony
Moved from original location in late
1980s and underwent succession of
remodelings that changed it dramatically. Featured in Baeder's *Diners* and
Bellink and Kaplan's *Diners of the Northeast* when it was still known as Larry's
Diner. Serves upscale Italian cuisine.

New Colony Diner
2321 Main St.
Bridgeport, CT
(203) 367-1217
1978 Swingle #478D
Mediterranean style.

New Colony V Diner
14 Stony Hill Rd., Rte. 6
Bethel, CT
(203) 791-2280
Unknown
Broad menu featuring American food
with Greek specialties. Twenty-four-
hour operation.

New England Country Collectibles
Rte. 5
Wethersfield, CT
1960 DeRaffele
Very large but much remodeled space-
age-style DeRaffele currently used as
retail store for collectibles. Formerly
Tina's Diner and San Remo Restaurant.
Suffered a fire that forced an interior
renovation.

New Star Diner
585 Lombard St.
New Haven, CT
(203) 562-5582
c. 1963 Fodero
In very good condition. Flared roof with
large plate glass windows. Formerly operating as the New State Diner in Ansonia.
Moved to New Haven in August 1995.
American food with Greek specialties.
Full menu on weekdays. Open twenty-
four hours on weekend.

Ninety-One Diner
Exit 8 off I-91
North Haven, CT
Unknown

Norm's Diner
171 Bridge St.
Groton, CT
(203) 445-5026
1954 Silk City
Very well-preserved, classic 1950s diner.
Simple Yankee menu open twenty-four
hours most days.

Old Saybrook Diner

809 Boston Post Rd. (Exit 67 off I-95)
Old Saybrook, CT
(860) 395-1079
1998 DeRaffele
Expansive ultramodern diner. American food with Greek specialties. Full menu on weekdays; open twenty-four hours on weekends.

Olympia Diner

3413 Berlin Tpk./Rte. 5
Newington, CT
(860) 666-9948
c. 1955 O'Mahony
Huge diner with spectacular, much-photographed neon sign. Possibly the largest diner built by O'Mahony. American food with Greek specialties.

Olympos Diner

1130 E. Main St.
Meriden, CT
(860) 235-5636
c. 1950 Silk City
Remodeled and expanded. Full menu of American food with Greek specialties. Sunday, breakfast and lunch only.

Orem's Diner

167 Danbury Rd./Rte. 7
Wilton, CT
(203) 762-7370
2003 DeRaffele
Big new diner with typical interior DeRaffele flourish, but almost no exterior stainless per town ordinance. Blue granite counter. Nice curves on ceiling stainless. Vaulted ceiling inset akin to old lunch wagon, complete with oak strips. Pink granite tile floors; no carpeting. Full menu of American food with Greek specialties.

O'Rourke's Diner

728 Main St.
Middletown, CT
(860) 346-6101
1946 Mountain View #223
Landmark diner that has made the pages of *Gourmet,* the *New York Times,* and many other publications. Noted for its creative brunch menu and steamed cheeseburgers. Breakfast and lunch only.

Parkway Diner

1066 High Ridge Rd.
Stamford, CT
(203) 321-8606
1957 DeRaffele
Grand space-age style exterior with flared roof. Some interior renovations. Clean and friendly operation. Full menu of American food with Mediterranean specialties. Homemade doughnuts. Open seven days.

Parthenon Diner

374 E. Main St.
Branford, CT
(203) 481-0333
www.parthenondiner.com
c. 1980 DeRaffele?
American food with Greek specialties. Open twenty-four hours, seven days.

Connecticut has few remaining Silk City diners, but Norm's in Groton is probably the best preserved.

Penny's Diner
212 East Ave.
Norwalk, CT
(203) 852-0326
1984 Swingle #784DKDR
Full menu featuring American food
with Greek specialties. Homemade
soups and daily specials. Excellent
meat loaf.

Penny's II Diner
2200 Black Rock Tpk.
Fairfield, CT
(203) 576-9884
c. 1970 DeRaffele?
Full menu featuring American food
with Greek specialties. Homemade
soups and daily specials. Excellent
meat loaf.

Post Road Diner
312 Connecticut Ave./Rte. 1
Norwalk, CT
(203) 866-9777
1947 Paramount
A restoration has been in progress. Interior completed in 2002 and looks wonderful. Easy access from I-95. Serves
extensive, innovative comfort-food
menu with daily specials and homemade desserts. Open twenty-four hours,
seven days.

Quaker Diner
319 Park Rd.
West Hartford, CT
(860) 232-5523
1931 on-site
Brick on-site construction, but closely
conforms to diner proportions. Restored
by third-generation owner in 1987. Features high-backed wooden booths and
glass counter. Breakfast and lunch only.
Smoke-free.

Quality Time Food & Spirits
999 Broad St.
Meriden, CT
(203) 634-9904
c. 1940 unknown build
Old diner converted into tavern.

Rajun Cajun
2790 N. Main St.
Hartford, CT
(860) 247-0453
1950 Paramount
Classic postwar styling. In good condition, but run down. Originally the Terry
Square Diner. Last operated as Hal's
Aquarius Cafe. Now closed but slated
to reopen as Cajun restaurant.

Red Colony Diner
121 Federal Rd./Rte. 202
Brookfield, CT
(203) 775-1182
c. 1970 Musi
Colonial style with hammered copper
hood. In very original condition. Full
menu of American food. Grilled diner
fare, homemade soups.

Rosie's Diner
145 Gold Star Hwy./Rte. 184
Groton, CT
(860) 445-9187
1954 Silk City #5412
Popular, well-kept classic. American
food. Open twenty-four hours,
seven days.

Route 66 Diner
Rte. 66
East Hampton, CT
1954 Mountain View #428
Former Berlin Diner of Berlin, New
Jersey. Moved in 2001 and is undergo-
ing some restoration. Currently closed.

Sandy Hook Diner
98 Church Hill Rd./Rte. 6
Sandy Hook, CT
(203) 270-5509
1920s Tierney?
Originally called Corrigan's Diner. Renovated but still retains vintage charm. Basic grilled diner fare with homemade desserts. Breakfast and lunch only.

Sherwood Diner
901 Post Rd.
Westport, CT
(203) 226-5535
1970s DeRaffele
Colonial style. Broad menu featuring American food with Greek specialties. Twenty-four-hour operation.

Shoreline Diner
345 Boston Post Rd.
Guilford, CT
(203) 458-7380
1994 DeRaffele
Mediterranean style. Vegetarian food plus American food with Greek specialties. Full menu. Late nights on weekends.

Silver Diner
3780 E. Main St.
Waterbury, CT
(203) 757-8140
1951 Mountain View/Manno
Moved in 1994 from Easton, Pennsylvania, where it operated as the Lafayette Diner. Built by Mountain View but has Manno tag, likely because of some minor renovations. Basic grilled diner fare. Full menu on weekdays; breakfast only on Sundays.

Silver Star Diner
210 Connecticut Ave.
Norwalk, CT

(203) 852-0023
1980 Kullman
World's first million-dollar diner. Modernistic styling and expansive. Broad menu featuring American food with Greek specialties. Twenty-four-hour-operation.

Skee's Diner
589 Main St.
Torrington, CT
1920s O'Mahony
Only diner in Connecticut to be listed on the National Register of Historic Places. Possibly the oldest viable diner in the country. Known only to have operated in Old Saybrook until 1944 and moved to current location in Torrington that year. Few interior modifications, which included removing a small section of the counter for a booth. Currently closed; future plans undetermined.

South Windham Diner
881 Rte. 32
South Windham, CT
(203) 456-9937
1958 Bramson
One of only two diners built by Bramson of Oyster Bay, New York. Last operated in 1994. Originally in East Hartford and moved to current location in 1960s. In good condition and for sale.

Squeak's Diner
CT
1941 Worcester #774
In storage. Rare Worcester streamliner model. Purchased in 2003 by a Canadian filmmaker and diner enthusiast for eventual restoration.

Stamford Diner
1625 Summer St.
Stamford, CT
(203) 325-2489
Unknown build
Broad menu featuring American food
with Greek specialties. Twenty-four-
hour operation.

Stonington Diner
Rte. 1 S.
Stonington, CT
c. 1930 unknown build
Dilapidated barrel-roof diner, last used
as a residence. Closed but clearly visible
from Route 1.

Tandoor
1226 Chapel St.
New Haven, CT
(203) 776-6620
1955 Mountain View #445
Beautiful, iconic 1950s diner that now
serves South Asian cuisine. In very good
condition. Once part of a failed upscale
diner operation known as the Elm City
Diner. Lunch and dinner only.

Maybe the only Ward & Dickinson car left
in New England, the Trolley Stop Restaurant
in Willimantic is mostly a tavern.

Ted's Diner
1503 Thomaston St.
Waterbury, CT
(203) 574-4439
c. 1920 Tierney
Rare diner, paneled over but otherwise
nicely preserved. Very clean operation.
Breakfast only.

Three Brothers
242 White St.
Danbury, CT
(203) 748-6008
c. 1990 DeRaffele
Mediterranean style. Broad menu
featuring American food with Greek
and Hispanic specialties. Twenty-four-
hour operation.

Three Brothers Diner
1088 Dixwell Ave.
Hamden, CT
(203) 777-9420
DeRaffele
Weathered colonial diner-restaurant.
Broad menu featuring American food
with Greek specialties. Twenty-four-
hour operation.

Tony's Diner
46 Columbus St.
Seymour, CT
(203) 888-7551
c. 1954 Kullman
Rare dinette model. Small with varied
breakfast menu. American food with
Italian specialties.

Triple A Diner
1209 Main St.
East Hartford, CT
(860) 289-1685
1970 Paramount
Colonial style. Some interior renovations. American food with Greek

specialties. Open twenty-four hours, seven days.

Trolley Stop Restaurant
Rte. 66
Willimantic, CT
c. 1930 Ward & Dickinson
One of only two possible Ward & Dickinsons in New England. Currently used as a tavern.

Twin Colony
Rte. 4 & Rte. 202
Torrington, CT
c. 1988 DeRaffele
Full menu featuring American food with Greek specialties. Open twenty-four hours, seven days.

Twin Pines Diner
34 Main St.
East Haven, CT
(203) 468-6887
unknown build

Two Guys Diner
495 Honeyspot Rd.
Stratford, CT
(203) 378-0278
c. 1970 DeRaffele
Colonial style. Closed in 2001.

Valley Diner
1047 S. Main St
Waterbury, CT
1950 Mountain View #281
Closed in 1998 and vandalized. Future in doubt.

Valley Diner
636 New Haven Ave./Rte. 34
Derby, CT
(203) 735-2445
1980s unknown build
Mediterranean style. American food with Greek specialties. Open twenty-four hours, seven days.

Washington Diner
175 Washington St.
Hartford, CT
(860) 247-6272
c. 1969 Paramount
Colonial style. Closed in 2001.

Waterbury Diner
625 Chase Ave.
Waterbury, CT
(203) 597-0032
c. 1987 unknown build
Broad menu featuring American food with Greek specialties. Twenty-four-hour operation.

Wethersfield Diner
718 Silas Deane Hwy./Rte. 99
Wethersfield, CT
(860) 529-9690
1951 Mountain View #308
Enveloped, with new tile floor and booths. New counter raised higher. Menu board missing. Full menu of American food with Greek specialties. Sunday, breakfast and lunch only.

White's Diner
280 Boston Ave./Rte. 1
Bridgeport, CT
(203) 366-7486
1957 DeRaffele
Preserved exterior, but interior renovations. Full menu of American and Italian food. Open seven days.

Windmill Diner
245 Danbury Rd.
New Milford, CT
(203) 354-1218
unknown build
Broad menu featuring American food with Greek specialties. Twenty-four-hour operation.

Windmill Diner
14 Mill Plain Rd./Rte. 6
Danbury, CT
(203) 743-6541
c. 1968 Manno?
Colonial style. American food with Greek specialties. Open twenty-four hours, seven days.

Winsted Diner
496 Main St./Rte. 44
Winsted, CT
(860) 379-4429
1931 Tierney
Encased with siding and pitched roof, but retains many original interior features. Renowned for its tasty "Ra-Doc-A-Doodle" Sandwich: scrambled eggs and American cheese with fresh Tennessee sausage on an English muffin. Grilled diner fare. Late-night to morning hours. Breakfast and lunch.

Zip's Diner
Rte. 12 & Rte. 101
Dayville, CT
(860) 774-6335
1954 O'Mahony
Spectacularly preserved diner with signature towering neon "EAT" sign above entrance. Replaced a 1946 model located in Killingly. Full menu of American food. Open seven days.

Index